February 1933

February 1933

The Winter of Literature

Uwe Wittstock

Translated by Daniel Bowles

polity

Originally published in German as *Februar 33. Der Winter der Literatur*
© Verlag C.H.Beck oHG, München 2018

This English edition © Polity Press, 2023

The translation of this book was supported by a grant from the Goethe-Institut

Polity Press
65 Bridge Street
Cambridge CB2 1UR, UK

Polity Press
111 River Street
Hoboken, NJ 07030, USA

ISBN-13: 978-1-5095-5379-2

A catalogue record for this book is available from the British Library.

Library of Congress Control Number: 2022945588

Typeset in 11.5 on 14 Adobe Garamond
by Fakenham Prepress Solutions, Fakenham, Norfolk NR21 8NL
Printed and bound in the UK by CPI Group (UK) Ltd, Croydon

For further information on Polity, visit our website: politybooks.com

Contents

Acknowledgments

Many people have assisted me in my work on this book in different ways. I would like to thank Karin Graf and Franziska Günther at the agency Graf & Graf; Stefanie Hölscher for outstanding copyediting and Martin Hielscher whose friendship means a great deal to me; the Brecht connoisseurs Jürgen Hillesheim and Stephen Parker for their reliable information; Joaquín Moreno, who provided me with unpublished material from the estate of Ferdinand Bruckner; Christoph Buchwald for advice in dealing with Walter Mehring's recollections; Thomas F. Schneider of the Erich Maria Remarque-Friedenszentrum at the Universität Osnabrück for his precise references; Marie Schmidt for the tip about Gabriele Tergit's visit to Carl von Ossietzky; Thomas Medicus for his support in searching for a letter from Carl Zuckmayer to Heinrich George; Holger Hof for information about Gottfried Benn; and Christoph Marschner, who ascertained for me life-saving train connections into exile from Germany in February and March 1933 with down-to-the-minute accuracy.

Without the vast treasury of holdings at the Deutsche National-bibliothek in Frankfurt am Main and the collections of the Deutsches Exilarchiv in Frankfurt am Main, it would have been impossible for me to write this book. Sylvia Asmus, Regina Elzner, Katrin Kokot, and Jörn Hasenclever supported me there with great patience and expertise. I give them my sincere thanks. I likewise used the archives of the Akademie der Künste in Berlin, the Monacensia at the Hildebrandhaus in Munich, and the Staatsbibliothek zu Berlin. I would also like to offer them my gratitude. And I thank Christine and Heinrich Michael Clausing for their esteem and for an incredible month at the Bleiche.

Figures

In memory of Gerta Wittstock (1930–2020)
who was two years old in February '33

Stepping off the Cliff
The month in which the die was cast

These are no tales of heroes. They are stories of people facing extreme peril. Many of them refused to acknowledge the danger, underestimated it, reacted too slowly, in short: they made mistakes. Of course, it is easy for anyone paging through history books today to say such people were fools if they could not comprehend in 1933 what Hitler meant for them. And yet such a notion would be unhistorical. If the claim that Hitler's crimes are unimaginable has any meaning, then it must hold true first and foremost for his contemporaries. They could not imagine or at best could only suspect what he and his people were capable of. Presumably it is in the very nature of a breach of civilization to be difficult to imagine.

Everything happened in a frenzy. Four weeks and two days elapsed between Hitler's accession to power and the *Emergency Decree for the Protection of People and State*, which abrogated all fundamental civil rights. It took only this one month to transform a state under the rule of law into a violent dictatorship without scruples. Killing on a grand scale did not begin until later. But in February '33 it was decided who would be its target: who would fear for her life and be forced to flee and who would step forward to launch his career in the slipstream of the perpetrators. Never before have so many writers and artists fled their homeland in such a short time. The first exodus of escapees, lasting into mid-March, is also the subject of this story.

From varying perspectives, historians of different stripes have described the political conditions that facilitated Hitler's seizure of power. Several common factors play a role in all analyses: the growing influence of extremist parties, which divided the country; overheated propaganda that drove the wedge deeper and deeper and inhibited compromise, together with the indecisiveness and weakness of the political center; the civil-war-like terror from right and left; the raging hatred of the Jews; the hardships of the global economic crisis; and the rise of nationalist regimes in other countries.

These days circumstances are different, happily. Yet parallels may be found to many elements: growing social divisions and the persistent indignation on the internet that exacerbates them; the cluelessness of the bourgeois center about how to rein in the appetite for extremism; the growing number of acts of terror committed by the right and sometimes by the left; increasing anti-Semitism; the risks for the global economy posed by the financial crisis and the coronavirus; the rise of nationalist regimes in other countries. Perhaps it is not a bad time to remind ourselves what can happen to a democracy after a catastrophic error in political decision-making.

In February '33 it wasn't just writers and artists staring down danger. The situation may have been even more perilous for others. The first casualty of the Nazis, the very night of Hitler's swearing-in as Reich Chancellor, was the Prussian police sergeant Josef Zauritz, a loyal republican and union man, according to the *Vossische Zeitung*. This story will recount his murder as well. But we know incomparably more personal details about writers and artists in February '33 than we do about any other group. Their diaries and letters have been collected, their notes archived, and their memoirs published and vetted by biographers with investigative zeal.

Their experiences give a sense of how people fared while attempting to defend democracy and the rule of law. They show how difficult it is to comprehend the point at which everyday life turns into a fight for survival and when a historical moment necessitates personal decisions about one's very existence.

For everything recounted here there are historical records. It is a factual report despite a few interpretative liberties, without which the historical or biographical contexts would not lend themselves to narrative. Of course, not everything that happened to writers and artists back then can be reproduced in this mosaic either. Thomas Mann, Else Lasker-Schüler, Bertolt Brecht, Alfred Döblin, Ricarda Huch, George Grosz, Heinrich Mann, Mascha Kaléko, Gabriele Tergit, Gottfried Benn, Klaus and Erika Mann, Harry Graf Kessler, Carl von Ossietzky, Carl Zuckmayer, or the Academy of the Arts in Berlin – all who appear here are merely exemplars. A complete panorama would be too large for any book.

Many a career that began so full of hope never recovered from this month. All too many writers faded into silence and vanished almost without a trace. It was a life-and-death turning point for everyone.

The Republic's Last Dance
Saturday, January 28

Berlin has been freezing for weeks. Shortly after New Year's Day a stinging frost set in – even the largest lakes, the Wannsee and Müggelsee, have disappeared beneath solid sheets of ice – and now, to add insult to injury, it has snowed. Carl Zuckmayer is standing before the mirror in his attic flat across from the Schöneberg district's municipal park, wearing a tuxedo and tugging his white bow tie into place over his shirt collar. The prospect of leaving the house tonight in eveningwear is not enticing.

Zuckmayer has no great love of large parties. He is usually bored and stays only just long enough to be able to vanish without a fuss into a random dive bar together with his friends. The Press Ball, however, is the most important social event of Berlin's winter season, a spectacle of the rich, the powerful, and the beautiful. It would be a mistake not to make an appearance; the ball will benefit his reputation as an up-and-coming star in the literature business with many irons in the fire.

The memory of the hardships during his first years as an author is all too vivid for Zuckmayer to turn his back on opportunities like this one. When he was completely broke, he got work as a barker, trolling adventure-hungry visitors to Berlin from the streets after curfew to conduct them to the illicit sideshow bars in backstreet courtyards. In some of these, the girls were half naked and not demure when it came to their guests' desires. Once he even dabbled as a dealer on Tauentzienstrasse by night with a few packets of cocaine in his pockets. It wasn't long before he called it quits; he's a sturdy fellow and unafraid, but even for him such business was too dangerous.

All that is behind him since *The Merry Vineyard*. After four pathos-laden and thoroughly miscarried dramas, all of which flopped, he tried his hand at his first comedic subject, a German screwball comedy about a vintner's daughter looking for marriage in the boondocks of Rhine-Hesse, Zuckmayer's homeland. In the milieu of wine growers

3

and merchants, he knows every detail. In his treatment the whole transformed into a kind of folk play in which every inflection clicked and
every joke landed. Initially, Berlin's stages were above such pastoral comic
fare, but when the Theater am Schiffbauerdamm hazarded the premiere
shortly before Christmas of 1925, the seemingly featherweight farce
bared its claws, to everyone's surprise. The vast majority of the audience
howled with laughter – and a smaller portion with rage – at the satiric
bite with which Zuckmayer mocked the *völkisch* prattle of bone-headed
war veterans and saber-rattling corps students. Their fury only made
The Merry Vineyard more famous and heightened its success. It became
a real blockbuster, perhaps the most staged play of the 1920s, and it was
adapted for film as well.

Now, seven years later, not one but three plays by Zuckmayer are
on the season schedules of Berlin theaters; the Freie Volksbühne will
stage *Schinderhannes*, at the Rose-Theater in Friedrichshain they're
showing his sensationally successful *Captain of Köpenick*, and at the
Schillertheater *Katharina Knie*. For Tobis Film he's working on a fairy-
tale picture, and the *Berliner Illustrirte* will soon begin serializing his tale
Eine Liebesgeschichte [A Love Story], which is to appear right afterward in
book form. Things are going swimmingly for him. Few authors in their
mid-thirties have enjoyed the success he's already had.

Gazing from his rooftop terrace he can see Berlin's lights, from the radio
tower to the cupola of the Cathedral. Together with the house outside
Salzburg he purchased with the royalties from *The Merry Vineyard*, the
apartment is Zuckmayer's second residence. It's of manageable size – an
office, two tiny bedrooms, a nursery, kitchen, bathroom, nothing more –
but he loves it and especially its views over the city rooftops. He bought
it off Otto Firle, the architect and graphic artist who designed, among
other things, the flying crane, Lufthansa's insignia. In recent years Firle
has become favorite architect to the wealthy Berlin Grand Burghers
and educated classes and no longer outfits attic apartments, instead
contriving villas by the dozen. In two years – although Zuckmayer of
course cannot anticipate such a thing tonight – Firle will build a country
home on the Darss peninsula in the Baltic Sea for a newly wealthy and
powerful minister named Hermann Göring.

The last Saturday in January is reserved for the Press Ball, a Berlin
tradition for years now. His publisher, Ullstein, sent Zuckmayer his

complimentary tickets, after which his wife Alice went about searching for a new evening gown straightaway. This year his mother has come from Mainz to visit for a week. She, too, is wearing a new dress, which he gave her for Christmas: silver gray with lace appliqué. It's her first big Berlin ball, and he can sense her excitement.

For now, though, they're planning to dine at a fine restaurant first. The evening will drag on, and it's better not to begin a night at the ball too early, and never on an empty stomach.

*

With regard to his evening plans, Klaus Mann has bet on the wrong horse: a masked party in Westend at a Frau Ruben's, quite normal and wretched. He feels out of place.

For three days now he's been in Berlin, living as usual in the guesthouse Fasaneneck. At Werner Finck's cabaret *Katakombe* he ran into Moni, his sister, who then encumbered him with the invitation to this Frau Ruben's. He found Finck's program wanting and without spark, but all the same he got to see Kadidja on stage again, the shy one of the two Wedekind sisters. He likes her. She's almost an ex-sister-in-law to him.

Klaus Mann has been frequenting cabarets of late, out of professional interest, since he himself is involved in one now in Munich, the *Pfeffermühle*, founded by his sister Erika, together with Therese Giehse and Magnus Henning. With Erika he writes couplets and sketches, Erika, Therese, and two others appear on stage, and Magnus furnishes the music. Klaus could really use inspiration for new scripts, but the acts in *Katakombe* left him empty-handed, and when Finck's actors started teasing him from the stage with interspersed taunts and little improvised jokes, it turned him off, and he left before the program ended.

He's making quick work of Frau Ruben's masked party as well. Instead of continuing to endure boredom, he leaves quite early despite knowing how unmannerly it is. A lame evening: so back to the guesthouse it shall be, where for his evening entertainment he will treat himself to a dose of morphine, and a large one at that.

*

In Erfurt's Reichshallentheater today, the premiere of Brecht's learning play *The Measures Taken*, with music by Hanns Eisler, is scheduled to take place. The police, however, terminate the performance by the *Kampfgemeinschaft der Arbeitersänger* [*Action Group of Worker-Singers*] with the justification that the play is "a communist-revolutionary depiction of the class struggle for the purpose of bringing about global revolution."

*

When Carl Zuckmayer pulls up in front of the Zoo Ballrooms with Alice and his mother, at first glance everything seems as it was in years past. Over 5,000 visitors are expected, of whom 1,500 are invited guests with complimentary tickets like himself. The others, well, they are curious onlookers who pay horrendous prices to mingle for a night among the country's celebrities.

In the foyer new arrivals must first squeeze past two magnificent automobiles, an Adler-Trumpf cabriolet and a DKW Meisterklasse, both polished to a high gloss: the grand prizes in the raffle for the welfare fund of the *Berliner Presseverein* [*Berlin Press Association*]. Just beyond the entrance, the stream of people disperses while tangos, waltzes, and boogie-woogie emanate from the ballrooms and corridors. Zuckmayer shepherds his ladies toward the waltzes. Provisions have been made for nearly every gastronomic predilection; there are bars with the ambience of a club, plush coffee parlors and beer counters, or quieter, more intimate side halls featuring solo musicians.

The grand two-story Marble Hall, festooned with fresh flowers and with antique Persian carpets draping the balustrades, has the most luxurious decorations. Couples twirl around the dancefloor in front of the stage with the orchestra. From above, in the gallery, one can watch as the parade of visitors elbows its way between the ballroom's side loges and the long rows of tables in the middle.

This year, a fact not to be overlooked, the most elegant ladies are sporting bright colors. And apparently the *dernier cri* is a long evening gown with small décolleté but a back neckline that plunges to the waistline, or even beyond.

Zuckmayer breaks off from the torrent of visitors as soon as they reach the Ullstein loge. There's more air here, less shoving, and right away the waiters procure him and his companions a table, glasses, and beverages. One of the publishing directors welcomes them with "Drink, drink up, who knows when you'll be drinking Champagne in an Ullstein loge again," thereby verbalizing what everyone is more or less feeling, while still all somewhat in denial about it.

Sometime around midday the cabinet of Kurt von Schleicher, who has only been Reich Chancellor since the beginning of December, stepped down: an absurdly brief tenure, not even two whole months, that, apart from new cabals, yielded the country not a whit – time lost during one of the most vicious economic crises. This evening, news spread that Reich President Paul von Hindenburg had, of all people, tasked Schleicher's predecessor in office, Franz von Papen, with forming a new government. The perplexity of these politicians is palpable. A member of the Centre Party, Papen nevertheless has no appreciable power base in parliament. Like Schleicher, he has landed in office solely by virtue of Hindenburg's good graces and via emergency decree after the parties were unable to rally a majority against the extremists in the KPD and the NSDAP. That pompous, politically unwitting Papen, however, is more liable to stage a coup d'état than to muster the aptitude for restoring the republic to reasonably stable democratic footing.

Just last summer, likewise with only the sanction of an emergency decree, he dismissed the Prussian government. Since then, the largest state in the empire has been administered by caretaker cabinets subordinate to the imperial government. Referred to as the "Preußenschlag," or Prussian putsch, that very act was a kind of coup that undermined the empire's federal foundations with the result that now, after Schleicher's resignation, Prussia is also left leaderless.

The government loge in the Marble Hall directly abuts the Ullstein partition. From his seat Zuckmayer can comfortably glance over at it and see it is nearly deserted. Idle waiters loiter about between the empty plush chairs as unopened bottles of sparkling wine jut from their ice buckets. In years past ministers or state secretaries would hold court there, drawing editors and columnists into conversation as if by chance and explaining to them the world as they saw it. Yet now, apparently, no one feels charged to attend to even such easygoing affairs of government anymore.

All that's left is the pleasure of keeping an eye out for famous faces in the throng. The tall, ascetic frame of Wilhelm Fürtwängler, conductor of the Berlin Philharmonic, is easy to spot, and with him, severe, almost always with a somewhat melancholic aspect, Arnold Schönberg, who gives the impression of being oddly out of place amid the festive hustle and bustle. Gustaf Gründgens and Werner Krauß have apparently made their way here just after their performance at the Schauspielhaus on Gendarmenmarkt where they're currently playing Mephisto and Faust. Also making an appearance: the hairless skull of Max von Schillings, a composer who hasn't produced anything new for quite some time and since recently holds the office of President of the Prussian Academy of the Arts.

A photographer intrudes, inviting Zuckmayer to exit the loge for a moment to pose in a group photo with a curiously motley cast: two young stage actresses along with the opera diva Mafalda Salvatini and Professor Bonn, a businessman and government advisor wearing on his chest, as rector of the Handelshochschule [College of Commerce], a rather silly gold chain of office with a medallion.

The director of *The Blue Angel*, Josef von Sternberg, emerges briefly from the crowd, surrounded, as would befit his station, by bright young blonde starlets. Marlene Dietrich stayed behind in Hollywood without him. In days gone by Zuckmayer had collaborated on the script for *The Blue Angel* and thereby came to know Heinrich Mann, who penned the novel upon which it was based, *Professor Unrat*. He likes that stuffy old boy and admires his book. And yet in his eyes Mann made a fool of himself by trying to replace Marlene Dietrich in the lead role with his then-mistress Trude Hesterberg. In his prim handwriting he drafted letters to the producers that revealed more about his infatuation with Hesterberg than about her qualities as an actor.

Back in the Ullstein loge Zuckmayer bumps into a stocky, exuberant man: Ernst Udet, and his companion Ehmi Bessel. Udet and Zuckmayer are overjoyed; they've known each other since the war. In those days Zuckmayer was often deployed to the foremost front lines as an observer, or he would repair shredded telephone lines while under fire. He's a man with steady nerves, but he'd never compare himself with Udet, a fighter pilot with the presence of a matador, elegant, cocky, cavalier – a mixture of a scoundrel and a gunslinger. When they met for the first time, Udet had already been given command of a fighter squadron at age twenty-two and been draped with medals by generals like a sacrificial animal is with flower garlands. He shot down his enemies in man-to-man dogfights: a modern-day knight riding off to the joust, an adrenaline junkie. By the time the war had ended, he'd brought down sixty-two planes. Only one other German pilot had been more successful in this deadly business: his commandant, Manfred von Richthofen, the "Red Baron." He, however, had died a few months before war's end from ground fire and was later replaced by a commandant named Hermann Göring. While not as talented a pilot, he had a surefire knack for making the right political connections.

Zuckmayer's mother especially is enraptured by Udet. Alice has known him for longer and is aware of the swashbuckling charm he exudes. As a real showman, Udet does not depend on his bleak wartime fame. These days he performs all over Europe and America in aerobatic shows, presenting nose dives, spirals, and loop-the-loops in which he turns off his propeller. Or he flies so close to the turf that he can pick

Figure 1: From left to right, Ernst Udet, Ehmi Bessel, and Carl Zuckmayer at the 1933 Berlin Press Ball

up handkerchiefs from the ground with his wing. He is and remains a jolly daredevil. UFA has discovered him independently and cast him in several adventure films with Leni Riefenstahl in which he lands in the high mountains on glaciers or flies through a hangar with his plane as bystanders fling themselves to the ground. Berlin's gossip rags love Udet, his affairs with actors like Ehmi Bessel, his sportscar known all over town, a Dodge, and his publicly celebrated friendships with film stars like Riefenstahl, Lilian Harvey, or Heinz Rühmann.

There's no possibility of boredom with Udet, but Zuckmayer never talks about the war with him, so when they meet up, they drink instead. Now, too, they're switching from Champagne to cognac. Udet notices with surprise how many ball guests are wearing their medals and badges on their tuxedos: "Take a look at those numskulls." In former years the Press Ball had a more civilian tone. Suddenly emphasis is placed on having a military past. Even Udet is wearing the highest order of merit he has, Pour le Merité, but since he never likes doing what everyone else is doing, he spirits it away into his pocket. "You know what," he suggests to Zuckmayer, "let's both pull down our pants now and hang our naked butts over the balustrade here."

Alice and Ehmi are alarmed at once. They don't put much past the men, especially when they're drunk and goading each other. And, in fact, they've gone straight to unbuttoning their suspenders. But Alice knows her role on such occasions and entreats the two not to cause a scandal, and thus, without losing face, the men may refrain from further disrobing.

Sometime after midnight, speculation spreads that Hitler is to be named Reich Chancellor. The calculation is simple. If Hindenburg finally intends to put the government back on halfway solid parliamentary footing but the SPD still will not participate under any circumstances, then in essence he and Papen are left with only the NSDAP as a partner. As leader of the largest parliamentary contingent in the Reichstag, Hitler, however, is unwilling to content himself with a ministerial position, as he has made categorically clear. He claims the chancellorship, or else he will remain in the opposition. It's all or nothing.

Such thoughts do not make the ball more cheerful. People dance and drink as in past years, but the unsettling feeling remains that something unforeseeable is headed their way. The mood is one of peculiarly phony gaiety. By now Sunday has long since begun, and Udet invites Zuckmayer and his two companions to an afterparty at his apartment. His conspicuous Dodge is parked in front of the Zoo Ballrooms like a billboard for himself. Outside, in the bitter cold, he seems sober, but everyone knows he is not. Zuckmayer and his wife prefer to hail a taxi. Only Ehmi and Zuckmayer's mother are brave enough to ride along in Udet's car and afterward report with effusive excitement that they didn't so much drive as fly through the streets.

Udet's flat is bursting with trophies from countries in which he's already filmed. Hanging just inside the foyer are a taxidermy rhinoceros and leopard head, along with a few sets of antlers. In the apartment there's even a shooting booth; several newspapers have been reporting that Udet shoots cigarettes out of the mouths of friends who trust him implicitly. That, however, is something for stag nights. Today Udet invites his guests to join him at a small bar he's set up, his "Propeller Bar," and entertains the ladies with anecdotes from the life of a pilot and about the film industry. Now and again Zuckmayer takes Udet's guitar from the wall and sings a few drinking songs as he did back when he bar-hopped through Berlin to earn a meal as a ballad minstrel.

These are good-humored but not carefree early morning hours, for in the end they mark a farewell. Only once more will Zuckmayer and Udet see one another after this night. In 1936 Zuckmayer musters considerable courage and a pinch of recklessness to travel to Berlin from his home outside Salzburg. The Nazis haven't forgotten how effectively he panned the military in *The Merry Vineyard* and *The Captain of Köpenick* and have long since listed his plays and books on their Index. Still, Zuckmayer cannot be dissuaded and travels anyway to meet actor friends Werner Krauß, Käthe Dorsch, and Ernst Udet, as well. The latter might always label himself an unpolitical person, but three months after the night of the Press Ball, he has joined the NSDAP and launched his career in the Ministry of Aviation under his old squadron commandant Göring.

It turns into a somber final encounter in a small, unobtrusive restaurant. The two luxuriate one more time in reminiscences, but then Udet implores his friend to leave the country as soon as possible: "Go out into the world and never come back." When Zuckmayer questions why he is staying, Udet replies that flying simply means the world to him and talks about the tremendous opportunities as a pilot that his work for the

Nazis provides him: "It's too late for me to quit. But one day the devil will come for us all."

In November 1941 Udet shoots himself in his Berlin apartment. Göring held him responsible for the failures of the Luftwaffe in the Battle of Britain. Someone has to be the scapegoat. Before Udet kills himself, he writes on the headboard of his bed in red chalk as a rebuke to Göring: "Iron One, you have forsaken me!"

The Nazis pass off his death as an accident, and Zuckmayer learns of it in exile on his farm in Vermont. The news bothers him for a long while, he later recalls, until he finally sits at his desk and writes the first act of his play *The Devil's General* in under three weeks. It tells the tale of a charismatic Luftwaffe general who despises Hitler but serves him out of a mistaken love of Germany and flying. When the war is over, the play is finished. It becomes one of Zuckmayer's greatest successes.

*

Kadidja Wedekind feels ill at ease. She allows the throngs of visitors to push her through the ballrooms, proud to number among the invitees already at just twenty-one, among the literati, but the crush in the corridors doesn't sit well with her. She likes to be by herself and in the background. She prefers to observe from a distance than to have to fight her way forward with the others.

That sort of shyness is otherwise unknown within her family. Her parents, Tilly and Frank Wedekind, once belonged to the towering figures of the German theater world and were always up for a bit of pandemonium. Her father Frank, who passed away back in 1918, was a tireless provocateur, a theater berserker who delighted in disparaging virtuous citizens' repressed rules of etiquette in his plays. There was not a taboo he didn't put on stage: prostitution, abortion, masturbation, sadism, homosexuality. He possessed the unerring talent of being able, anytime and anywhere, to unleash an impromptu scandal. Not even his friends were safe from his flashes of temper. Over some years Tilly was a much-sought-after actor who primarily performed in her husband's plays and shone in the role of Wedekind's Lulu, an uninhibitedly libidinous girl who both abuses men for her pleasure and lets herself be abused by them. Together Tilly and Frank could have enjoyed the life of an admired and feared theatrical couple. But Wedekind made life a hell for his wife

– and thus also for himself – with fits of rabid jealousy. Twice he drove Tilly to attempt suicide. She has been widowed for fifteen years now.

Kadidja's sister Pamela, five years her senior, inherited some of their parents' temperament as well as some of their talent. Since her youth she's felt at ease on stage, has a pretty voice, and likes to perform her father's songs, which she sings as he used to with lute accompaniment. She has everything Kadidja lacks: courage, initiative, assertiveness. "Pamela," Kadidja writes one day in her diary, "is quite a strong personality and tremendously talented; with my meekness I've got to take a backseat to her."

After their father's death in 1918, Pamela and Kadidja made the acquaintance of the oldest Mann children in Munich, Erika and Klaus. They almost lived in the same neighborhood, not a half hour on foot from one house to the other. The Mann siblings were entranced by Pamela's abilities and fell instantly in love with her. Kadidja was as yet too young to be able to keep up with the others. The three formed a precocious (to the adults: somewhat sinister) trio and impelled each other to ever more novel dandyish actions. Klaus, who wore makeup and made no pretense about being gay, got engaged to Pamela in 1924 and within two weeks had written the chamber play *Anja and Esther*, which was brimming with allusions to the lesbian love affair between Pamela and Erika. The play didn't account for much – it was just a sketch, not a well-thought-out work; a couple of boarding-school pupils wallow in their melancholy search for love and the meaning of life. But Gustaf Gründgens, one of the greatest theater talents in the country, was enthusiastic about it, sent an ardent telegram, and persuaded the three to stage the early work together with him and take it on tour throughout Germany.

The play garnered scathing reviews, with critics unwilling to forgive the son of the great Thomas Mann any youthful indiscretion. Nevertheless, the theatrical sensation was perfect, and every theater sold out. The lively activities of these poets' progeny and their scarcely clear-cut erotic entanglements stoked the public's curiosity, particularly as Erika then also married Gründgens despite his notorious attraction rather to men. For several weeks the four featured in all entertainment columns and society pages; they tugged at the strings, and every newspaper jumped like a marionette. Who or what might better have embodied the wild, the lustful, the uninhibited twenties than this *ménage-à-quatre*?

Figure 2: Kadidja Wedekind in 1932

Kadidja is neither able nor willing to keep in step with her sister's pace of life. Even her mother, engaged more and more seldom by the great stages and for important roles, throws herself into one new love affair after the other. For a time Udet the pilot, whom Kadidja saw in the loge of Ullstein Verlag, was Tilly's favorite. Zuckmayer, who's sitting with Udet, also visited her mother now and then. Kadidja was twelve at the time, and Zuckmayer would play Cowboys and Indians with her. She would waylay him in the dim foyer right after he came in, leaping onto his neck from the linen closet, while holding a long kitchen knife to scalp him.

For a few years now, though, her mother has maintained a more solid relationship with a doctor who is also an author, named Gottfried Benn. Tilly is rather infatuated with him, but Benn keeps her at a distance. Whenever he finally has time for her and they go out, Tilly is as excited as a little girl. She even earned her driver's license, bought a little cabriolet, an Opel, and went on excursions with Benn to the country over the summer. Once, Benn's daughter Nele was also there. Kadidja got along famously with her.

But Kadidja does not care for this dismal Benn. One time she visited him in his Berlin flat on Belle-Alliance-Strasse at the corner of Yorckstrasse, which he also uses as his medical practice. Granted, he is an interesting man, but ultimately he sickens her. For the most part there is nothing about Benn's and her mother's relationship she understands. Once, when she arrived home at night unannounced, the lights were on in every room, but no one was around – until Hans Albers stepped out of her mother's bedroom.

Such affairs are not for her. Kadidja thinks differently and wants above all to be a good person who makes others' lives easier. And yet she often lacks the energy necessary for that. She cannot understand where others derive the strength to attend to their work every day. This was a problem for her back in school, and then all the more so when in 1928 she went off to the Academy of Fine Arts in Dresden. She could, her teachers attested, become a remarkable painter, if she would work more. But she finds it insanely difficult; self-discipline and diligence are not her strong suits, this she knows.

She felt happiest during the holidays in Ammerland on Lake Starnberg. An actress friend of her mother's, Lilly Ackermann, keeps a house there, and a few years earlier Kadidja regularly spent her days there in reverie or playing with Georg, Lilly's son. At the time he was ten, but that didn't matter to Kadidja. On a whim she established a kingdom with him called Kalumina. Here, in this fantasy realm, things would finally unfold according to her ideas. Her will was law, and so she had herself crowned Empress Carola I by Georg and his friends. Together they designed a flag and a constitution. Georg was named chief of the general staff and had to muster an army. It continued on like that for three whole weeks, and when they met again for the subsequent holidays, they kept tinkering with their fantasy world.

It is this time she recalls when she is about to continue her studies at the Berlin Academy. She has been recommended to Emil Orlik, who counts George Grosz among his students. The very attempt to compile a portfolio of her work from Dresden, however, fills her with pure dread. The stink of sheer aversion washes over her with every single page. She'd rather sit down and write the story of her kingdom Kalumina. That might turn into a novel, she thinks. After all, it's about ancient, classical themes: taking leave of one's youth, the travails of becoming an adult, the first premonitions of love. Her father had always wanted to write a novel, but he never managed to. Her ambition is all the greater, and for the first time she cultivates self-discipline and willpower. She senses the old themes in her manuscript taking on a new, an airily light allure.

To her own surprise Kadidja has uncovered a talent in herself she never imagined she had. She can write. She has, if she is given time, a poetic sensibility. Scherl Verlag is convinced by her ability, too, and has added her book to its catalogue: *Kalumina: The Novel of a Summer*. A thousand-mark advance! Nine hundred of that she passes along to her mother who earns less and less acting and has already secretly had to pawn jewelry to be able to make rent.

What is much more important to Kadidja than money is her newly sprouted talent, together with the hope that it may meet with favorable weather in the future and might blossom. All the acquaintances she runs into between loges and tables amid the tumult of the ball buoy her. Initially she won't believe what she hears, embarrassed and ashamed as she so often is. But then she enjoys herself more and more. Resisting so much encouragement is impossible. For a moment she allows herself to be persuaded that even she might be something special. She senses unimagined confidence, overconfidence even. I am, she thinks, I am the Empress of the Press Ball.

*

Erich Maria Remarque was also unable to resist the invitation, especially since he has just completed the rough draft of a new novel, *Three Comrades*. He's treating himself to a little relaxation after such a slog. He hasn't been living in Germany for months now, but there is always plenty of business to take care of in Berlin, and so he has traveled here to meet people, to check off appointments, and, finally, to fight his way through the ball crowd.

He glimpses Zuckmayer in the Ullstein area, but he seems to be fully engrossed in Ernst Udet. Remarque and Zuckmayer have known each other for almost exactly four years. When Remarque was almost finished with his war novel *All Quiet on the Western Front* in 1928, he sent the manuscript first to the most important German publishing house, S. Fischer, but they passed. At Ullstein, however, the editors were enthusiastic and mobilized the entire company to give the book the launch it deserved in their eyes. First, it was serialized in the *Vossische Zeitung*, which belonged to Ullstein. Then, when the novel arrived in bookstores, the *Berliner Illustrirte*, likewise part of the Ullstein concern, moved up its usual publication date by a few days, from Sunday to Thursday, in order to print an article on Remarque's book by Ullstein author Zuckmayer in time for the first date of sale.

It was not a review in the customary sense, nor was it the standard effusive praise from among authorial colleagues. Zuckmayer's article was a drumroll, a fanfare, a clarion call, and also a prophecy: "There is now a book, written by a man named Erich Maria Remarque, lived by millions, and it will be read by millions too, now and for all time … This book belongs in schoolrooms, reading rooms, universities, in every newspaper, on every radio broadcaster, and all that is still not enough."

All Quiet on the Western Front tells the story of a frontline soldier in the First World War, from his emergency early graduation in 1914 to his death in 1918. Remarque had written it in terse, unpoetic, and yet emotion-laden sentences, had recounted the panic and dying in the trenches, the dread of spending entire nights under a barrage of detonating grenades, of the madness of storming into enemy machine-gun fire, and of bayonet slaughter in close combat.

Zuckmayer had experienced much of this himself but had never been able to find a viable language for it. His excitement for *All Quiet on the Western Front* was all the more intense now: "This is what Remarque offers here, for the first time, clear and indelible – what went through the minds of these people, what was happening internally …" The novel gave literary form to the confused, murderous, nerve-wracking experiences of an entire generation and in this way made them communicable. For Zuckmayer – and he suspected not only for him – this was akin to being liberated from an incubus. "We all have experienced time and again that nothing can be said about the war. There is nothing more deplorable than when someone recounts his wartime experiences. That's why we remain silent and wait … Here with Remarque, however, fate itself – the entirety of it – takes on a form for the first time. What was behind it, what was burning underneath – what remains. And written, crafted, lived in such a way that it becomes more than reality: truth. Pure, valid truth."

Indeed, hundreds of thousands of people felt as Zuckmayer did, not only former frontline fighters, but others, too, who hadn't been soldiers, yet who'd wanted to comprehend the experiences these veterans lived with. After only a few weeks the novel had reached a print run of half a million. That same year it was translated into twenty-six languages. An international hit.

And a provocation for all who were trying to sugarcoat war and the death of soldiers, meaning mostly for the German Nationalists and National Socialists. They did battle with the novel and its author with populist lies obstinately repeated and thus hammered into the public imagination; the book debases the fallen, mocks their sacrifice for the Fatherland, drags everything noble about being a soldier through the mud. Because Remarque only spent seven weeks at the front and lay wounded in a field hospital after that, he is a fraud who never really participated in the war, who doesn't know war at all in fact. Because his name was originally Remark, they called him a traitor to the people who derived his pen name Remarque from, of all places, the language of France, the language of the archenemy. Such a one as he has no right to write about the heroism of men who gave their young lives for Germany's honor.

The propaganda battle escalated when the 1930 American film adaptation of *All Quiet on the Western Front* arrived in German cinemas. The day after the premiere, Goebbels sent his SA thugs into movie theaters in Berlin and other cities where they threw stink bombs, released white mice, and threatened or beat viewers until the showings had to be cut short. Instead of protecting the film and its audiences, however, the authorities bowed to pressure and after five days banned further showings "for endangering German prestige." Goebbels triumphantly celebrated the Nazis' first large campaign success: "It was a battle for power between Marxist asphalt democracy and German-conscious state morality. And for the first time in Berlin, we are able to record the fact that asphalt democracy was brought to its knees."

Months afterward, the film will in fact be released again in a considerably abridged version. That, however, can no longer assuage Remarque's disappointment in his country. And regardless of what he

Figure 3: Erich Maria Remarque in 1929

does, says, or writes, he remains a favorite enemy of the right wing. Luckily, *All Quiet on the Western Front* made him a rich man. He purchases a villa on Lago Maggiore in Switzerland, a few kilometers outside Ascona, and puts behind him a Germany he finds more and more alien.

That's why, after the Press Ball, Remarque spends only one brief night in a hotel. Who the new chancellor after Schleicher will be basically no longer affects him at all, no more than the question of whether this ball is the last dance of the republic. Early Sunday morning right after breakfast he gets in his car, a Lancia Dilambda – he loves fast cars and high speeds – and sets off toward the Swiss border. It is a long, cold drive, from north to south, through wintery Germany. It will be almost twenty years before he sees his homeland again.

In just a few weeks, emigrants will circulate his address on Lago Maggiore among themselves like an insider tip. Remarque is known as a generous man. He gives shelter to refugees, slips money into their hands, procures tickets for them to Italy or France. Ernst Toller visits him. The Jewish journalist Felix Manuel Mendelssohn numbers among his guests as well. He stays with him for a few days. In mid-April he is found dead in a ditch near Remarque's estate, with a fractured skull. Did he fall, or was he beaten to death? Swiss newspapers write of an accident. Reading the accounts, Thomas Mann is certain: it was a Nazi attack gone awry. In the dark, young Mendelssohn was "probably mistaken for Remarque" by the assassins.

Hell Reigns

Monday, January 30

Joseph Roth does not intend to wait for the news the day will bring. First thing in the morning he heads to the station and boards a train to Paris. Saying goodbye to Berlin comes easily to him. For years he has worked as a reporter for the *Frankfurter Zeitung*, and being on the road has become second nature for him. He has been living out of hotels and guesthouses for years. "I believe," he once claimed boastfully, "that I would be unable to write if I had a permanent residence."

Four months earlier, toward the end of September 1932, Roth's *The Radetsky March* appeared in print, a masterful novel that, like Thomas Mann's *Buddenbrooks*, tells the story of a family's downfall over the course of several generations: that of the Trottas, who rise under Franz Joseph I, ruler of Austria-Hungary, and perish with him in the First World War. It is one of his most significant books. Roth worked hard on it and thus has reason to restrain himself from making political statements so as neither to inflame anyone against him, nor to endanger the sale of his novel in Germany.

Delicate maneuvering does not, however, number among his talents. In questions of morality he is inclined to drastic decisions. Perhaps it is also because of his latent propensity for self-destruction, but when it comes to the Nazis, Roth does not want to mince words. He wants to go to battle with them, unquestioning, even if he knows that they are endlessly superior in force: "Every shred of hope must be renounced, once and for all, with calm and strength, as is right and proper." In one of his letters to Stefan Zweig, he writes: "By now it will have become clear to you that we drift toward great calamities. Aside from the private ones – our literary and material existence is of course obliterated – the whole thing will lead to a new war. I fear the worst for our lives. Letting barbarism assume rule bore fruit. Do not delude yourself. Hell reigns." Roth's incentive is not survival. He marches off to battle, armed with pen and paper and with a firm belief in his downfall.

*

Changing of the guard among journalists: Joseph Roth leaves the city, and Egon Erwin Kisch arrives. He again lives up to his sobriquet, self-conferred, "the raging reporter." Over the previous year he has been in China, which is being torn apart by civil war, has seen some of the most miserable places there, visited a home for elderly former imperial eunuchs, came across defenseless beggarwomen in the streets who are not even admitted to the guild for beggars, was shown a tuberculosis hospice for female workers, half-children still, waiting hopelessly for death. Then he traveled to Moscow, in a manic frenzy recorded his experiences in the book *Secret China*, and immediately set out to be punctually on the scene for Hitler's accession to power in Germany today.

Kisch is an international star. Even in China, he claims, people recognized him – although none of his books has been translated into any of the Chinese languages. He is a Jew from Prague who, like Rilke and Kafka, belongs to the city's German-speaking minority. He enjoys making himself the central character of his stories and gives his readers the impression they are standing shoulder to shoulder with him at key venues around the globe. And he possesses great skill in styling himself the epitome of the journalist-as-adventurer and hardcore man: ever in transit to some hotspot or battlefield, ever chain-smoking, ever on the trail of some secret by semi-legal means.

Initially he was a frontline soldier in the First World War, then later, after being severely wounded, a press officer. That multi-ethnic massacre honed his sense of political responsibility. He became a member of illegal soldiers' councils, organized strikes and peace demonstrations, and joined the Communist Party.

That changed him as an author, too. At first he swore allegiance to the ideal of the independent journalist: "The reporter has no bias, is not obligated to justify anything, and has no point of view. His task is to be an impartial witness and provide impartial testimony." After joining the party, however, he grew more and more into the role of an activist who wants to use his articles to serve purposes deemed politically correct.

His reports read with the same thrill and vividness as before, but their propagandistic overtones can hardly fail to go unheard.

Kisch disembarks at Anhalter Bahnhof. Until now he's scarcely concerned himself with the Nazis. As a staunch communist he knows the direction world history will take: the path to proletarian revolution. Fascism or National Socialism are just waystations on it. Now, though, he wants to get a closer look and experience for himself the – ultimately victorious – battle for power by the KPD.

He rides to his new apartment on Motzstrasse, near Nollendorfplatz. It's only a sublet room, and he normally lives better. He hails from a wealthy Jewish family and is a successful author, which he doesn't deny. He may have committed himself to the cause of the proletarians, but he doesn't live like one. Why would he? His library is in storage here in Berlin, forty boxes with a total of four thousand volumes, which are worth a small fortune by themselves. He considers shipping his books to his mother in Prague for safety's sake; it would be a shame if they were to be lost in the chaos of the coming political battles. Maybe that will be the second big task of his stay in Berlin.

*

Anhalter Bahnhof is massive, a place you can easily miss someone in passing. On the same morning Kisch arrives, Lieutenant General Werner von Blomberg steps off the night train arriving from Geneva. There he was participating as the German delegate in an international disarmament conference where Germany, absurdly, wanted to push through an enlargement of its Reichswehr, which the Treaty of Versailles limited to 100,000 men. Yesterday, however, he was surprised in Geneva by a telegram from Hindenburg summoning him to Berlin immediately.

A brouhaha is raging there behind the scenes of power, hardly in check, and almost anything could happen. Kurt von Hammerstein, chief of the army command, wants to prevent Hitler's nomination as chancellor at any cost and over the prior week has received assurances in conversation with Hindenburg that the "Austrian private" has no chance of being appointed to that office. Not two days later, however, Hammerstein is forced to realize that Papen has changed the Reich President's mind and that Hitler is in fact moments away from assuming power. As a last resort he proposes a putsch to Schleicher, who already

Figure 4: Anhalter Bahnhof

resigned and is only conducting business as chancellor and Minister of the Reichswehr on a provisional basis. The Potsdam garrison is to be put on alert, Hitler arrested, a state of emergency declared, and the obviously no longer sane Hindenburg deposed. Since Schleicher rejects his plan, Hammerstein attempts to salvage what can still be salvaged; he meets with Hitler and urges him to concede that Schleicher remain Minister of the Reichswehr in the new cabinet and thus retain hold of the country's military might. Hitler assures him he will, likely to sideline him for the next few hours, although Hindenburg and he have long since arranged to replace Schleicher with Blomberg.

And so, when he arrives that morning from Geneva, Blomberg is welcomed on the platform by two gentlemen at once: by Hammerstein's adjutant, who is to intercept him to summon him to the Ministry of the Reichswehr, and by Oskar von Hindenburg, son of the Reich President, who is tasked with bringing him to his father as quickly as possible. Faced with the orders of both his military superiors and the head of state, Blomberg decides to follow Hindenburg's directive. Shortly thereafter, around 9 a.m., the Reich President swears him in as Minister of the Reichswehr in a government that doesn't even exist yet. He thereby flouts the constitution of the republic, according to which ministers may only be appointed at the suggestion of the chancellor. Hitler may agree that Blomberg be Minister of the Reichswehr, but at this stage he is not yet chancellor. Yet no one bothers about such juridical subtleties anymore now.

In order to make Blomberg's appointment more plausible and so as not to upset the rank structure of the Wehrmacht all too much, Hindenburg promotes him to general of the infantry in the same breath. After the ceremony, Oskar von Hindenburg nevertheless urgently advises him not to go right away to the Ministry of the Reichswehr on Bendlerstrasse, which he now heads. For Hammerstein is waiting there, and he will presumably arrest him promptly upon his arrival.

*

Klaus Mann was woken up around 10 a.m. and then had Hans Feist take him to Anhalter Bahnhof. Feist is almost twenty years older than Klaus Mann and not his preferred lover, but he is wealthy, often quite generous, and, aside from his primary occupation as translator, is also a doctor, which greatly facilitates Klaus' access to morphine.

Yesterday Mann indulged in another injection together with Feist and his friend Wolfgang Hellmert, a somewhat idly unproductive poet who means more to him than Feist. No wonder he isn't fully well this morning. Only with great effort did he manage to pack his suitcase. Nevertheless, he feels as if he is being propelled forward by some malevolent premonition. He's in a bad mood, and he doesn't wish to stay a moment longer, but rather to travel to Leipzig to see Erich Ebermayer, an author friend of his with whom he's working on a theatrical adaptation of Saint-Exupéry's novel *Night Flight*. He will not likely win any literary laurels with this enterprise, but he might improve his financial situation; the Frenchman Saint-Exupéry is currently a popular man among Germany's young people.

The customary parting lamentations from Feist, who incessantly courts him, are a bit irksome. Klaus Mann is glad when he can finally collapse alone into his compartment seat and the train departs. But then, to make matters worse, he gets sick.

*

Last night Hitler heard the rumor that the Reichswehr could stage a coup against Hindenburg. Hammerstein and Schleicher are said to be behind the plan. As a countermeasure he put Berlin's SA and SS units on alert and, inflamed with rage, demands that a police officer devoted to him prepare to occupy the government quarter with several police battalions. Hitler of course does not have official authority over the battalions, but that is hardly of any consequence since it is not entirely clear which battalions Hitler, in his fury, means and whether they even exist. Until five in the morning he remains in Goebbels' apartment on Reichskanzlerplatz, debating with his entourage how he might respond to his opponents' potential attempts to prevent his appointment. Then, to get a bit of shuteye, he has himself taken to his suite at the hotel *Kaiserhof*.

In the morning the members of the new governing coalition between NSDAP and the German Nationalist DNVP gradually turn up at vice-chancellor-elect Papen's flat. He still resides in the annex of the Reich Chancellery. While he was forced to resign as chancellor two months earlier, to date he has not vacated the chancellor's apartment for Schleicher, his successor. He scorns the rules of the republic and attempts at any cost, even that of being ridiculous, to cling to his claim to power.

Not everything has gone smoothly in the preparations to swear in the government over the past few days. Franz Seldte, head of the *Stahlhelm*, the militia organization of the German Nationalists, is to inherit the Ministry of Labor. But he was not told the date and time of his appointment. When Hindenburg's state secretary Otto Meissner telephones him to ask where he is, he is still lying in bed, and it is expected that he will scarcely be able to make it on time to the swearing-in ceremony. And so his deputy Theodor Duesterberg is to step in for him as a replacement. That, in turn, is awkward because only months earlier, while campaigning to be elected Reich President, he was labeled "racially inferior" by Nazi newspapers on account of his Jewish grandfather and assailed with the vilest insults for weeks afterward. Duesterberg promptly asks whether it is absolutely necessary that the government be ushered into office under such time pressure, whether a postponement might be possible. At this, Papen turns the rumors circulating about a coup to good account, fearing for the painstakingly arranged coalition and his office as vice-chancellor, and claims a military dictatorship under

Schleicher and Hammerstein is looming: "If a government isn't formed by eleven o'clock, the Reichswehr will march."

Meanwhile, Hitler is chauffeured in an open Mercedes some hundred meters from the *Kaiserhof* to the annex of the Reich Chancellery, along with his future ministers Göring and Wilhelm Frick. Because of the cold they are wearing heavy, dark coats and have pulled their hats down over their faces; they look a bit like gangsters on their way to extort protection money. When they arrive at Papen's, Hitler again proves himself to be a quick-witted improvisational actor. He goes straight up to Duesterberg, takes his hand, and with wavering voice and tears in his eyes declares to him: "I regret the insults inflicted upon you by my press. I assure you on my word that I did not instigate them."

From Papen's chancellor flat the route is not a long one. At around 10:45 the group of men sets out. Because press photographers are waiting in the cold in front of the building, Papen leads them through a rear exit and via the wintry ministerial gardens to the Reich Chancellery. It is there that Hindenburg provisionally maintains his offices, as the presidential palace has been under renovation since the summer. This brief peregrination takes place, as it were, before the eyes of the Prussian Academy of the Arts, whose seat is but a hundred meters north on Pariser Platz. If they'd wanted, the Academy members could watch from their building's rear windows as the politicians trudge through the snow in their solemn, dark garb.

There is one central point Papen has not yet resolved during their coalition negotiations, however. Hitler insists on asking Hindenburg to dissolve parliament and announce new elections immediately after he takes office. The people, Hitler maintains, ought to confirm the new cabinet democratically. He doesn't say it aloud, but he's banking on a landslide victory for the NSDAP because as head of government he's planning to fund his campaign propaganda out of the public purse. The chairman of the German Nationalists, Alfred Hugenberg, wants to avoid this very scenario though because his party expended great effort to gain just under two and a half percent in the most recent election, which he fears losing again to the superior competition of a Chancellor Hitler with his quadruply large NSDAP.

Not until they are in the office of Hindenburg's state secretary Meissner do Hitler and Papen lay their cards on the table. Hugenberg is furious, feels blindsided, and refuses all the more vehemently. From his perspective, new elections are unnecessary, and he is not willing to accede to this stipulation. Papen and Hitler take Hugenberg aside to a window bay and argue fiercely. To ease his misgivings, Hitler infuses his voice with pathos again and gives his solemn word of honor that he will change nothing in the government coalition or the composition of the cabinet after the elections, regardless of whatever balance of power prevails in parliament. In this Papen sees a near ultimatum as an argument for it: "You couldn't doubt a German man's solemn word of honor." Hugenberg stands pat, however. He would rather topple the laboriously negotiated coalition at the actual last minute. At that moment State Secretary Meissner enters the room, pocket watch in hand, with the admonishment not to keep the Reich President waiting, for it is already 11:15.

It is these words that overcome Hugenberg's resistance. The thought of appearing disrespectful to an authority figure like Hindenburg he finds unbearable. For him, as for all German Nationalists, the president is a hero of the world war, and not at any price does he intend to stand in the way of the president's schedule. Acting contrary to his own interests and all rules of political reason, he agrees to Hitler's stipulation, and the assembled can now finally proceed to the swearing-in.

At the last minute, Franz Seidte, the designated Minister of Labor, shows up after all. And so the certificate of appointment is taken from Duesterberg's hands and ripped up. The group ascends the stairs to the reception hall, Hindenburg enters, reads aloud the oath of office for each and every member of cabinet, and has them repeat it. First of all, Hitler: "I will use my power for the well-being of the German people, uphold the constitution and the laws of the empire, conscientiously fulfill the duties incumbent upon me, and conduct my affairs impartially and fairly toward everyone." Afterward Hitler gives a short speech, which is not planned, wherein he emphasizes his intention to return to normal parliamentary democracy after the period of emergency decrees. He schedules the first cabinet meeting for that afternoon. By twelve o'clock it is all over.

From a nationalistic perspective, the cabinet appears moderate: Franz von Papen is vice-chancellor and provisional head of state for Prussia, for which the Reich government has likewise been responsible since the "Preußenschlag." It is he who enjoys Hindenburg's trust. Without Papen's presence Hitler may not discuss any government business with Hindenburg, which is supposed to prevent intrigue. Furthermore, Reich President Hindenburg can at any time send the new chancellor packing. After all, Hitler also heads a minority government only. Important departments like the Foreign, Finance, and Justice Ministries are going to experts without party affiliation, Hugenberg is getting a super ministry for economics, agriculture, and food, and Seldte is Minister of Labor. By contrast, the National Socialists receive only the Ministry of the Interior for Wilhelm Frick and for Göring a ministerial posting without portfolio as well as the Prussian state Ministry of the Interior. It would appear as if Papen's plan to "box in" Hitler with established right-wing powers and thereby restrain him politically had worked. To a critic who accuses him of having handed over the country to a dictator, Papen replies: "What do you want? In two months we've squeezed Hitler into a corner and made him squeal."

The usual NSDAP potentates are waiting at the *Kaiserhof*, vacillating between anticipation and final doubts. They have convened quite a few of the rank and file on the streets between the hotel and the Reich Chancellery. For his retinue and himself Hitler has leased an entire floor of the hotel at a price the party hasn't been able to afford for a long while. The numerous election campaigns in recent years have emptied their coffers dramatically and accumulated precarious debts. Should the government takeover fail, bankruptcy is imminent. The *Kaiserhof*, however, is not merely the finest hotel in the city, but by virtue of its location at the center of the government district, it also has a semi-official air to it. Hitler has been staying here for years whenever he is in Berlin, not least because the owners are staunch right-wingers who fly the black, white, and red colors of the German Empire instead of the black, red, and gold flag of the republic. If Hitler had opted for other, cheaper lodgings because of strained finances, it would have come across as an admission of his party's weakness.

With field glasses Ernst Röhm, Chief of Staff to the SA, observes the entrance of the Reich Chancellery from a hotel window. Göring steps out of the building first, shouting the news to the bystanders. Then he, Frick, and Hitler board the Mercedes and ride to the *Kaiserhof* at an idle, straight through the throngs of people surging right up to the vehicle, cheering the freshly appointed chancellor with right arms raised erect and ecstatic cries. This short stretch takes the car several minutes. As soon as Hitler has alighted, his entourage surrounds him and accompanies him into the hotel. Goebbels, Heß, and Röhm shake his hand, moved, while many have tears in their eyes. Their greatest aim has finally been achieved; their Führer is chancellor. The noise of the jubilant crowd on the street can be heard through the windows of the *Kaiserhof*, but the men encircling Hitler are struck silent, overcome with emotion.

*

In the Café Kranzler outpost on Kurfürstendamm, Georg Kaiser has made an appointment for lunch with his editor and publisher Fritz Landshoff. In his mid-fifties, Kaiser is already a living legend of Expressionism. He writes plays at a frenetic speed that do not put on stage characters so much as theories poorly disguised as characters. His works give the impression of being literary laboratory experiments; they are games for the mind, not dramatic spectacles. Still, audiences like them, and Kaiser enjoys astonishing success with them. Whoever goes to the theater to see one of his dramas knows what to expect: a dense succession of scenes, laconic, fervently sermonizing language, and images of isolation in a modern world dominated by technology.

Business is good for Kaiser, and in a few days his winter fairy tale *Silver Lake*, with music by Kurt Weill, will celebrate its world premiere simultaneously in three city theaters: in Leipzig, Magdeburg, and Erfurt. On the other hand, Landshoff is plagued by serious financial difficulties. Together with his partner Gustav Kiepenheuer, who lent his name to their publishing house, he must prepare for a tricky meeting with creditors. Debts have accrued with printers, bookbinders, and paper suppliers, the mood is poor, and a declaration of bankruptcy is likely unavoidable at this point. Although Kaiser possesses a phenomenal talent for blocking out all the unpleasant facts of life in order to plunge fully into his literary world of archetypes, he worries about the publishing house and about young Landshoff. He'd like nothing more than to discourage him from facing up to his creditors. It awakens far too many memories of the time he was taken to court in 1921. Back then Kaiser had rented a sumptuously furnished house to be able to work on his plays without interruption, sold off the furniture piece by piece, and lived off the proceeds. That anyone dared to sue him, a poet, for such a mundane transgression he considered a national disaster. He demanded flags be flown at half-staff throughout the country and his colleagues Heinrich von Kleist and Georg Büchner, who both met an untimely demise, be considered his defense counsel. The judge showed staggering patience with him and sentenced Kaiser to a year in prison for misappropriation.

When Landshoff now appears at Café Kranzler, however, the financial misery of his publishing house all at once becomes incidental. A newspaper boy is waving around the *B. Z. am Mittag*, whose title page proclaims in the usual giant lettering: "Adolf Hitler, Reich Chancellor." Landshoff is dumbstruck. Horrified, he buys one of the newspapers. Kiepenheuer Verlag has never left any doubt about its anti-Hitler leanings. If the Nazis come to power now, what chances of survival can their battered enterprise possibly have? Landshoff has invested a great deal of money in the press from his reserves – will he, at just over thirty, soon be not just unemployed, but ruined, to boot?

After hurrying to Kaiser's table at the Kranzler, he holds out the newspaper for him, agitated. Yet Kaiser has not the slightest desire to get involved in the political quarrels of the day; over the last few months the chancellors have alternated too often and too quickly. Kaiser can no longer take it seriously. The travesty of politics is among the pesky aspects of reality he blocks out. "A bowling league diversifies its board of directors," he says to Landshoff with a shrug, taking the paper from him and tossing it into one of the empty chairs at their table. He doesn't want to discuss such matters now.

By contrast, Hermann Kesten, the deputy editor at Kiepenheuer Verlag, does not doubt for a second that their lives have changed once and for all with the headline in the *B. Z. am Mittag*. He has an appointment with Landshoff and has promised to fetch him after his lunch with Kaiser. He enters the Kranzler at the moment they have the waiter bring them their coffee. He joins them at their table for a moment, orders a cup for himself as well, but he no longer possesses the calm to drink it. He leaps up and runs home.

His whole family – his mother, his sister Gina, and his wife Toni – is in bed with the flu. He himself has only just recovered. Only fifteen years after the Spanish flu took the lives of millions of people between 1918 and 1920, no one takes this illness lightly. Newspapers report the number of new infections each day, and today, in Berlin alone, there are 373. In a city like Frankfurt am Main there are over 2,000 infected persons, but schools are to be closed only in the direst of emergencies because many schoolchildren live in such cramped housing conditions that they would otherwise have to spend their days on the streets despite the cold.

Kesten knows he cannot, therefore, leave Germany at the moment. All the same, he grabs his and his wife's passports at home and heads to the French consulate to apply for visas for them both. Afterward he withdraws as much travel money from his bank as he is permitted to take abroad under the Foreign Currency Act. When he enters his flat again, he runs into the doctor treating the family, who issues an emphatic warning; his wife will be ready to travel in eight days at the earliest. Their escape must be postponed.

*

Around midday Erich Ebermayer receives Klaus Mann's telegram in Leipzig: "Arriving today 14:14. Regards Klaus." Around 2 p.m. Ebermayer drives to the train station. It is a gray, dreary winter's day. When Ebermayer steps into the gigantic front hall, the voices of the newspaper salesmen are already echoing toward him: "Adolf Hitler, Reich Chancellor." He purchases a *B. Z. am Mittag* and is still pallid when he receives his visitor on the platform.

At first Klaus Mann smiles but then startles the second he has deciphered the headline from the newspaper Ebermayer is handing him. He'd never have thought it possible. He stares at the page without reading it. "This is terrible …" He begins walking slowly, then faster and faster without even knowing where. His very next thought concerns his father. "It will also be terrible for the Magician …"

He and Ebermayer go to a restaurant, dine, try to calm themselves, and aim to work on their *Night Flight* project at Ebermayer's afterward because nothing better occurs to them. For today they have planned to sketch out the third act in broad strokes, but they are absent-minded and make no progress. At all once their work has taken on a spurious aspect. Amid the new political situation, it is obvious no theater in the country will be interested in a dramatization of a French novel by the homosexual Nazi-adversary Klaus Mann and his likewise gay friend Ebermayer. Why waste more time on it? "You're going to have to leave my name off of it …," Mann suggests. "Nonsense! We'll put the play on ice for a year," Ebermayer reassures him.

They end their work early and head to the theater where they see *Lob des Landes* [*Praise for the Land*], a comedy by the Austrian Richard Billinger, who has enjoyed so much success recently and shared the Kleist Prize with Else Lasker-Schüler the previous year. Klaus Mann is curious but quickly realizes he doesn't like the piece. For a metropolitan man like himself, there's far too much nature mysticism in it. What's more, the actors can't crack the Austrian dialect.

Around midnight, Ebermayer takes him to the train station. They say their goodbyes outside the sleeping coach and arrange for Ebermayer to visit Klaus Mann in Munich two weeks later so they can make further progress on *Night Flight*. It is one of those visits that is agreed upon without those involved seriously believing they'll be able to keep the engagement. Klaus plops into his compartment seat, waving to his friend on the platform. The train then vanishes into the night. They never see each other again.

*

That afternoon Hitler has himself photographed standing behind the chancellor's desk: the official picture of his inauguration. In the photo he stares off sideways into space beyond the camera with both hands tucked into the pockets of his double-breasted blazer, an oddly defiant gesture. It is intended to show decisiveness, of course, but it rather seems like he has something in his hands to hide. He hasn't left himself much elbowroom: before him the nearly empty chancellor's desk, to the left the chancellor's chair upholstered in velvet, behind him a half-height file cabinet, to the right a side table. To lend the picture a bright, genial air in spite of the stiff, imposing scenery, the photographer has placed a basket with lilies of the valley on the file cabinet at Hitler's back.

Later, during the first cabinet meeting, the argument between Hitler and Hugenberg about new elections erupts again. Hugenberg's opposition no longer carries any weight now, so nothing remains for him to do but place the decision in Hindenburg's hands, who as Reich President can order or disallow the dissolution of parliament.

That evening, people begin gathering on Pariser Platz and along Wilhelmstrasse. The new government has announced a torchlight parade. Street vendors show up to sell sausages and warming beverages.

From 8:30 p.m., SA and SS units as well as detachments of the German Nationalist *Stahlhelm* march in long columns through the Tiergarten toward the Brandenburg Gate. There are said to be 25,000 men altogether. On Charlottenburger Chaussee, which leads arrow-straight through the nocturnal park, the raised torches of the uniformed men to the right and left of the parade line look like two slender glowing ribbons. Drums boom, and the smell of kerosene lingers in the air. Marching between the columns are flagbearers and brass bands playing the German or Prussian anthems. But as soon as they have passed the Brandenburg Gate and step onto Pariser Platz, where the French embassy is also located, some of the bands cease playing, follow with a drumroll, and strike up the melody of an old soldier's ballad, the main line of which goes: "Victorious we shall vanquish France."

Also located on Pariser Platz, just beside the Brandenburg Gate, is Max Liebermann's villa. He is now eighty-five years old, just like Hindenburg, whose portrait he painted a few years earlier. At the time it almost became an affair of state. Why, some of the right-wing nationalist newspapers criticized, did the Jew Liebermann of all people receive the commission to paint the German head of state? At the time, Liebermann took it in his stride. After all, he was not only one of Germany's most respected painters, an Impressionist of international stature, but also most favorably networked among the country's intellectual and artistically inclined society, very wealthy, and not least President of the Prussian Academy of the Arts. He did not want to let his feathers get ruffled by a few right-wing yappers who were incapable of detracting from his fame anyway. He is not a religious Jew, having not visited a synagogue since his parents' death. It goes without saying that he feels himself to be a German and a Berliner; he is convinced of the success of Jewish assimilation.

The attitude toward Jews has changed rapidly, however. Liebermann is a conservative, a bourgeois man through and through who firmly believes he can rely on the old Prussian tolerance and the liberality of the republic. In the past several years, though, he couldn't help but take note of an ever more aggressive strain of anti-Semitism running rampant even in supposedly better, more cultured social circles.

Last summer, after twelve years, he relinquished his role as President of the Academy. In gratitude for his efforts, the Academic Senate

appointed him Honorary President. Max von Schillings was elected as
his successor, however: the composer who no longer composes and who
openly professes his hostility toward the state and toward Jews whenever
he refers to the Weimar Republic disparagingly as "Semitania." This
much is clear to Liebermann: with Hitler's victory, his dream of assimilation is spent. "I cannot fill my belly," he says, "nearly as much as I'd
like to puke."

At Pariser Platz the line of marchers veers to the right down
Wilhelmstrasse. The torches cast an uneasy light on the buildings and
the people on the curb. Behind an illuminated window of the old Reich
Chancellery, Hindenburg reviews the parade, bolstered by his cane
which he occasionally taps to the rhythm of the march music. One
building farther on, Hitler is standing in an open window of his new
official seat. He is illumined by spotlights from across the street and,
surrounded by Rudolf Heß and his ministers Göring and Frick, salutes
the crowd below again and again with his raised right arm. At one point,
men break loose from their column, form a human ladder, and hand
Hitler a rose through his window. Later he has to slip on a brown SA
jacket because of the cold, but he is delighted by the hours-long parade
review and by Goebbels, who organized it all: "Where in the world did
he get ahold of so many torches in such a short time?"

Goebbels takes care of everything. He forced a radio broadcast of the
torchlight parade; all stations part of Reich Broadcasting join, some of
them against the will of those responsible. Only Bayerischer Rundfunk
successfully refuses. He and Göring give ebullient speeches that also have
to be broadcast. Not until around midnight does he dismiss the steadfast
final few still in the streets defying the freezing cold with shouts of *Heil*
to Hitler and Hindenburg.

A gargantuan propaganda production. In Goebbels' eyes, however,
it still wasn't large or successful enough. The few film recordings that
are made – low-contrast and often jittery – disappoint him above all as
they generate too little visual intensity for the cinematic newsreels. He
wants to present the public with a true victory parade that looks as if
it could steamroll over anything in its way. That summer he therefore
decides to stage the torchlight parade for the cameras one more time
and even more impressively: more men, more torches, more compact
columns, better camera angles. This time the men march in extra-wide

Figure 5: Torchlight parade in Berlin on the evening of January 30, 1933

rows, and almost everyone carries a torch, not just those along the sides, such that the parade gushes through the Brandenburg Gate like a river of fire. Whoever looks closely at these images will notice that there is no large crush of people along the street curbs in this post-hoc shoot. But Goebbels doesn't much care about that; with skillful cutting that will no longer be apparent.

*

Carl von Ossietzky, editor-in-chief of the *Weltbühne*, is indefatigable as ever. While the editorial staff was working, news came that Hitler had been sworn in as Reich Chancellor. Late that afternoon Ossietzky sets out for a meeting of the *Schutzverband deutscher Schriftsteller* [*Association for the Protection of German Writers*] in a bar at Hallesches Tor. The *Schutzverband* is something like the authors' union. Fiery as ever, Erich Mühsam talks himself into a rage and demands systematic resistance to the Nazis. Most of the other authors smirk at Mühsam's indignation; this Hitler nightmare will be over just as soon as it began. Then Ossietzky rises, everyone in the bar falls silent, and in a quiet voice he says: "This will last a great deal longer than you think. Perhaps years. We are powerless against it. But each of us can promise not to cede a single inch to those now in power."

After the meeting, Ossietzky makes his way by U-Bahn to the convention of the *Liga für Menschenrechte* [*League for Human Rights*] on Monbijouplatz. When the train enters Kaiserhof subway station, he gets out to see the Nazi fuss for himself. Ascending the stairs, he sees the immeasurable ranks of brownshirts marching past, the flickering torchlight on their faces. Ossietzky watches the pageantry for a moment, purses his lips, then turns around, and heads back down the stairs. The *Liga* wants to organize a rally in the Beethovensaal the following Friday at which Ossietzky is to give a speech.

*

This evening Harry Graf Kessler is going to the hotel *Kaiserhof*, though not to celebrate the new chancellor, but to attend a long-planned dinner with subsequent lecture. The speaker is Richard Nikolaus Graf Coudenhove-Kalergi, an Austrian writer with a Japanese mother, who promotes an economically and politically united, federalist Europe wherever his speaking engagements take him.

Kessler knows of these pan-European proposals, which he finds congenial but ultimately unpersuasive. Coudenhove-Kalergi may be able to describe the advantages of a united Europe with impressive loquaciousness, but he all too easily skips over the infinitely many conflicts and political antagonisms dividing the continent. And Kessler knows a thing or two about this eternal quarreling. After the end of the world war, he devoted a few years of his life to politics, advocating for the idea of a different league of nations in which not states are to be represented, but supranational institutions, which is to say, trade associations, religious communities, workers' organizations, or academies. Its purpose was to have been combating the egotism of nations and above all placing more power in the hands of transnational forces. Resistance to his plan was too great, however, so it remained a utopia, and Kessler ultimately gave it up.

Tenacity does not rank among his greatest virtues. Kessler doesn't need it. His family is filthy rich. His mother is British, his father was German, he grew up in France, and then went to school in Ascot and Hamburg – a pedigree that is both a blessing and a curse for him at once. He pursued neither his legal education nor his diplomatic and political ambitions with consistency, instead spending the majority of his time as a collector and patron of the arts and as an international traveler. There are but few significant European artists and writers he doesn't know personally; it is said his notebook lists ten thousand names and addresses.

Many people who don't know him very well see in him the perfect example of a dandy: unconstrained, highly intelligent, and endowed with an immaculate sense of style. But he also suffers from his unconstraint. He feels the need for a foundation or a meaning that might give his life direction, and since he anxiously conceals his homosexuality, he has also never found a stable life partner. He lacks the playful lightheartedness that is part of the ideal of the dandy.

When Kessler leaves the *Kaiserhof* after Coudenhove-Kalergi's lecture, he has the feeling of having gotten caught up in a kind of military carnival. Even in the hotel corridors he runs across SA and SS people on patrol. In the lobby and in front of the entrance, SS men in uniform are standing in a line. When he steps into the street, he sees SA columns marching past the hotel from Wilhelmsplatz. On a balcony above the *Kaiserhof* entrance, Röhm is standing together with the Berlin SA chief Graf von Helldorff and a few others from the second ranks of the NSDAP. They cannot resist the temptation to emulate their great Führer and review the parade as well. Like him, they stand there hour after hour, watching the people marching by and shooting their right arms into the air to salute the crowd again and again.

The sidewalks and Wilhelmsplatz itself are bursting with gawkers. Kessler and his friends had wanted to have a beer at Fürstenberg-Bräu on Potsdamer Platz, but their progress through the crush of people is laborious. Even on Potsdamer Platz the squad leaders have their people marching in military formation, but no one knows where to exactly, so they stick with a constant back-and-forth. Kessler has no desire to watch this and disappears with his companions into Fürstenberg-Bräu. Here, too, pure carnival ambiance, but here it's apt.

*

Shortly after 10 p.m., Erich Kästner and Hermann Kesten meet in the *Weinstube Schwanneke*, not far from Tauentzien. Here in the western part of the city all is quiet, with at most the odd man in the streets returning home from the torchlight parade. The wine bar is actually named *Stephanie*, but most of the guests call it after the owner, actor Viktor Schwanneke. It is not a large venue, just twenty tables, some of them set in window nooks. Among theater folk and authors Schwanneke is well known, so his wine bar quickly became one of the most important meeting places in the city for artists. Dramatists like Brecht, Zuckmayer, or Ödön von Horváth, critics like Alfred Kerr, publishers like Ernst Rowohlt, actors like Fritz Kortner, Werner Krauß, or Elisabeth Bergner and Käthe Dorsch sit together here, not all at the same table – their ideological or personal sensibilities are too ample for that – but in the same room at any rate.

"We have to leave Germany," Kesten presses his friend. "We can't write here anymore, can't print anything anymore. Hitler's waging a dictatorship, chopping off heads, waging war."

"No," Kästner says, "you have to leave, I have to stay." Kesten is Jewish, but he isn't. He declares his intent to write *the* novel about the Third Reich. Someone has to bear witness and tell the stories of this coming age. That's what he's taken upon himself to do.

*

Sturm 33 of Charlottenburg's SA has the worst reputation imaginable. It is a household name throughout Berlin; wherever it shows up, blood flows. The heads of the unit are Fritz Hahn and Hans Maikowski, both only in their mid-twenties but experts in street terror for years now. It ranks among the favorite activities of *Sturm 33* to go to Kurfürstendamm on Sunday, together with other SA divisions, and harass passersby. A uniformed portion of the storm troopers walks into the middle of the street, shouting slogans and waving Nazi flags. They are accompanied on each side of the street by particularly burly comrades in plainclothes who jostle or thrash anyone on the sidewalks they take for a Jew or who doesn't display the enthusiasm for their deployment and flags they'd hoped.

Hahn and Maikowski do not content themselves with brawling alone, however. Both have already shot and killed communists during street battles, and ever since their brigade has been known as the "Murderer *Sturm*." After these murders Hahn and Maikowski each went into hiding for a few months abroad but later returned to Berlin largely scot-free.

The SA's attacks are not tracked by the police with very much persistence. When Maikowski was forced to confess under questioning the previous year to having killed a communist, he was arrested, to be sure, but released a few weeks later by the Christmas amnesty Hindenburg ordered. As though homicide were a trivial offense.

Obviously, *Sturm 33* is also participating in the torchlight parade to honor Hitler. The men would have insisted on it, come hell or high water. After the pass in review by Hindenburg and the various Nazi bigwigs, however, Maikowski and his people have no desire to go home just yet. Now they are especially bent on causing a ruckus and march into the "red neighborhood," a district in Charlottenburg considered the stronghold of communists. Here they shout slogans, accost passersby, break windows, and finally run into men from the *Häuserschutzstaffeln*, groups formed for self-defense to protect homes against such SA incursions. Neither Maikowski nor Hahn, known as the "Roter Hahn," or "Red Cock," because of his eye-catching hair color, are anonymous strangers here; people know them, hate them, scream insults at them. The circumstances are explosive.

Then, on Wallstrasse, shots are fired. Maikowski collapses, as does a police officer beside him, Sergeant Josef Zauritz. He had been observing *Sturm 33* and was about to call for backup because he sensed the situation escalating. Both men are lying in front of the building at Wallstrasse 24. Ambulances are called, but help arrives too late; both die in hospital shortly thereafter.

Now, finally, several police units move in and search the adjoining buildings. Officers find three residents with gunshot wounds and arrest fifteen men in total whom they label as suspects. Living in the building at Wallstrasse 24, right at the scene of the crime, is Rudi Carius, a precision mechanic. He is still young, twenty-six years old, an operative of the KPD, and he is noted by investigators as a suspect, too, but they are unable to arrest him because he went straight to ground after the shooting and cannot be found.

Those now in power are breathing down the police's necks and want to see results, but Carius seems to have vanished from the face of the earth. He has a girlfriend, a strawberry blonde, voluptuous beauty working as a hostess at the night club *Bajadere* or at the bar *Kakadu* near Kurfürstendamm. Her real name is Emmy Westphal, but she goes

by Nelly Kröger and at thirty-five years of age does not number among
the youngest in her profession. She likes to drink quite a bit, but alcohol
hasn't yet bloated her so she is as attractive as ever. In June of 1929, Nelly
met a stocky man of almost sixty at *Bajadere*. With his graying mustache
and thin goatee, he resembles a Spanish grandee. He is the author
Heinrich Mann, who has just broken things off with Trude Hesterberg
or she with him. He is a bit lonesome and, like his novel's protagonist
Professor Unrat, likes to spend evenings in night clubs. As the daughter
of a fisherman and a maid, Nelly comes from a very different world than
Heinrich Mann, the son of patricians. She has little to say about art or
literature. That doesn't bother him, though. He likes it when she chats
so informally – some would say chatters – and both hail from the region
around Lübeck, a fact that initially bridges the divide between them.
Mann also has stories to tell that sound to Nelly like they come from the
society pages of magazines: not just about that cheeky Trude Hesterberg,
but also about the UFA film studios in Neubabelsberg where the principal
photography for *The Blue Angel* is being prepared. Then, in autumn of
1929, to top it off, Heinrich's brother Thomas receives the Nobel Prize for
Literature, and the newspapers are full of photos of him and his family.

No wonder Nelly feels as though she has hit the jackpot. She, a
barmaid, and Heinrich Mann, one of the most famous writers in the
country. In the spring he's invited her to Nice for a few weeks where
they'll stay in the *Hôtel de Nice*, a grand hotel in the center of town.

But that's why Nelly did not break up with young Carius. Heinrich
and Rudi know about one another, and they get along surprisingly well.
Now and again they meet in Nelly's little flat on Kantstrasse and talk
politics, an opportunity Mann likes to take advantage of to get a sense
for the milieu of proletarian party communists to whom he otherwise
has no access. Heinrich Mann is generous, though he can imagine that
some of the money he gives Nelly ends up with Rudi Carius. That,
at least, is how Rudi's money troubles are held in check now that he
must disappear from the police's radar for a good long while after Hans
Maikowski's death.

*

After the end of the torchlight parade, Goebbels also discusses with
Hitler the schedule for the envisaged new elections. If Hindenburg plays

along, they are due to take place on March 5. Then Goebbels travels to Potsdam to Prince August Wilhelm of Prussia to celebrate with him the accession to power. It isn't until around three in the morning that he arrives home. There, Fritz Hahn from the Murderer *Sturm* is waiting for him and is debriefed: Maikowski is dead. A police officer named Josef Zauritz was also shot and killed. Goebbels is too exhausted to talk for long, dismissing Hahn: good that he can rely on him. Then he collapses into bed.

Axes at the Door
Tuesday, January 31

Thomas Mann is nervous, albeit not so much on account of the political decision of the day prior, but rather for literary reasons. His son Klaus, just back from Berlin and Leipzig, wants to talk about Hitler. At the moment, however, he has other things on his mind.

In the past several weeks he was forced to set aside the manuscript for his Joseph novel once again in order to concoct a speech he is scheduled to give on February 10 at the University of Munich for the fiftieth anniversary of Richard Wagner's death. He has already written a great deal about Wagner's music theater, one of the great artistic experiences of his life. At the outset he figured he would proceed quickly with the project, but then the lecture swelled more and more into an essay, indeed, even a short book. His thoughts and ideas surge onto the paper with such force that he struggles to give them a viable form.

But that wasn't the whole story. After he consented to speak about Wagner in Munich, the Dutch *Wagner-Vereeniging* [*Wagner Association*] asked him to repeat his lecture in the Concertgebouw in Amsterdam. Then came two further invitations to give the speech in French: from the Belgian PEN-Club in Brussels and the Théâtre des Ambassadeurs in Paris – where he is to deliver it yet again, but the second time in German. A short, honorable European tour, which nevertheless carries with it additional headaches for Thomas Mann. While still working on the manuscript, he had to ask his French friend and Germanist Félix Bertraux to translate it. He only completed the essay a couple of days ago. Now he must hurry and shorten it to an appropriate length for a lecture, steadfastly cutting off his nose to spite his face, as it were, and, as soon as the translation arrives, rehearse the French version of the text until he can present it with the requisite facility.

That leaves little time for political matters. Besides, in various articles and speeches from the previous year, he left not the shadow of a doubt what he thinks of National Socialism, this defrauding of an entire people

Figure 6: Thomas Mann in his Munich villa, 1932

that attempts to lie its way to a revolution. He cannot keep repeating himself over and over again. And yet tomorrow or the next day he was also planning to draft for former Prussian Minister of Culture Adolf Grimme – who wants to lure him to an SPD election campaign event in Berlin – an extensive *Avowal of Socialism* that Grimme is to read aloud at the rally. What more can he do?

At the dinner table discussions about politics cannot be avoided. Erika and Klaus are palpably tense; Klaus has obviously read all the newspapers, even the *Völkischer Beobachter*, and he sneers at the modest lamentation the left-wing press raises in light of this change of government. After the meal the two children set off for the dress rehearsal of Erika's *Pfeffermühle*, the February lineup of which is to be premiered tomorrow. Hitler's accession to power is of course a field day for a cabaret.

*

Goebbels first gets a good night's rest, then discusses strategy for the upcoming campaign with his staff. An initial propaganda highlight will be the memorial service for Maikowski and Zauritz. The two, he declares, are martyrs of the nationalist movement, treacherously shot and killed on the night of triumph by red murderers. He wants a huge staged spectacle for them in the Berlin Cathedral, with all the requisite pomp and with robust mobilizations of people. Although the Cathedral is a Protestant church and Zauritz was Catholic, Goebbels cannot make any allowances for that.

And especially not for Maikowski and the true story of his death. Over the last few weeks many in the SA feared that although the NSDAP was having them do its dirty work in the years-long street fights against the communists, the party bosses, now that their political aims were finally within reach, were trying to cast them aside to secure all the advantages of victory for themselves. Shortly after Christmas over sixty Charlottenburg SA leaders met and discussed how they thought him, Goebbels, particularly capable of such a rotten scheme. At that point Maikowski did not hesitate, Goebbels' informants reported, roaring that in such a case he would take it upon himself to kill Goebbels.

For Goebbels it was thus an act of political savvy to take corrective measures. As *Gauleiter* of Berlin he is always surrounded by SA men; he has to be able to trust them implicitly. Maikowski's swaggering that he'd put a bullet in his head must not remain without consequences. Goebbels had to make it clear to every single storm trooper that even thinking about an attempt on his life would not go unpunished. Luckily, Fritz Hahn knew his people from *Sturm 33* inside and out and knew there was one among them, Alfred Buske, who would reliably dispose of Maikowski for good money. Yesterday Buske took care of it at the right moment and eliminated Zauritz, the only police witness, right along with him. If the other men in the squad saw what happened, then all the better for Goebbels. This warning will get around. He is not a man to be threatened.

He also likes the thought of exploiting Maikowski for his own ends, especially now that he's had him liquidated. It'll be child's play to declare him a martyr. He'll have Maikowski buried like a king and speak at his coffin himself. Hitler and Göring present in the Cathedral too, wreath-laying, solemn moments of silence, organ music, moving speeches, and then a funeral procession through the city. Major state theater.

*

That evening an SA commando storms the building at Trautenaustrasse 12, in placid Wilmersdorf. As soon as the men have gathered in front of the apartment they're after, they kick down the door, rush in – and find themselves standing in emptied rooms. No renters, no furniture, no pictures, no nothing. Just bare walls. The men hesitate for a moment, forced to come to terms with the shock. Then they race back onto the street, running straight toward Nassauische Strasse. There, too, they storm into one of the buildings, break down a door with axes, and find an empty art studio. No one home, everything abandoned: they've arrived too late.

The SA squad is looking for George Grosz, painter, graphic artist, caricaturist. The Nazis hate him as they hate few other artists. With his drawings he not only attacks everything they believe and consider sacred – their Führer, their male societies, their enthusiasm for war – but he also subjects them to ridicule, showing them as pompous buffoons, drunkards, vacuous goons, whoremongers, gangsters. No one who wants to be taken seriously in political combat may underestimate such an opponent. Satire can be lethal. But even lawsuits over slandering the Reichswehr or offences against common decency don't help. A court case against Grosz and his publisher Wieland Herzfelde for blasphemy dragged on for four years, from 1928 to 1931, prompted by protests against his drawing *Maul halten und weiter dienen* [*Shut up and do your duty*] depicting Christ on the Cross wearing a gas mask and soldier's boots.

The trials ended with acquittals or paltry fines and made Grosz even more famous, which sent the Nazis into a burning rage. The constant legal attacks, however, also wore him down. The atmosphere of hate and incessant petty feuds did not do Grosz any good. His doubts about whether reason can ever prevail grew larger, as did his doubts about the internal motivations of his art. Was the impact of satire, however well crafted it may be, not exorbitantly overestimated in the end? Could he ever hope to open the eyes of a furious multitude precisely by means of furious art?

Then the letter from New York arrived. The *Art Students League* was offering him a teaching position for Summer 1932. Grosz was delighted. America had been enticing him since he was a child. He accepted right away. It was like an escape from utterly desperate circumstances. And when five months later he returned to Germany on one of those gigantic transatlantic steamships, he greeted his wife Eva from the very gangway with the news that he had come only in order to emigrate to America with her and their children once and for all. Just after Christmas.

This is quite a gamble for him. In Germany he is an established artist with the very best connections, and in America virtually a nobody. They will be hard times. He'll have to work again as a teacher at the art school for 150 dollars a month. Whether he'll be able to make a name for himself again as a painter is uncertain. Nothing can dissuade him from his plan, though, not even his own doubts. He wants out of this country.

Eva and he liquidate the apartment, packing only a few things. Grosz gives away the furniture, clears out the studio, and stores pictures and books with his mother-in-law. He is propelled onward like a block of wood on an unknown, underground current. On January 12, 1933, the *Stuttgart* puts out to sea in Bremerhaven with Grosz and Eva on board. They've left the children with Grosz's sister in Germany until the summer. The crossing is more than just turbulent – a storm with Beaufort force 12 gets hold of them off Newfoundland – but when they go ashore in New York on January 23, mild spring weather greets them: a week before Hitler becomes Reich Chancellor, eight days before the SA stands before their old apartment and the studio with axes.

*

On this day a group of ten or twelve National Socialists chases after Reichstag deputy Julius Leber, a Social Democrat, who is on his way home at night with two bodyguards. They ultimately attack Leber's vehicle, and one of Leber's men fatally wounds one of the Nazis. During the struggle Leber is also injured. After the ambush the police arrest him, ostensibly for his own protection.

In Breslau [present-day Wrocław], a police lieutenant shoots at a marching communist demonstration, killing one of the demonstrators.

In a street fight between communists and National Socialists in Duisburg-Hamborn, a National Socialist and a *Landjäger* constable are killed. Three other officers are wounded by gunfire.

While attempting to tear down a swastika flag, a communist in Velbert (near Essen) is beaten to death. That evening communists storm an SA home. Two National Socialists suffer injuries.

At the railway inspector's office in Harburg (by Hamburg), a rail official kills a colleague in a political argument. The culprit shoots himself thereafter.

In Zittau, the local agent for the National Socialist newspaper *Oberlausitzer Frühpost* is found murdered.

Influenza cases rise rapidly. In Berlin alone, 572 new infections are reported.

Inferior Foreign-Blooded Trash

Thursday, February 2

Trouble for Brecht in Darmstadt. The NSDAP is protesting against the planned premiere of Brecht's *Saint Joan of the Stockyards* at the Hessian State Theater. In the crucial city council meeting the Nazi deputies are lent support by the German People's Party and the Catholic Centre Party. Together they demand the police ban the production. A closed performance for the *Verein der Theaterfreunde [Association of Friends of the Theater]* is prohibited as well. Only the SPD defends theater director Gustav Hartung's right to program his repertory ad libitum.

Hartung is considered one of the country's most important directors and innovators of theater. Brecht knows him and his work. Hartung was head of the Renaissance-Theater in Berlin for three years before moving to Darmstadt in 1931. *Saint Joan*, Brecht's half parody, half learning play reckoning with the Church and capitalism, had been drafted three years ago but until now could only be broadcast in an abridged radio play version, with voice work actors as brilliant as Carola Neher, Helene Weigel, Fritz Kortner, and Peter Lorre.

As was his wont in Berlin as well, Gustav Hartung has not included any *völkisch* authors on his program in Darmstadt, having instead planned plays by Else Lasker-Schüler, Erich Kästner, Franz Werfel, or Carl Zuckmayer. Brecht's *Saint Joan* is supposed to continue this series with a particularly prominent world premiere. For the Nazis that is reason enough for a smear campaign in the *Hessische Landeszeitung*. They accuse Hartung of producing "inferior foreign-blooded trash and fusty bogus art" and of being predisposed to employ Jews in his theater.

Instead of rebuffing any encroachment upon the artistic freedom guaranteed by the constitution, Lord Mayor Rudolf Mueller of the liberal German State Party approaches the outraged city council delegates with a compromise. He condemns the Marxist and anticlerical leanings in Brecht's play, but defends Gustav Hartung's work as director. The Nazis' anti-Semitic accusations are, in his view, absurd. From among the 361 employees of the state theater, thirteen are Jews. That, he says, can hardly be called a "Jewification."

*

The flu continues to spread apace. Today in Berlin, for instance, 800 new cases are reported, and the city has now had to close over 200 school classrooms. In Great Britain over a thousand lives have already been lost. From Japan the writer Hans Michaelis gives an account of a new means of protection against contagion in the *Berliner Morgenpost*: "The bacillus mask. A black piece of cloth cut into an oval is tied over one's nose and mouth and has the onerous task of denying entry to the germs." To Michaelis' surprise, however, the face covering is only worn in the open air. On trains and in offices the Japanese remove their masks. They are of the belief that flu pathogens spread primarily on the street, not in enclosed spaces.

*

The wounded Reichstag deputy, Julius Leber of the SPD, is provisionally released. Armed men ambush him in front of police headquarters and fire at the vehicle meant to take him to the hospital. A short while later Leber is arrested again. Prompted by this, Lübeck workers decide to strike for twenty-four hours in protest.

In Altona, a shootout ensues between communists and National Socialists. A passerby on a walk with his wife suffers a shot to the lung and dies in hospital. Ten other people are injured, some critically.

In a scuffle with National Socialists in Berlin-Charlottenburg, one communist is stabbed to death and a second one wounded.

Tongue-Tied

Friday, February 3

Else Lasker-Schüler also lives on Motzstrasse, where Kisch has found his sublet. She has a tiny room in Hotel Sächsischer Hof. From here it isn't far to the Romanisches Café at the Gedächtniskirche, to the restaurant *Schlichter*, or to *Weinstube Schwanneke*. Else Lasker-Schüler loves places where writers, artists, publishers, gallerists, and actors gather. For her they provide a refuge from too much reality. For a couple of years she was the undisputed queen of Berlin's bohemian society, boyishly slight, her black hair cut noticeably short, garbed mostly in baggy clothes and velvet jackets with glass-bead necklaces, clattering bangles, and rings on every finger. She came across as a dancer from the Orient, but also bestowed upon herself the male fairy-tale name and noble title Prince Jussuf of Thebes, for boundaries did not apply to her, neither those of fiction, nor of social status, nor of gender.

She is now sixty-three – she turns sixty-four next week – and has a tough period behind her. Five years ago her son Paul died of tuberculosis. Even Ferdinand Sauerbruch, chief physician at the Charité, was unable to save him. That caused her to lose her footing. For a long time she earned almost nothing, forced, as she puts it, to live off fifteen pfennigs a day, while owing the hotel rent.

Now things are looking up again, though. She's enjoying something akin to a comeback. In the previous year not one but two books of hers have appeared with Rowohlt: new poems and a story. In addition, she completed her new play *Arthur Aronymus and His Ancestors* and was awarded the Kleist Prize together with Richard Billinger. At first she took offense that she was to receive only half the prize and only half the prize money, 750 Reichsmarks, but then she set aside her pride, dutifully submitted to the honor, and paid off her hotel debts.

One of her former lovers, Gottfried Benn, cabled to congratulate her: "the kleist prize so often defiled both by those bestowing it and by those awarded it was ennobled once more by being conferred on you." Their

Figure 7: Else Lasker-Schüler around 1933

affair now lies twenty years in the past. Back then, in 1913, they were a very unevenly matched couple: he twenty-six years old and at the very beginning of his career, she forty-four and already a central figure of the German avant-garde; he an irreligious son of a pastor with aspirations of extinguishing the last glimmer of religious hope from his literature, she the granddaughter of a rabbi whose poetry is steeped in faith and assurance seemingly as a matter of course. In spite of or perhaps precisely because of this, a passionate love bound them together for several months, a "beastly love" she wrote about in her poems. "You snatch with your teeth what you crave," Benn wrote, and Lasker-Schüler: "I carry you around always / Between my teeth." Their separation they also memorialized in verse: "I am the edge of your path," she insisted, and he, just as staunchly: "No one will be the edge of my path."

That was a long time ago. Today Else Lasker-Schüler is writing to her "finance minister," Klaus Gebhard, in Wuppertal. He helps her when she has to negotiate contracts; she can't be bothered with such things. Sometimes Gebhard also sends warnings to publishers who are too slow to disburse fees. That's why she has dubbed him her finance minister. She likes to gives new names to people important to her, thereby transforming them into characters in her poetic world. Benn, for instance, she calls "Giselheer the Barbarian" or "Giselheer the Tiger."

It turns into a feisty letter, outspoken and spirited. This she can do well, and she writes to almost everyone in this way. She has an invitation to a reading in Elberfeld, the city of her birth, and Gebhard, she requests, is to arrange a fee of 200 Reichsmarks. Aside from that, she raves about the "collllosssal efforts" the Schillertheater is making in its rehearsals for the premiere of *Arthur Aronymus*: "A huge production."

How she is really doing, however, she reveals in writing neither to Gebhard, nor to anyone else. After all, her successes from the prior year do not have only pleasant repercussions. She had almost vanished completely from public life, but it was the Kleist Prize that brought her back to the Nazis' attention. She is Jewish, she has the bearing of a phantom from the East, she writes modernist, expressive poetry – all this is unforgiveable in the eyes of National Socialists. The *Völkischer Beobachter* is up in arms: "The daughter of a Bedouin sheikh receives the Kleist Prize!" and in no time a couple of men turn up, occasionally waylaying her in front of her hotel to insult her and push her around, until she takes a tumble and is lying on the ground. In one of those falls she bit her tongue so hard that it needed stitches. A tongue-tied poetess.

There are troubles with *Arthur Aronymus*, too. When the play was finished last spring, the big-name stage and artistic directors pounced on it. Gustav Hartung responded quickest, writing from Darmstadt how delighted he was and asking her to grant him the rights of first performance. She agreed. Then came Max Reinhardt, who wanted to place her play with the Deutsches Theater in Berlin, and Leopold Jessner, who wanted to stage it at the Schauspielhaus on Gendarmenmarkt, two of the country's most prominent theaters. Both of them now have to wait for Hartung's premiere, and stars like Reinhardt and Jessner don't like waiting.

But only the day before yesterday Gustav Hartung wrote her with a heavy heart; unfortunately, he will have to postpone the premiere. At the moment he is fighting a difficult battle against the NSDAP in

Darmstadt because he's programmed Brecht's *Saint Joan* and because he allegedly employs too many Jews in his theater. If he were to debut *Arthur Aronymus* under these circumstances, a play written by a Jew, which takes as its subject conflicts between Christians and Jews to boot, it would come across as an open provocation, and he cannot afford that at the moment. He asks for patience.

And so she is now banking on the Schillertheater where Jessner is currently rehearsing the play. Either February 12 or February 19 is under discussion for the premiere, but nothing is yet set in stone. At any rate, she is bowled over by the energy with which Jessner has thrown himself into working on a play that especially now, after Hitler's rise to power, might take on enormous significance. *Arthur Aronymus* tells the story of a looming anti-Semitic massacre in a Westphalian village about a hundred years earlier. The pogrom is able to be averted through the combined efforts of a Jewish landowner, his charismatic young son Arthur Aronymus, and the Bishop of Paderborn. In the final scene the wise bishop demonstratively takes part in a Pesach Seder at the landowner's home and blesses the people of Israel. While the Nazis show fewer and fewer inhibitions in blanketing Germany with their hatred of the Jews, Else Lasker-Schüler celebrates the reconciliation between religions in her play. No wonder that Jessner, himself a Jew and a politically alert theater man, promises her to make "colllllosssal efforts" with the production.

*

Carl von Ossietzky is supposed to give his speech for the *Liga für Menschenrechte* this evening. The *Liga's* executive director, Kurt Grossmann, is proud to have snagged the Beethovensaal for the event, a gigantic space, an extension building of the Berliner Philharmonie. Normally concerts take place here, framed by opulent frescoes, crystal chandeliers, and columns decorated in plasterwork. When Grossmann arrives there with his entourage an hour and a half before admission, all the doors to the hall are locked. Nervously he buzzes the custodian out of his office, who hands him a missive from the Superintendent of Police: the rally is prohibited. The preposterous rationale reads that in light of the heated political situation, participants "of a different opinion" could take offense at Ossietzky's speech. With this argument any speech in any location could be prohibited during the weeks of campaigning.

Time is already running too short, however, to cancel the event. On the spur of the moment, Grossmann has arriving attendees redirected to Café Friediger on Potsdamer Platz, just a few steps away. Until a few years ago it was called Café Josty, and it is still one of the city's most popular coffeehouses. He also diverts Ossietzky there, who, as a friendly police captain makes clear to him, however, may under no circumstances give a speech there. And so Ossietzky improvises, sitting at one of the café tables and beginning a very loud conversation with friends about the united front of SPD and KPD that guests at other tables listen to with interest. The police captain cannot have any objection to that.

For many democrats and pacifists Ossietzky has become an important political rallying figure in recent years, a sort of hero of the republic. In April 1929 an article appeared in the *Weltbühne* exposing the secret plans of the German military to establish an air force despite the explicit prohibition of the Treaty of Versailles. It was not the Reichswehr officers responsible who were subsequently brought to trial, however, but the author of the article and Ossietzky as the responsible editor. They were

Figure 8: Carl von Ossietzky reports for his jail term in Tegel Prison on May 10, 1932. The photo shows, from left to right, Kurt Grossmann, the journalist Rudolf Olden, Carl von Ossietzky, and the two attorneys Alfred Apfel and Kurt Rosenfeld

sentenced to eighteen months in prison for treason. The trial caused an international stir since Germany ultimately attested in it to purposefully violating the Versailles restrictions.

Many friends and political allies warned Ossietzky against actually serving out his sentence and implored him to abscond abroad. But he chose differently. Not out of respect for the court, but rather, he wrote, as a "living demonstration" against a case of wrongful justice did he report for his term of imprisonment in May 1932. He put his personal freedom into the service of political combat. Quite a few colleagues, writers, and celebrities accompanied him on his way to Tegel Prison, among them Albert Einstein, Erich Mühsam, Leonhard Frank, Lion Feuchtwanger, Ernst Toller, and the satirist Alexander Roda Roda. Thus, they transformed the first day of his detention into a protest rally against the scandalous verdict.

Only six weeks ago Ossietzky was released from prison early through Hindenburg's usual Christmas amnesty. Today's speech is actually supposed to be his first public appearance since his release. His audience wants to hear his take on the new Hitler government.

*

In Annaberg in the Erz Mountains, a man from the democratic *Reichsbanner* is shot and killed by National Socialists in front of the People's House.

In a brawl in Duisburg-Hamborn, National Socialists injure a communist so gravely that he dies at the police precinct.

National Socialists shoot and kill an eighteen-year-old communist in Berlin-Moabit and a twenty-one-year-old communist in Berlin-Neukölln.

Not Sure What to Do
Saturday, February 4

Early this morning, on his desk at the office of the *Liga für Menschenrechte* on Monbijouplatz, Kurt Grossmann finds the written order banning yesterday's rally in the Beethovensaal. For a moment he is tempted to lodge a complaint with the Superintendent of Police, but he knows how futile that would be. Around 11 a.m. he receives a call from Willi Münzenberg, who tells of two French reporters who allegedly want to interview Grossmann. He is surprised, but agrees and arranges to meet Münzenberg that afternoon in a café on Kurfürstendamm.

Münzenberg is a communist and member of the Central Committee of the KPD, but above all he is a brilliant publisher and an undogmatic thinker. During the First World War he lived in Switzerland where he became acquainted with and worked for Lenin, which made him a kind of unimpeachable saintly figure to many communists for the rest of his life. Since then, under his own steam and largely without the support of his party, Münzenberg has built one of Germany's largest media concerns from the ground up, one that controls quite a few newspapers, book publishers, and film production companies. Its papers are politically one-sided but well made, lively, entertaining, and governed according to journalistic principles, not stubbornly according to the party line. Münzenberg cares little for the proletarian affectations and Moscow-minded insularity of most KPD functionaries. A scintillating man, stout and broad-shouldered, he likes to live well and has himself chauffeured around in a bulky American limousine by a driver who doubles as his bodyguard.

When Grossmann meets him in the appointed café, there is no more talk of the two French journalists. They were just a smokescreen. Instead, Münzenberg reminds him of the committee *Das freie Wort* [*The Free Word*] that Grossmann founded quite some time ago now along with numerous authors. Perhaps he might like to convene a committee congress, Münzenberg asks, as a substitute for the prohibited *Liga* event yesterday? His newspapers would support him in such an endeavor in every respect, including financially. Not wanting to be idle in the middle of the electoral campaign, Grossmann is quickly on board. In order not to make the communist influence too plain, he agrees with Münzenberg to name as organizers a slew of famous men who have nothing to do with the KPD: Albert Einstein, Heinrich Mann, Harry Graf Kessler, and one of the most high-profile Berlin journalists, Rudolf Olden of the *Berliner Tageblatt*, in addition to Thomas Mann as the opening speaker.

Münzenberg nods, noting down the names, and passes along the list to his papers' editorial teams as soon as he has returned to his publishing company. The next day it is printed in Münzenberg's Sunday editions without even one of those named having agreed to participate.

*

Berlin's cultural scene is alarmed. The *Vossische Zeitung* reports that Bernhard Rust, a founding member of the Nazi party and a former secondary school teacher, will take over the Prussian Ministry of Education. Additionally, the writer Hanns Johst, an admirer of Hitler and a close friend of SS chief Heinrich Himmler, is to become head of the state theater. Klaus Mann is also horrified when he learns of it in Munich. As a playwright, he knows how much power the artistic director of Berlin's most important stage has.

Klaus Mann has indirectly been a witness to Johst's career development from an early age. The name was occasionally mentioned in family circles. Klaus was still a precocious twelve-year-old when his father made Johst's acquaintance in Munich in 1918. Only a few days earlier, the workers' and soldiers' councils had usurped power in the city. Quite against his will, Thomas Mann felt entangled in the political turmoil of the incipient November Revolution. Among other things, a *Rat der geistigen Arbeit* [*Council of Intellectual Work*] had been established in which there were arguments about various manifestos for or against the abdicated Kaiser, for or against the coming republic. Thomas Mann took the streetcar into town to participate in these debates. At that time, he himself still advocated strictly aestheticist views; art and literature shaped his philosophy, not the analysis of economic or social concerns. During the discussions in the *Rat*, he met Hanns Johst, a massive Saxon with curly dark hair, a large nose, just under thirty years old, and got along swimmingly with him. Both were of the mind that democracy and Western civilization stood in profound contradiction to everything they recognized as German *Geist* and German culture.

Johst lived on Lake Starnberg, had married a well-heeled woman, and was therefore able to devote his full attention to literature. His most important work to date, the play *Der Einsame* [*The Solitary Man*], had made him a minor celebrity. It depicts the suffering of a genius, far ahead of his time, who amounts to nothing due to his world's incomprehension. One can already discern in it, however, notes of German chauvinism, *völkisch* ideology, and anti-Semitism. In the initial period of their acquaintanceship, Thomas Mann was not bothered by this in the slightest. "I adore you very much and rejoice at your existence," he wrote to Johst.

Bertolt Brecht had keener senses here. To be sure, he was only eighteen when he saw *Der Einsame* at the Munich Kammerspiele, but in his eyes Johst's hymn of praise to the outsized, brilliant maverick beyond all criticism was so very far from reality and outmoded that he wrote his first play *Baal* as a foil, in which he made fun of Johst's gushing veneration for the artist figure, among other things.

A fascinating constellation: three writers whose paths cross in Munich after the First World War and whose later development could not be more different. Klaus Mann is all too familiar with their careers as he holds the press notice about Johst's potential appointment as artistic director and general manager in Berlin. Now Brecht numbers among the most important Marxist authors of the age. Having broken with his early aestheticism, Thomas Mann, an author of international stature, has become the most prominent bourgeois defender of the Weimar Republic. And Hanns Johst, now a member of the NSDAP, pledges himself as resolutely as few other authors have to Adolf Hitler.

Like an itinerant preacher, Johst travels the country delivering lectures to promote his party's ideas with tremulous pathos and a mellifluent, oddly seductive voice: the individual is nothing, the community of the *Volk* everything. Between nations and races there rages a merciless, murderous battle for power and survival; such is the lesson of history, in his view. For that reason alone, a superior people like the Germans had to ruthlessly defend their ethnic purity and cultural identity against all external influences, which could only be enfeebling. Each and every form of tolerance, pluralism, or willingness to compromise that ran counter to the country's identitarian unity are, for Johst, nothing but the symptoms of a decadent decline. His notion of ideal social organization resembles the structure of a bee colony in its simplicity. The nation's great, solitary Führer stands beyond reproach and guides the destiny of his people with superhuman, almost godly, insight. The individual is to be obedient and subservient to this Führer, or he will die out as soon as he fails in his duty.

Thomas Mann and Hanns Johst have also made their ideological differences public. After Mann demonstratively committed himself to democracy and the new German state in his 1922 speech *The German Republic*, Johst accused him in an open letter of treason against Germanness, to which belonged precisely not faith in reason, justice, and humaneness, but wholehearted devotion to the ethnic community and to mythic-mystical ideas like fate, blood, or destiny. Thomas Mann in turn lent the fanatical character Naphta in his *The Magic Mountain* some of Johst's features, making him rave in crazed enthusiasm about his passion for obedience and disavowal of the self. Naphta is, moreover, a Jew, a detail which especially aggrieved the anti-Semite Johst.

His plays, his political disposition, and his family background, Klaus Mann understands right away, will never stand a chance with an artistic director like Johst. And Johst is only the first symptom, which Klaus Mann also realizes at once. Now, after Hitler has come to power, the cards are being reshuffled in the cultural scene. Throughout the country people with nary a political scruple are waiting in the wings, aligning themselves with the Nazis in order to snatch up positions, and such people are certainly no friends of his. He has just turned twenty-six, works hard and fast, and has already published eight books and five plays, but he is by no means an established author who could assert himself against the pushback from a politically prejudiced literary system. He still needs support, or at least a certain amiable goodwill, for his books' success, but he can no longer count on that now. It won't be easy for him in the coming years. When he picks up his diary the following evening, he writes: "Not sure what to do."

*

Toward the end of his first week in government, Hitler tests Hindenburg's willingness to fundamentally change the country and abrogate constitutional rights. He places before him an emergency decree to sign, which Franz von Papen's cabinet had already drafted but not implemented: the *Verordnung des Reichspräsidenten zum Schutze des Deutschen Volkes* [*Decree of the Reich President for the Protection of the German People*]. Hindenburg doesn't hesitate and signs it. With this decree, the freedoms of assembly and of the press are placed under the discretion of the Ministry of the Interior, which since Monday is headed by Nazi crony Wilhelm Frick. Four weeks before the new elections on March 5, all political rallies and newspapers can now be banned according to vaguely worded criteria. Any single article that supposedly incites the disobeying of laws, glorifies acts of violence, or calls for strikes is sufficient grounds to issue a publication ban for the entire newspaper. And the decree is no mere saber-rattling. It is applied with such intensity that during the election campaign the KPD and SPD in particular can hardly hold any events and their newspapers are not permitted to appear in print for weeks.

*

Berlin reports 1,055 new cases of flu within a single day. The city's hospitals are so overcrowded that resident physicians and auxiliary physicians are sought through newspaper appeals to begin work at once.

In Staßfurt (outside Magdeburg), the Social Democratic mayor Hermann Kasten is shot dead at the gate to his yard. The police arrest, as the alleged perpetrator, a seventeen-year-old high-school student who avows himself a National Socialist. The schoolboy disputes the deed and is released a short time later. Further investigations are not carried out.

In Bochum-Gerthe, an SA leader is shot five times and murdered by communists; in Berlin National Socialists shoot and kill two communists in a scuffle.

Burial in the Rain

Sunday, February 5

At 1 p.m. the memorial service in Berlin Cathedral for Maikowski and Zauritz begins. Goebbels' plan to stage the ceremony as a piece of grand propaganda theater is working. The Cathedral council did prevent the deceased from publicly lying in state before the start of the ceremony and did demand that the Cathedral must not be misused for a political party event, nor do the relatives of Zauritz, a Catholic, want his funeral rites to take place in a Protestant cathedral. But Goebbels has brushed all that aside. The church is festooned with swastika flags, storm troopers are in uniform throughout, and Hitler is riding up in an open Mercedes. In the Cathedral he is saluted by his devotees with raised right arms and lays down two wreaths at the caskets; the former Hohenzollern crown prince, Wilhelm of Prussia, follows him with one wreath.

After the memorial liturgy Zauritz is transported to his hometown in Upper Silesia, and Maikowski's coffin is driven in a black hearse from the Cathedral to the Invalidenfriedhof [Invalids' Cemetery]. Mounted divisions of the constabulary accompany it through pouring rain. Six hundred thousand Berliners line the streets, among them several film units recording the funeral procession for the newsreels. Goebbels, Göring, and Berlin SA chief Graf von Helldorff deliver graveside speeches.

Almost unnoticed, a small memorial ceremony begins in Charlottenburg at nearly the same time. Members of communist organizations lay two wreaths in front of the building at Wallstrasse 24, where the murders took place. They bear the inscription: "The revolutionary workers of Charlottenburg, for their friend, murdered by the NSDAP, the police officer Josef Zauritz." A short while later the wreaths are confiscated and removed by the police.

*

Christiane Grautoff is only fifteen, but already a full-fledged beauty, slender, blonde, a bit tomboyish, and highly talented. She is regarded as

Berlin's theater prodigy. When she was twelve, Max Reinhardt put her on stage, and at fourteen she was shooting her first film alongside Henny Porten and Gustaf Gründgens. More even than these stars, however, it is Ernst Toller, dramatist, poet, and revolutionary, who has made an impression on her. Despite his fame he comes across to her as still so vulnerable, as though he needed help.

Her acting coach Lilly Ackermann, a friend of Tilly and Kadidja Wedekind, introduced her to Toller a year ago. The writer is almost forty, a full twenty-three years older than Christiane. Nevertheless, she has fallen in love with him, which has turned into a gigantic headache for all involved. This love plunged not just Christiane into endlessly new emotional turmoil, but Toller, too. She would often visit him, and he would read aloud to her from his still-unfinished manuscripts and ask what she as an actor thought of them. Of course, they tried to keep their relationship a secret, but after several months Christiane confessed to one of her sisters that she had met the man she wanted to marry. She assured her parents her friendship with Toller was strictly platonic, but they do not believe her, staid conservative people that they are. Her father, Otto Grautoff, is an art historian, president of the *Deutsch-Französische Gesellschaft* [*German-French Society*], and a friend of Thomas Mann since their schooldays. Her mother Erna is a writer and translates poetry from French and English. Understandably, both harbor concerns about Christiane's friendship with a man so much older than she and would like to bring her back into the fold to keep her from making premature decisions – which drives the girl out of the house once and for all.

Toller has always been a man of extremes. He registered for war service and voluntary duty on the frontline straightaway in 1914. As a Jew, he wanted finally to belong and cease being an outsider. He was on deployment in Verdun, in the battles that cost hundreds of thousands their lives, and fought to the point of total physical and mental breakdown. He left the field hospital a radical opponent of war, defended the Munich Soviet Republic against the nationalist *Freikorps* in 1919, together with authors like Erich Mühsam or Oskar Maria Graf, and for this was sentenced to five years' imprisonment.

Never again was he literarily as productive and original as in his prison cell. He wrote plays that riled up a disoriented postwar Germany, making him the most famous prisoner in the country. The

Bavarian government offered him an early reprieve, but he refused, not wanting to receive better treatment than his former revolutionary comrades-in-arms.

Since his release from prison, he has written five more plays, in addition to countless radio plays, travelogues, speeches, and newspaper articles. There is scarcely a politically fraught topic about which he has not written. But he no longer captures the tone of the times, the blistering human pathos of his prison plays having gone out of style. Although he no longer belongs to a party now, he is branded as a socialistic moralist. The left considers him politically unreliable while the right sees in him a subversive and a radical.

When his friend and editor Landshoff separates from his wife in 1931, Toller moves in with him in Wilmersdorf. It is apparent to both of them, however, that they need to be careful. The name plate on their apartment door reads "Schwarzkopf," and they keep it that way. In times like these it is better to be hard to track down.

In January, Christiane applied to be an actor under Gustav Hartung in Darmstadt. She simply cannot stand being at home with her parents

Figure 9: Christiane Grautoff and Ernst Toller

64

anymore. And, in fact, Hartung has sent her a contract for his troupe; he doesn't want to pass up Berlin's child prodigy. From now on, Christiane has decided, she will live in Darmstadt but use any opportunity for side trips to Berlin to see Toller.

Soon after, Toller sets off for Switzerland on a lecture tour. Not a long trip, just two weeks, but even the brief separation is tough for lovestruck Christiane. Toller was intending to come back to Berlin on January 31, but now, after Hitler's appointment as chancellor, he doesn't dare hazard a return to Germany.

Christiane has gone without word from him for five days now. That perplexes and troubles her. Today she saw the matinee performance at the Theater am Schiffbauerdamm, Schiller's *The Robbers*. Afterward she feels horribly lonely but doesn't want to go home where there's only strife with her parents anyway. It is still raining. Berlin is dreary and gray. She walks to the nearest telephone booth, dials the number for Toller's and Landshoff's flat, but no one picks up. Crestfallen, she clutches the receiver and lets it ring and ring, endlessly. What should she do? She doesn't know where to go. Suddenly there's a crackle on the line. Then another, and a strident voice shouts: "Who is this? Identify yourself immediately! Where are you calling from?! Hello? Hello! Who's there?"

Christiane recoils. It is neither Toller's voice nor Landshoff's. She is unable to breathe and drops the receiver. Horrified, she leaps out of the phone booth and runs pell-mell down the street. Her parents' and Toller's fear of the Nazis has always struck her as excessive and a bit ridiculous. Now their warnings flash through her mind. She is in a panic. She runs and runs through the rain, farther and farther, down all of Schiffbauerdamm, as fast as she can, gasping for breath. Where in the world is she supposed to run to?

*

Following rallies by the SPD-affiliated *Iron Front* in Breslau [present-day Wrocław] and Chemnitz, Nazis stab two of the attendees to death.

At a pub in Hamburg frequented by National Socialists, an apprentice metal worker is killed as he enters the restroom by a gunshot fired from the courtyard through the open window.

In Dormagen, a KPD man shoots dead a National Socialist during an argument. The perpetrator is killed by the police while fleeing.

During the SA attack on *Pappschachtel*, a pub in Berlin-Schöneberg where communists socialize, the landlady is shot and killed.

Meeting Routine
Monday, February 6

Heinrich Mann now resides at Fasanenstrasse 61, a stately, upper-class apartment building on Berlin's west side. In December Nelly and he moved in; this is their first apartment together. For the most part they have purchased all new furniture for themselves, so a lot of it is still fresh and a bit alien. This is where they intend to settle for the long term, and the new address is supposed to provide the foundation for a new stage of life.

Heinrich has turbulent years in his wake. Divorcing his wife Mimi was difficult. The newspapers milked his liaison with Trude Hesterberg for everything it was worth, which of course strained matters even more. When the first rumors began flying, Mimi traveled from Munich to Berlin in a fury and assailed her rival in a hotel. Afterward she hounded Heinrich for weeks with telephone calls and letters, now infuriated, now distraught. Ultimately, though, she was unable to refuse the divorce – at best their marriage consisted in mutual regard for one another – and she, too, had had her love affairs. They include the much-idolized Ernst Udet, who travels around everywhere in Germany with his air show and would now and again send Mimi confidential notes relaying in which city and hotel he was staying at the time.

After having lived in guesthouses and hotels for several years, Heinrich Mann would now prefer to give his life a more reliable structure, not out of deference for so-called polite society which he, *épater le bourgeois*, has always enjoyed scandalizing. By now, however, he is over sixty and beginning to feel the gravitational pull of age. The international hit *The Blue Angel* revived his fame, which had been at risk of fading among large audiences, and certainly his esteem on the literary scene is, as ever, unabating. If he is honest, though, he must admit that his books from recent years made hardly more than respectable showings. His two large, triumphantly celebrated novels *Professor Unrat* and *Der Untertan* [*The Man of Straw*] date back quite a bit now. He does not intend to resign himself to these circumstances and would, at long last, like to refocus all his efforts on his literary work.

Besides, his writer colleagues elected him two years earlier as President of the Division for the Art of Poetry in the Prussian Academy of the Arts. Considering the ideologically charged situation in the country, it is virtually a political office that demands a settled rhythm of life. The climate of conflict does not frighten him; on the contrary, he cannot keep himself from meddling in the debates of the age. It is part of his authorial temperament. He suffered far too much under the narrow-mindedness and parochial militarism of the German Empire to now want to keep his enthusiasm for republic and democracy under his hat. More so than his brother, he advocated in newspaper articles and by appending his signature to public appeals and manifestos that Germany finally orient itself more strongly toward Western standards – and toward socialist ideals. He loves France, speaks the language perfectly, even writes in French for French papers, and, like Coudenhove-Kalergi, has outlined a vision for a European federation. It is no wonder, therefore, if for years now he has been a *bête noire* for right-wingers and dyed-in-the-wool nationalists. And yet there may be another reason for the very particular rage with which the National Socialists pursue him.

In 1931 Heinrich Mann and his writer friend Wilhelm Herzog requested a private audience in the Prussian Ministry of the Interior and were received by State Secretary Wilhelm Abegg, a well-known man, a liberal and defender of the unloved Weimar Republic, the epitome of the punctilious civil servant, with a pince-nez and a fastidiously trimmed handlebar mustache. With prudence and flair, he had built the Prussian police into a hard-hitting, almost militaristically equipped outfit. And it was precisely in his function as the person responsible for the police that the two wanted to speak with him. They were alarmed by a speech in which Hitler had blatantly proclaimed his desire to come to power with legal means, to be sure, but afterward to establish a national tribunal that would settle scores with his adversaries and make "heads roll."

Mann and Herzog pleaded with Abegg not to stand by and tolerate threats of a kind that mocked all the rules of democracy. The Republic, they demanded, must mount a tough response, with all constitutional means. They made detailed suggestions of how the armed Prussian police ought to intervene against the Nazi goon squads and end the terror in the streets.

Abegg listened patiently to his guests and ultimately asked them to dictate their suggestions to his secretary, whom Wilhelm Herzog recalled as a German Gretchen figure somewhat past her prime with a coiled braid of blonde hair. What neither Abegg nor the two authors could have known at the time, however, was that this blonde Gretchen was a friend of Rudolf Diels, a handsome young career official who headed the department tasked with countering communist underground activities – and who secretly fostered close connections with Göring. Diels knew he needed benefactors if he wanted to advance professionally, so he willingly supplied Göring with information on everything that took place within the ministry, especially on what was discussed and planned in the office of Abegg, the head of the police. A week ago, just after his own swearing-in as minister, as thanks Göring made Diels the head of the Prussian Political Police in the Ministry of the Interior.

The hate with which the Nazis persecute Heinrich Mann has recently gotten even more unscrupulous. Just the other day, when his brother Thomas was passing through to Berlin, the two acknowledged to each other suffering from the political attacks more severely than they wanted to admit. All the same, for himself Heinrich Mann had chanced upon a protector, who shields him a bit and attracts a good portion of the threats. The guardian angel's name is Heinrich Mann, a retired insurance clerk and church cantor. Because his address and telephone number are listed in the Berlin telephone book, countless abusive phone calls and letters arrive at his home, though in actuality they target Heinrich Mann the author. Naturally, his namesake is shocked at the boundless animosity spewed at him, but he is brave enough to continue fulfilling his role as a lightning rod.

By late afternoon today, Heinrich Mann is making his way to the Academy; as chairman of the literary division, he has two meetings today. Given that Hitler holds the reins of the Reich Chancellery in his hands, though, the topics to be discussed now seem unfathomably harmless and distant from reality. Precisely the usual routine. Heinrich Mann can change nothing about that. Even as chairman he cannot take whatever action he wants with his academy of poets and send out declarations of protest into the world. According to his understanding of the democratic rules of the game, he must implement the resolutions of the majority. That, however, is what makes the Academy tremendously ponderous.

That is essentially how it has always been. Now quite a bit more than 200 years old, it is an honorable, renowned institution that lives more in its past than in the present. The section for literature was not founded until about six years ago, in 1926, and is thus a genuine child of the Weimar Republic, which, Heinrich Mann thinks, it ought to champion as well. Nevertheless, only with the greatest effort can consensus be reached among its members about even a fundamental question such as this.

Does the new division want to be something akin to the intellectual voice of the nation? Among the public it is often understood in this way and thus eyed with mistrust, criticized, and opposed. Internally, however, it is perpetually at odds with itself. It first began with a scandal. The poet and dramatist Arno Holz, a difficult, intolerant man, admittedly felt flattered to be appointed to the section's small, just five-person founding circle, but then he read the statutes and picked them to pieces in a memorandum, item by item. The Academy's constitution is indeed full of defects in its construction because it did not unhitch itself decisively enough from Prussia's old feudal structures. Unlike what one might expect a new republican state to condone, Academy members are not truly independent in their activities. While the Academy may appoint its own president and the divisions their own chairpersons, all elections, as well as all other decisions, must be confirmed by the Prussian Minister of Education, who as trustee bears political responsibility.

Even in the composition of the new literature section there were inconsistencies. Although the Academy calls itself "Prussian," writers belong to it who don't even reside in Prussia, like Thomas Mann for instance, who is from Lübeck and lives in Munich. To all intents and purposes, the country could have used a German Academy, and the re-established body is supposed to, and aims to, be just that. For strictly legal reasons, however, Prussia is not authorized to call into being an institution for all of Germany. To bring the absurdities to a head, on many key questions only members who live in Berlin and its periphery are entitled to vote, which is to say, those who can easily be convened for meetings. All the others have a say in matters only in plenary sessions.

In other words, it is nominally a Prussian Academy that would like to be regarded as a German Academy but is administered like a Berliner Academy.

Naturally, overt inanities like these can be counterbalanced with a degree of nonchalance among members who deal with one another in fairness and trust. That was precisely what Max Liebermann, President of the Academy at the time, suggested to a blustering Arno Holz when he assured him that the statutes were administered quite liberally and that, aside from Holz, not a single other member had ever read them, much less complied with them. But what is possible in the other divisions for fine art and music does not work for the writers. From the outset they split into two blocs whose disagreements, instead of weakening over time, deepen more and more and become freighted with ideological resentments.

The eternal battle revolves around shifting terms, but ultimately always comes down to the very same questions: whether it is the section's task to combat new, modern currents in literature or to leverage them, whether it espouses a literature that represents specifically German, timeless values or a contemporaneous, worldly literature in which the nation's traditions are redefined from a European perspective. If the first camp fights against the foreignization of the book market and theatrical programming by means of cheap entertainment from abroad, the other camp cautions against retreating into intellectual provincialism. If some criticize metropolitan literary life – primarily in the metropolis of Berlin – as "business for business' sake," others polemicize against the complacency and parochialism of the "completely vacuous countryside." The former see in the poet something like a visionary or priest who, with his works, provides an inner coherence and identity for his people. The latter view the writer as an intellectual who can no longer assume a unifying function in an increasingly technologized and highly differentiated society, but who instead plays the role of an intellectually independent critic beholden only to himself.

Of course at the same time, what's behind these controversies around artistic self-understanding are political proclamations – that's patently obvious to any observer. Right versus left, antidemocrats versus republicans, nationalists versus internationalists, devotees of myth versus adherents of the Enlightenment. The former spit venom at "cultural

Bolshevism," the latter against "cultural backwardness." Perhaps the intransigence with which ideological extremes are disputed here constitutes what is best about the literary Academy. Perhaps it is precisely this endlessly smoldering conflict that actually makes the section a sort of proxy for the nation; the rift that divides the populace also polarizes the writers.

Two years ago, the dispute escalated. The nationalist-conservative wing surprisingly pushed through a new set of bylaws that was promptly nullified by its opponents by dint of a somewhat dubious legal opinion. At this, the emphatically *völkisch* members Erwin Guido Kolbenheyer, Emil Strauss, and Wilhelm Schäfter resigned in protest, which the newspapers reported as a triumph for the leftist authors. While collaboration within the Academy grew more harmonious from that point, it made the division all the more assailable to its right-wing, nationalist adversaries.

At around 6 p.m. Mann arrives at Pariser Platz. It is a forbidding, rainy winter's evening, but even so the punishing freeze of recent days has subsided. The Academy lies wedged between the sprawling Hotel Adlon

Figure 10: November 1929 meeting of the Division for the Art of Poetry in the Prussian Academy of the Arts, from left to right: Alfred Döblin, Thomas Mann, Ricarda Huch, Bernhard Kellermann, Hermann Stehr, Alfred Mombert, Eduard Stucken

and the resplendent façade of the Palais Wrangel, but it isn't exactly modest either. Its building is located on one of the most prestigious city squares and once belonged to the family of Chamberlain von Arnim. His son, the poet Achim von Arnim, grew up here. The house has been rebuilt from the bottom up since, but it has maintained its stately, aristocratic aura. Mann takes the side entrance with its formal wide steps, crosses the front hall, and climbs the main staircase to the upper vestibule and conference halls.

Of the thirty-four members of the poetry division, five have come, plus Alexander Amersdorffer who as First Secretary of the Academy has a bit of the bearing of a chaperone. Heinrich Mann is not really disappointed. He had no great expectations. Assemblies are seldom better attended. In light of the political earthquake of the prior week, however, the disinterest on the part of members to meet with colleagues and perhaps vote with them is indeed a bit striking.

After the small circle is seated in the much-too-large meeting room, the agenda items are checked off quickly. Alfred Döblin has drafted a short note of protest. He reads it aloud himself but advises against publishing it. It concerns an important, perhaps even central topic with which the division ultimately never really came to grips. A short while back the critic Paul Fechter published a literary history with the title *Dichtung der Deutschen* [*Poetry of the Germans*]. The hefty volume is being distributed to readers in large numbers by a book club. The tome reeks of such unbridled anti-Semitism and *völkisch* tendentiousness, however, that the Academy feels obliged to issue a warning about it. Some of the most important and most read Jewish authors, like Lion Feuchtwanger, Stefan Zweig, or Kurt Tucholsky, don't appear in it at all, while others like Ernst Toller, Carl Sternheim, or Jakob Wassermann receive brief, dismissive mentions. The first few drafts of a protest note granted Fechter's book so much import, though, that it seemed as if the Academy had wanted to celebrate it instead of criticize it. Gottfried Benn then wrote a version from a very lofty perspective directed not solely at Fechter, but at reactionary cultural tendencies in general. Then the text sounded so complicated and stilted in certain passages that Alfred Döblin was asked to rework it again.

A delicate request, because Benn is a highly sensitive man with an elitist self-assurance who has little sympathy for the view that a

73

text written by him could need reworking. Consequently, he has not even come to today's proceedings. Döblin has dutifully cleared up the opaque passages in Benn's draft, but in the meantime the general political climate has shifted completely, and what was a statement of cultural policy a few days ago would now inevitably be perceived as a frontal assault on the new Reich Chancellor. Thus, Döblin has no option but to caution against the note of protest he himself wrote, and for that he garners universal approval from his colleagues. The literary Academy must admit to itself that it wasted its time in the final weeks before Hitler's rise to power with discussions about a response to a substandard book, a response it doesn't even dare publish now that it is finished.

Later, when Heinrich Mann sits down to write a letter to his brother in Munich about the section's resolutions, it is all so embarrassing to him that he only mentions the declaration, buried without a whimper, in a single sentence. Instead, he gives an account of the evening's second meeting which concerned negotiations with the Prussian Ministry of Education for a new literary prize. The composition of the jury was the subject of constant argument.

What most preoccupies him in his letter are not the affairs of the Academy, however, but the congress *Das freie Wort*, whose organizers are labeling him a co-organizer without having asked him. "The whole thing is brazen exploitation," he writes to his brother, warning him that he is also being drawn into the situation: "On the program you are 'presumably' delivering the opening address." He urges him not to participate in the event; it could only be a flop. "The best thing that could happen would be a ban of the congress. But perhaps it will be allowed to proceed to show how ineffectual our dissent is these days."

*

Hindenburg issues the emergency decree *Zur Herstellung geordneter Regierungsverhältnisse in Preußen* [*On Establishing Orderly Governing Conditions in Prussia*] and dissolves the Prussian state legislature. New elections are to take place on March 5 together with the Reichstag election. By virtue of the emergency decree, Göring, as provisional Prussian Minister of the Interior, is granted authority over the Prussian police and administration.

In Duisburg, the funeral procession of an SS man murdered on February 1 is shot at. The police and funeral attendees return fire. An innocent bystander dies in the crossfire. In Harburg-Wilhelmsburg three National Socialists kill a twenty-seven-year-old worker as he is leaving a Social Democratic Party-affiliated pub.

Hideous, Violent Little Creatures

Friday, February 10

From 8 p.m. Hitler gives his first big speech of the election campaign before around 10,000 audience members at the Sportpalast in Potsdamer Strasse. He wears an SA uniform, speaking thus not as Reich Chancellor, but as the head of the NSDAP promoting his party. And yet Goebbels has succeeded in compelling all German radio stations to broadcast it nationwide.

Hitler's speech sounds programmatic but reveals hardly anything concrete about his program. Instead, he relies on pompous metaphors and the sound of grand words, signal words he repeats rhythmically, even if quite a few sentences thereby lose their meaning. He intends, he solemnly attests, "to build up this *Volk* upon the German farmer as the cornerstone of each *völkisch* life. By fighting for the German future, I must fight for this German patch of soil and must fight for the German farmer. He renews us, he peoples our cities, he has been the perpetual fountainhead for millennia, and he must be preserved. Then onto the second pillar of our nationhood, the German worker, that German worker who in the future ought not and must no longer be an alien in our German Reich, whom we intend to lead back into the community of our people, for whom we will pry open the gates and burst them open so that he may enter into the community of the German *Volk* as the backbone of the German nation."

Between it all, like a random stray bullet, a vaguely worded but concrete political threat: Hitler also wants to fight "against the symptoms of our parliamentary, democratic system."

Then it continues in the swaying rhythm of lofty diction. His aim, he hammers into his listeners, is the "restoration of cleanliness in our *Volk*. Cleanliness in all areas of our life, cleanliness in our administration, cleanliness in public life, but also cleanliness in our culture." He will, he proclaims, favor the people once again "with a truly German culture, with a German art, with a German architecture, a German music that ought to reflect our soul." He wants to "inspire reverence for the grand traditions of our people, inspire deep reverence for the achievements of the past, the humble admiration of the great men in German history."

The terms can't sound sublime enough: reverence, cleanliness, *Volk*, *völkisch*, *Volkstum* [nationhood], *Volksgemeinschaft* [community of the *Volk*], and again and again German, German, German. Not a word about the fact that a homogeneous *Volk* in concord about fundamental questions doesn't even exist, but that the nation's populace has by now fanned out into classes, strata, and milieus with contrary interests and opinions between which compromises must be brokered. Hitler the populist maps out for his audience this fantasy-construct of an organic "Volksgemeinschaft" in which all distinctions and individualities coalesce into monolithic collectives like "the" German farmer and "the" German worker, or into hard-to-define ideas like "the" German culture and "the" great men of German history.

*

At the same time, 8 p.m., Thomas Mann delivers his speech on Richard Wagner in the main lecture hall of the University of Munich. Katia accompanies him. Klaus and Elisabeth, the youngest daughter, are also present. Biographers will later claim that listeners had filled the rows of seats to capacity. Klaus Mann's view of the matter is more sober; looking around the hall in which his father is to speak, he notes: "Not very full, but good-sized audience."

Thomas Mann has worked on his essay *Leiden und Größe Richard Wagners* [*Sufferings and Greatness of Richard Wagner*] since mid-December and then trimmed it down to a barely tenable length for a lecture. He leaves no doubt about his enthusiasm and love for Wagner: "What I owe him as one who relishes and learns I can never forget, never the hours of profound, solitary bliss amid the multitude of theatergoers, hours replete with thrills and raptures of the senses and intellect, with insights into matters of such poignant and grand significance as only this artform can vouchsafe." In order to intimate Wagner's stature as artist, he ranks him among a pantheon of peerless authors: Tolstoy, Zola, Ibsen, Dostoyevsky, Schopenhauer, Nietzsche. He pays tribute to him as the discoverer of myth for opera, as an arch-Romantic, a great psychologist, and an ardent master of theatrics.

77

He does not restrict himself to invoking illustrious names and lofty merits. He aims to paint a nuanced portrait and present his very individualistic view of Wagner the artistic personality. Thomas Mann describes Wagner as the forerunner of the poets of Decadence who at the fin-de-siècle celebrated ecstasy and decay, the morbid and the bizarre. In the very enumeration of characters with whom Wagner populates the stage in *Parsifal* he sees striking proof of this: "What an accretion of extreme and offensive outlandishness! A sorcerer emasculated at his own hand; a desperate hybrid creature comprised of corrupter and penitent Mary Magdalene with cataleptic transition states between both forms of existence; a lovesick high priest awaiting redemption from a chaste young boy ..." In other words, Mann does not limit himself to a white-washed glorification of Wagner, but rather gets to the root of his operatic art's secret psychic drives, which have nothing to do with homespun notions of decency and sexual morals – and nothing whatsoever with the insistence upon "cleanliness" in German culture that Hitler is exalting in Berlin at the same time.

This is a provocation, no, a sacrilege. For adherents of *völkisch* art, Wagner's oeuvre is a sanctum. His passion for ostentatiously German cultural traditions and Nordic mythology makes him an unassailable figure of identification for them. Hardly anything could be more offensive in their eyes than seeing Wagner of all people occupy the role of a modernist artist driven by exotic desires, conjuring extreme crises of the psyche in his operas.

Most of all, though, Thomas Mann comes to Wagner's defense against all nationalists among the Wagnerians. In so doing he directly targets, without naming names, Hitler himself. After all, he adorns his lecture with a whole array of dog whistles from the current political battles. He calls Wagner a "socialist and cultural utopian," speaks about the "cosmo-politan" spirit of his music, praises not his German but his "European artistry," and even claims that by now Wagner would "most assuredly be called a cultural Bolshevik." As if that weren't enough, Thomas Mann finally attacks the allegedly decisive "great men" of history whom Hitler celebrates at the Berlin Sportpalast in parallel. He calls them, employing a prophetic phrase of Wagner's that anticipates much of the psychological analysis of narcissistic Führer figures, "hideous, violent little creatures, insatiable – because they have nothing whatsoever inside themselves and thus must always devour their way into themselves from without."

The applause is considerable and Thomas Mann satisfied. Karl Vossler, the university's most famous scholar of Romance languages, walks up to him and praises him to the skies; it was the best lecture he had ever heard in this auditorium. This delights Thomas Mann so much that he invites Vossler to join him and his family in the bar of the Hotel Vier Jahreszeiten afterward. There is, after all, not just the success of the speech to celebrate, but also, after midnight, his and Katia's twenty-eighth wedding anniversary, as well as the impending departure for his little tour of Europe. The following afternoon at 4 p.m. he will set off for Amsterdam with Katia, the Wagner manuscript in his suitcase, and then later add on some weeks of vacation in Switzerland. All in all, a happy conclusion to a good six weeks of hard work. Elisabeth, the fourteen-year-old, is in a bar for the first time, looking around, excited and intimidated, and Klaus is amused at her bashful curiosity at the nocturnal lives of adults.

Two months later, however, the happy evening has a serious epilogue. For a long time no word of dissent is lodged in public against Thomas Mann's lecture, but as soon as the essay is published in its entirety in April, Thomas Mann is in for a bitter surprise. At first, only rumors about an attack directed against him reach him by radio broadcast. Then two days later he has the Easter edition of the *Münchner Neueste Nachrichten* before him with a declaration of protest in it that inveighs against his Wagner lecture. He knows quite a few of the signatories well: Olaf Gulbransson, for example, the caricaturist for the satirical magazine *Simplicissimus*, or composers like Richard Strauss or Hans Pfitzner.

His adversaries have waited, they write, until "Germany's nationalist uprising assumed a sturdy framework" to finally accuse Thomas Mann of having denigrated in his speech "the memory of the great German master Richard Wagner," which is to say, they first wanted to be certain of having the power of the new Nazi state behind them before moving against Thomas Mann in their open letter. His portrait of Wagner as a decadent and cosmopolitan is intolerable to them and their nationalist pride. If Mann hears in Wagner's music not just Germanness, but also "worldly conformity, worldly palatability," then they view that as tanta-mount to a disparagement "of our great German musical genius."

Among the peculiarities of this literary scandal is the fact that fifteen or twenty years earlier Thomas Mann would likely have added his own signature to quite a few passages of this protest declaration. Until some time after the end of the German Empire, he, too, numbered among the artists and intellectuals who enjoyed pitting German culture against international and especially Western civilization. At that time they were scared by the notion that elite culture as the benchmark standard could be superseded by mass entertainment as it was beginning to develop in the United States, Great Britain, and France.

Back then Thomas Mann saw himself as the proponent of a specifically German art, the "mission" of which consisted not least in cleaving to an aristocratic, upper-class understanding of culture, in opposition to the trend of the increasing democratization of all social relations. He saw himself expressly as an artist who felt beholden solely to the laws of aesthetics and who didn't want to be bothered with politics. What's more, in his eyes the Germans were, as a whole, an unpolitical people for whom democratic circumstances were essentially foreign and who had found their proper system of government in the "much-decried authoritarian state."

A position that brought with it political consequences, however. With the outbreak of the First World War, Thomas Mann lost himself in a frenzy of nationalism. His 600-page essay, *Reflections of a Nonpolitical Man*, struck *völkisch* notes in places; Mann defended not only the particular traditions and colorations of German culture, but also worked himself into a feeling of superiority over other national cultures, against the backdrop of Weimar Classicism, German Idealism, and the aesthetics of German Romanticism. In this sense he necessarily understood any borrowing of impulses from abroad as an attenuation, a degradation of the German ideal. For a time, the cosmopolitans among those artists who viewed culture as a seamless network of influences and traditions, such as his brother Heinrich, turned into doggedly combated bogeymen for him.

Not until 1922, a good ten years ago, did he espouse democratic values and an international culture in his speech *The German Republic*, a shift prompted more by political reasons than aesthetic ones. Thomas Mann was horrified at the nationalist violence of the initial postwar years that erupted in assassinations and coup attempts. Given the flood of such bloody acts, he discovered for himself the core of the democratic, republican ideal, namely, settling disputes peacefully through compromise. Precisely this, he then emphasized, accorded with the nature of "Germanness," for it was "liberal in the humane sense, clement in culture, dignified, peaceable," and not at all aggressive, marginalizing, and destructive.

Yet as the protestation against his Wagner lecture now unequivocally shows him, he himself has become the target of an aggressive, marginalizing nationalism. He, the man who understands himself to be the ambassador of Germany and German culture, has quite a bit of trouble coping with this. Despite always having been repelled by Nazi brutality and anti-Semitism, he is starting to bargain with himself now that he has been driven into emigration, secretly, in moments of weakness, about whether and under what circumstances an arrangement with Hitler's people might just be possible. They are depressing deliberations that he logs in his diary, and they sound terrible: "To a certain extent, the revolt against the Jews would have my sympathy," he writes there, "if the cessation of control by the Jewish spirit over what is German weren't so perilous for the latter and this Germanness weren't so dumb as to lump my sort together in the same pot and drive me out along with them."

A frightening, egotistical, anti-Semitic thought that sounds as though Thomas Mann were in fact ready to accept the expulsion of the Jews from Germany if he weren't thrown in the same pot with them and would get to stay in the country unmolested. The extent to which he has remained so alien to politics despite his affirmation of the Republic is shown by his preposterous formulation about the "control by the Jewish spirit over what is German." This note from a candid, desperate moment becomes even more inscrutable when one realizes that Thomas Mann's wife and his parents-in-law are of Jewish ancestry.

*

The wave of influenza is receding. The number of daily new infections in Berlin has sunk below one thousand.

In Berlin-Wedding, a forty-six-year-old communist metal worker is attacked by four men and shot dead.

Schutzstaffel for Writers

Sunday, February 12

Bernard Rust, the new man at the helm of the Prussian Ministry of Education, has come to a decision. He will tap Franz Ulbrich, hitherto artistic director in Weimar and an experienced theater manager, as chief of the Schauspielhaus on Gendarmenmarkt. Hanns Johst, rumored to become artistic director and general manager, will serve alongside Ulbrich as head dramaturg and will see to a nationalist-minded repertory. Last year Ulbrich staged Benito Mussolini's and Giovacchino Forzano's drama *Napoleon: The Hundred Days*, which was premiered in the presence of Adolf Hitler. As their first large production, the new leadership duo is planning to stage the world premiere of Johst's play *Schlageter* for Hitler's birthday on April 20.

*

Bernhard von Brentano cannot accept the crippling inaction since January 30. He wants to do something, just doesn't know what. Now thirty-one years old, he is a wiry, somewhat insecure man and still not a famous author, but he has outstanding connections. His father was the Justice and Interior Minister in Hesse, and it is from him he learned the importance of cultivating one's networks. Brentano's first mentor was Joseph Roth, who procured him a job in the Berlin editorial office of the *Frankfurter Zeitung* in 1925. But then Brentano met Brecht, developed a passion for Marxism, and flirted with joining the KPD, which Joseph Roth opposed as radically as he did the Nazis. As usual Roth reacted irascibly, breaking off his friendship with Brentano and proclaiming him a favorite villain: "He is one of the three or four people I could murder with the casual disregard with which one stubs out a cigarette."

Through his friendship with Brecht – they planned to establish a magazine together – quite a few doors opened for Brentano among left-wing writers and journalists. He quickly had excellent relationships with Anna Seghers, Leonhard Frank, Alfred Döblin, and Johannes R. Becher, who recently ascended to the Central Committee of the KPD, or even with Helene Weigel, Heinrich Mann, Hermann Kesten, and Rudolf Olden of the *Berliner Tageblatt*.

He has invited all of them for a private meeting of writers today at his home, on Budapester Strasse between Kurfürstendamm and Tiergarten, and all of them have come. The apartment occupies a quiet location in the rear building, with high ceilings and wide, luminous windows looking out onto a grassy inner courtyard.

It has been two weeks now since Hitler has been in power and left no doubt he plans to use it. How can they as writers respond? That is what Brentano wants to know. As soon as he opens the newspapers, he finds damn good reasons for being afraid. Last year he published a book of reportage: *Der Beginn der Barbarei in Deutschland* [*The Beginning of Barbarism in Germany*], a singular polemic against the Nazis. He of course must bank on now ranking quite highly on the list of authors with whom Hitler wants to get even. What can they as writers do? What strategies are out there? How are they supposed to act?

The most combative reaction comes from Brecht. He has already clearly felt the effects of the change of government. It's not just that a production of *The Measures Taken* was canceled by the police in Erfurt and the premiere of his *Saint Joan* was banned in Darmstadt. A few days ago, Helene Weigel, Brecht's wife, was arrested while performing his *Wiegenlieder einer proletarischen Mutter* [*Lullabies of a Proletarian Mother*] at a communist event. Brecht was alerted right away and fortunately was able to secure her release quickly. But the situation had been dangerous enough.

He is ready any time, Brecht proclaims to the assembly at Brentano's. He'll write anything needed now before the election: proclamations, appeals, speeches, plays. That he can do, that is his purpose. But he needs protection. He has already received several threatening letters notifying him of the arrival of five SA men. He does not want to wait until they are actually standing at his door. Wouldn't it be possible, Brecht asks the circle, "to get a *Schutzstaffel* for threatened writers?" He envisions, he says, a couple of hard-nosed bodyguards, four or five guys, practiced in brawling and, if possible, armed.

A suggestion that fits splendidly into the world of his *Threepenny Opera*: Brecht as soapbox orator shielded during his appearances by bodyguards like gangster boss Mack the Knife is by his entourage.

Rudolf Olden yanks Brecht back down to earth, however; how exactly does he picture this working? In his apartment, for instance: "You can't just install a guardhouse there." Heinrich Mann, too, can do little but smile ironically at the suggestion. Will Brecht's *Schutzstaffel* guard or surveil the writers, protect them or put them into protective custody, defend them or betray them?

Violence, Heinrich Mann submits, cannot be a reasonable strategy for writers because ultimately violence will always turn against them. Violence is the weapon of the Nazis, who can mobilize tens of thousands of storm troopers. In the face of such a force, a *Schutzstaffel* for authors and artists will always end up on the losing side. The only reasonable prospect lies not in civil-war-like street fights, but in a return to civilized political circumstances.

Perhaps they should call a large rally, Leonhard Frank says, a convocation of writers with the most illustrious names who object to Hitler as Reich Chancellor. Even a tiny remark from a writer like Gerhart Hauptmann would echo around the globe! It would nevertheless have to be an ideologically neutral rally of the largest possible size, which is to say, not one limited only to left-wing or even just liberal bourgeois authors, but one committed to ideals everyone can agree to: "As far as I'm concerned, for the freedom of the spirit or some such mumbo jumbo."

Not exactly a very original proposal, the idea garners little more than a shrug from the others. A protest event of the most important, most renowned writers has in fact already been convened under Olden's direction for February 19: the convention of *Das freie Wort*. A venue for the event has since been found, too: the large ballroom of the Krolloper across from the Reichstag. Unfortunately, Heinrich Mann has already declined because he doesn't want to be co-opted into being a co-organizer without his consent. Thomas Mann's opening speech will also probably come to naught because he is currently on tour abroad with his Wagner lecture.

Frank doesn't have it easy in this group as it is. He is either viewed with mistrust or derided by many writers oriented around the KPD. To be sure, he is a genuine proletarian, the son of a journeyman carpenter, and has been able to eke out a university education only at great personal sacrifice. For several years, however, he's been practically spoiled by success and recognition. The reviews of his books are glowing, as are the sales figures, and the Prussian Academy has admitted him to their ranks. The success of his novella *Carl and Anna*, the love story of a soldier returning from war who adopts the name of a comrade to win over the latter's wife, made him a well-to-do man – a newly acquired wealth he enjoys displaying. He clothes himself after the English fashion in tailored suits and handmade shoes, and loves good food and expensive hotels.

The others have a hard time reconciling themselves to that. All of them – Brecht, Anna Seghers, Johannes R. Becher, Helene Weigel, Alfred Döblin – grew up in bourgeois families, attended good schools and universities, but now often cut an explicitly un-bourgeois figure. Brecht has made the proletarian leather jacket his trademark, likes to appear unshaven wearing his flat cap and wire-rimmed glasses, and thereby inspires many emulators among younger left-wing authors. But it's not just about outer appearances. The others ultimately insinuate that

Figure 11: Leonhard Frank in his study, 1930

Frank is a renegade, that he has sacrificed his convictions for success. When Leonhard Frank notices how indecisive and dejected Brentano's guests are today, he says in surprise to Brecht: "I thought we wanted to start a revolution here." Brecht's snarky reply: "Then you'll be pleasantly disappointed."

In the end Brentano hasn't thought enough about the impact of the meeting he's called. There are no proposals or plans on which they are able to agree, and so a feeling of helplessness takes hold fast, which does not improve the mood, but lowers it more. At a very similar meeting perhaps four weeks earlier when Hitler was not yet in power, Brecht, Feuchtwanger, Becher, and Frank had spoken about potential exile, almost as a matter of course. Back then Brecht had adjured the others that they mustn't lose contact with one another under any circumstances: "The worst thing facing us in our emigration is being separated. We have to try to stick together." Now that the danger has grown significantly, however, no one apparently wants to bring up the topic of exile or make concrete arrangements – not even Hermann Kesten, even though he has had a visa for France in his pocket for two weeks now.

Only Johannes R. Becher makes one last attempt to cheer up the assembly. The situation, he says, isn't all that bad. The worst thing that could happen to them would be for the Nazis to dump them all in a train and ship them off to Moscow. And Becher sees no harm in that.

For him, as a leading member of the KPD, it probably wouldn't be, either. By contrast, this vision of the future instills surprisingly little optimism in all the others, although they do view themselves as communists. Despondent, they say their goodbyes and head off.

*

On this day Egon Erwin Kisch receives an order from the Berlin Chief of Police. He was born in Prague and has a Czechoslovakian passport. This enables the authorities to deport him. He must, the document reads, leave the country within two weeks because he has acted "subversively toward the German Empire." Kisch did in fact participate in several events that weren't exactly pro-government. If he does not leave willingly, the order threatens with deportation and, if he should return to Germany without authorization, six weeks' imprisonment. Kisch enjoys such situations. Of course he won't leave. He'd much rather be forcibly deported, which would provide him with the material for his next story, which will then automatically turn into an indictment of the Nazi regime.

*

Pasted to the advertising columns is an *Urgent Call for Unity!* of the *Internationaler sozialistischer Kampfbund* [*International Socialist Militant League*] that opposes the inability of the SPD and KPD to take a common stand against the NSDAP despite their ideological differences. The placard reads:

"The obliteration of all personal and political freedom in Germany is imminent if it is not possible at the last minute to combine all forces united in their rejection of fascism, irrespective of their differences in principles. The next opportunity to do so is March 5 … We appeal to anyone who shares this conviction with us to help realize a fusion of the SPD and KPD for this election campaign … Let us ensure that idleness of character and cowardice of heart do not allow us to sink into barbarism!"

The appeal bears sixteen signatures, among them those of the painter Käthe Kollwitz and of the writer Heinrich Mann.

*

In Eisleben, west of Halle, a propaganda march of around 600 SA and SS men takes place. During the march they attack two buildings used by the city's communists with pistols and spades. Three communists are shot dead, twenty-four wounded by blows from spades. An SS man dies, too. And in a street battle in Hesse's Bensheim between communists and National Socialists, an innocent passerby is killed by a shot to the chest.

Men in Black

Monday, February 13

Wilhelm Herzog has been back in Germany since December. The *Liga für Menschenrechte* has invited him to Berlin for some lectures. For three years now he has been living in a fishing village called Sanary-sur-Mer, a bit east of Marseille. The Nazis' harassment of the Jews and outbursts of hatred had become unbearable for him. Sooner or later, he reckoned, they would seize power for themselves. And so he rented a cheap little house in Sanary and has since been enjoying the beauties of the Côte d'Azur, glad to be spared the daily reports of terrorism in Germany. He hasn't, however, neglected his old contacts, particularly his friend Heinrich Mann.

On the agenda this evening is his final lecture, which he entitled *Die Generäle der Republik* [*The Generals of the Republic*]. If one were to think of Schleicher, it sounds politically quite relevant, but the reference is to the generals of the French Republic at the time of the Dreyfus Affair. The parallels between the scheming, anti-Semitic French military officers of that period and the German generals of the Weimar Republic are so glaring, however, that Herzog doesn't need to point them out explicitly to his listeners.

The event venue is the assembly hall in the Ministry of Economics. Heinrich Mann walks on stage first and introduces Herzog to the audience in a few sentences. When he descends to make room for his friend behind the lecture podium, he whispers a brief remark about two men in black in the first row he takes for informers. Indeed, Herzog notices that the two assiduously take notes as soon as he begins speaking.

Herzog is stunned and alarmed. He interrupts his lecture to address the two men: "I have had quite a few attentive listeners before, but none this attentive." Some people from the audience stand up to get a better look at them both, but they show no signs of bother and continue taking notes as soon as Herzog resumes speaking.

After the lecture, a Reichstag deputy, the socialist Oskar Cohn, takes Herzog aside and counsels him to leave Germany as soon as possible, preferably this very night, he urges. There's another train departing for Marseille just after twelve.

Herzog deems this excessive, waving him off. He'd planned to stay overnight in Berlin and not leave until the following day around noon. When Cohn very forcefully advises him once more against any delay, Herzog realizes that the two informants portend a very real danger. Straightaway, his mind is made up. Even if it looks like a precipitous getaway, he shall take the night train to France. In his agitation he suggests to Heinrich Mann that he accompany him. After all, it is possible the two suspicious men were also supposed to monitor him.

Mann shakes his head: "No, alas, I can't. I have to give a speech in the Academy on April 3 to celebrate the sixtieth birthday of Jakob Wassermann."

"You won't be giving that speech," Herzog says.

"Why not?"

"You will not be giving that speech," Herzog repeats.

"Oh, don't you look on the black side," Mann replies.

"I don't know if I see black, but I do see brown. Anyhow: I'll expect you in Sanary. You can stay with me. Telegraph me upon your arrival."

*

Bernhard Rust, the provisional Education Minister of Prussia, delivers a lecture at the University of Berlin on the "Kulturwillen der Nationalsozialisten" ["National Socialists' Will to Culture"]. He announces the future strict alignment of all forms of schooling, education, and culture according to *völkisch* viewpoints: "Let me provide an example with which I can demonstrate what I intend to do: There is, for instance, an academy of writers. It also has a director. In the past few days, the name of this man has been seen flaunted from the advertising columns, calling on Social Democrats and communists to form a 'joint defensive front.' It seems to me it is not just that director who is guilty, but equally guilty are all those who chose this man, Herr Heinrich Mann, as director of their Academy. Do not worry! I will put an end to the scandal at the Academy."

*

During political altercations in Dortmund, Bochum, Braunschweig, and Hecklingen (outside Dessau), four men are killed and two women sustain serious injuries.

Fever and Flight
Tuesday, February 14

Alfred Kerr is sick with a nasty case of flu. It was only January 29 that he was in the theater and saw Frenchman René Fauchois' comedy *Prenez garde à la peinture* [*Caution! Wet paint*] on Schiffbauerdamm. Without a doubt, Kerr is Germany's most influential, often most merciless, and not infrequently most supercilious theater critic, but he likes such light, short fare: "Delightfully wrought comedy. Radiant cast. Huge laughs," reads his summary in the *Berliner Tageblatt*.

Kerr is also trying to find cheer in his illness. In a short poem written from his sickbed, he informs *Tageblatt* readers about the "Verlauf und Heilung der Grippe" ["Progression and Healing of the Flu"]. For him this isn't out of the ordinary. In his eyes he is an important enough author that his audience very well ought to take an interest in his illnesses too. He is now sixty-five years old and writes not only for the *Berliner Tageblatt*, but also for the *Frankfurter Zeitung*, which is to say, for the country's two most sophisticated newspapers. For his pieces he is paid so terrifically well that he can afford a rather impressive villa in Grunewald, at Douglasstrasse 10.

Kerr is a Jew and has never left any doubt about what he thinks of Hitler and the NSDAP. In the papers as well as on the radio, he warns against them, polemicizes against them, makes fun of them. One of his poems published a year earlier reads:

"We who truly back our nation / Brutalize and go berserk.
Just for public acclamation / Do we vote for Hindenburk.
If through our election riots / Germany should go to hell, –
Deutschland, Deutschland über alles, / Über alles in der Welt."

Last year he was elected President of the German PEN Centre alongside the ailing poet and novelist Theodor Däubler – a position that may lend even more weight to his warnings about the Nazis among liberal readers.

This afternoon the telephone rings. Influenza still has Kerr firmly in its grasp. A police officer requests to speak with him. Kerr struggles over to the phone, weary. Evidently the officer is no Nazi but means well. He warns him that the very next day his passport is to be revoked by the authorities, and from that moment on he will be unable to leave Germany again. It is obvious the new masters of the Interior Ministry do not under any circumstances want to let him escape and want to be certain they can arrest him whenever they deem the moment ripe.

Kerr does not delay. Despite a fever of 39°C (102°F), he gets up, within minutes has packed a rucksack with the barest of necessities, grabs his still-valid passport, and catches a ride to Anhalter Bahnhof. There he boards the next train to Prague and within three and a half hours of the considerate officer's call is in Czechoslovakia, without any money, without a job, without his wife and their two children. He will see Germany again fourteen years later.

*

This evening around 8 p.m.: a large throng of celebrities at *Capitol* cinema on Budapester Strasse, not far from the house where Bernhard von Brentano lives. It's pouring with rain, and in the street taxis and hulking limousines are nudging their way as closely as possible to the cinema foyer so that their passengers can get out. The film *Grand Hotel* is celebrating its premiere, a Hollywood production for which no expense was spared, having won the Oscar for the year's best film and starring Greta Garbo, Joan Crawford, and John Barrymore.

The host is the Stage Guild, which organized the evening to bring in money for its unemployed members. No one who wants to be somebody in the film industry can afford to pass up this screening. Gentlemen in tuxedos, ladies in spectacular eveningwear, the hall decked out in splendor. The Italian soprano Mafalda Salvatini, who posed for the photographers with Carl Zuckmayer at the Press Ball two weeks ago, is singing as the opening act. The ballet of the Staatsoper Unter den Linden is performing on stage, and Richard Lert – referred to by the *B. Z. am Mittag* with some facetiousness as "Herr Vicki Baum" – is conducting its orchestra.

Vicki Baum, Richard Lert's wife, is the actual star of the evening, after all. Until recently she was an editor at Ullstein and supplied the press's various newspapers with reviews and news coverage. On the side, she knocked out stories and novels year after year like it was nothing. They also appeared with Ullstein and have secured her a devoted community of readers. A petite woman with large eyes, and as one of the country's more popular star authors, she has a remarkable flair for characters representative of the age: men who have lost their footing in war and ensconce themselves behind a façade of callousness, or young women carving out a new, independent life for themselves while incurring bitter wounds for doing so. In her books she is always hard on the heels of the latest fashions. She depicts the spirit of the times without turning up her nose at it and as a result has always enjoyed tremendous success, but all of her triumphs were nothing compared to what was in store for her when she published the novel *Grand Hotel* in 1929.

She didn't start off as an author, but as a musician. A highly talented, very busy harpist, she played in Vienna in Gustav Mahler's and Bruno Walter's orchestras. It was by accident that she discovered her literary talent when she wrote articles for her first husband, a journalist with writer's block, which he then published under his own name. When she had children with Richard Lert, her second husband, she called it quits in her vocation as a harpist and focused on her career as an author.

Vicki Baum describes herself as an author in the first row of the second-raters. She writes breathtakingly fast: a novel in three months or even in only a couple of weeks. Sentences and ideas just come to her. With *Grand Hotel*, however, the idea gestated for a long time before she set down to work on it.

It is a novel that makes do without a central protagonist. In it, Vicki Baum brings together characters from the most varied social strata and milieus in a classy hotel, artfully linking their fates for a brief moment in their lives before their paths again diverge. A formerly world-famous prima ballerina rebels against the decline of her career, a secretary gets involved with a company boss fighting the bankruptcy of his business, a terminally ill accountant wants to spend his last days amid the luxury of a ritzy hotel, and a very style-conscious young baron who forfeited his fortune as a soldier during the war wants to rob the aging prima ballerina but falls in love with her instead.

The novel skates hard along the edge of low-brow writing. Guiding her readers at high speed through a venturesome mixture of society, mystery, and romance novel, Vicki Baum eschews no melodramatic effect, but her book is not superficial. She writes with coolness and sobriety and has an exacting eye for people living under the impression that they have to battle their way through a society without morals or bearings.

As with Remarque's *All Quiet on the Western Front*, Ullstein Verlag has the savvy to jump-start her novel with effective marketing, too. Once again the book is serialized in Ullstein's *Berliner Illustrirte*, and once again the other Ullstein newspapers are roped in for a vigorous PR campaign. Vicki Baum tells reporters she worked as a chambermaid at the luxury hotel *Bristol* for weeks to do research for her novel and poses for fabulous photos: Vicki Baum in a fur coat, Vicki Baum in a Charleston dress, Vicki Baum at her desk with an absurdly long peacock feather as a quill pen, or even while training at a boxing ring.

The success is overwhelming. The book sells hundreds of thousands of copies, foreign publishers scramble for the translation rights, and a theatrical adaptation under the direction of Gustav Gründgens becomes a huge nationwide event. Broadway in New York restages the play, and Hollywood buys the film rights. It is a novel's victory march.

Ultimately her American publisher Doubleday invites her to the United States on a promotional tour. The plan entails a couple of weeks, but she stays for seven months. She enjoys life in the United States. Paramount Pictures offers her a highly remunerative contract as a screenwriter; with directorial genius Ernst Lubitsch she is to develop the topic for a new film, set this time not in a hotel, but in a department store. Her script is rejected, alas, and her contract abruptly terminated, but even setbacks can scarcely tarnish her enthusiasm for America, especially as she can now read in German newspapers that the Nazis consider her a typical Jewish asphalt writer whose activities they need to put a stop to at once since she was ruining German culture with her shallow sensationalist novels.

Like George Grosz, Vicki Baum also returns to Germany in 1932 solely to arrange her family's relocation to America. In Santa Monica, California, she rents a house and plans to construct a villa nearby with the fortune *Grand Hotel* is earning her.

Now Vicki Baum is working on her first American book for Doubleday. With Richard Lert and their children, she left Germany behind without much melancholy; sentimentalities don't suit her. It was in fact supposed to be a permanent farewell for them, though her husband has now traveled to Berlin once more to conduct the Staatsoper's orchestra at this film premiere. Persistent rumors abound, however, that Vicki Baum is also in town. There are people who stubbornly claim they saw her sitting in the Ullstein Verlag loge at the Press Ball just over two weeks ago, not far from Zuckmayer, Udet, and Remarque.

As the lights go back up now in the *Capitol* cinema after the gala premiere of *Grand Hotel* and the clapping crescendos at the end, though, the British director Edmund Goulding steps out before the screen without her and accepts the applause. Did Vicki Baum stay in America after all? Did she send her husband by himself to launch her film? Or can she no longer risk being seen in public now, fifteen days after the NSDAP seized the reins in the country?

*

Two of the communists who suffered severe injuries during the SA attack on the KPD bookstore in Eisleben the day before yesterday die in hospital. An SS man is shot dead in front of the People's House in Siegburg.

Slamming the Door
Wednesday, February 15

Max von Schillings is summoned to the ministry by Bernhard Rust, Prussia's provisional Education Minister. Schillings knows about summonses like these. When he was artistic director of the Staatsoper Unter den Linden in the mid-twenties, he argued bitterly with then-Education Minister, Carl Heinrich Becker, a liberal man without party affiliation. The topic was money. A "theater without a deficit," Schillings claimed at the time, is "in times like these a downright utopia." Eventually the Staatsoper's budget was so heavily overdrawn that Becker fired him without notice. But even that could not intimidate Schillings. He filed suit against his dismissal and received a settlement.

Now circumstances are different. Max von Schillings feels weary and sick, having never achieved as a composer what he expected of himself after following in the footsteps of his great idol Richard Wagner. For years nothing new has turned out well for him, and sometimes he thinks he knows what has caused him to fail; the Jew-dominated music world didn't give him, the Aryan and proponent of a pointedly German musical language, a chance to develop his talent. "It is no wonder," he writes after a revised version of his opera *The Piper's Day* attracted little attention in 1931, "that my dear critics, to whom any music emanating from one's heartstrings and emotion is anathema, derail the work. A piece that pledges itself to the German soul, to the German homeland, and even to an 'earnestness of art,' as Wagner revealed to us was possible, must of course be trampled underfoot."

A little more than three months ago, Schillings took over his office as President of the Academy from Max Liebermann. He is regarded as a skillful negotiator, but he still has little experience in his new role, and when Rust confronts him now in the ministry with accusations against the Academy, he offers almost no resistance. Rust is enraged about the signatures of Käthe Kollwitz and Heinrich Mann beneath the *Urgent Call for Unity*, which hangs from the advertising columns demanding a unified front of SPD and KPD against fascism and barbarism. Rust also interprets the matter as a direct assault on himself, a National Socialist. Here, he insinuates, he is vilified by members of the Academy as a barbarian although he, as trustee, is principal of this Academy.

The incongruities in the Academy bylaws inherited from the German Empire, which Max Liebermann was able to gloss over with nonchalance, now reveal their explosive power. The Academy is not truly free in its decisions; its statutes cede too much authority to the minister who happens to be in office. Rust demands the resignation or expulsion of Kollwitz and Mann, and forthwith, lest he dissolve the Academy altogether or, at a minimum, the Division for the Art of Poetry.

Schillings needn't let this ultimatum fool him. After all, Kollwitz and Mann signed the *Urgent Call for Unity* not as Academy members, but as citizens with the constitutionally guaranteed right to freedom of expression. They are world-renowned artists and not employees of the Academy under an obligation to maintain political neutrality.

Figure 12: Max von Schillings (center foreground), with Hermann Göring standing behind him

Of course, it is not clear whether a Nazi minister like Rust would be responsive to discussing such subtle differences. But for him, too, quite a bit is at stake. Were he actually to attempt to shut down the long-standing and illustrious Prussian Academy of the Arts after just ten days at the helm of his ministry because two of its members signed their names to a political appeal during an election campaign, such a move would pose nearly incalculable risks for him. The uproar that would invariably follow such a decision could also flush him out of office.

In the end, however, it never even occurs to Schillings to defend these two members of his Academy. Like many others who have felt short-changed in the past or have failed in the face of Jewish competitors, he sympathizes with the new anti-Semitic rulers. In his view, as well, any public campaigning for a people's front consisting of SPD and KPD is a political provocation. Schillings tries merely to protect the Academy as an institution. He announces his immediate resignation should Rust pursue its disbanding. This resignation would cause a considerable stir and would have to be confirmed by the Prussian Minister of State, thus involving Rust's cabinet chief, Franz von Papen. Apart from that, Schillings accepts Rust's accusations against Kollwitz and Mann, declares he will see to their resignation, and hastens back to the Academy.

*

On his way from the ministry to the Academy building on Pariser Platz, Schillings could, if he took the time, purchase at a newsstand a copy of today's *Deutsche Kultur-Wacht* containing a short article by Hanns Johst. The newspaper is the mouthpiece of the *Kampfbund für deutsche Kultur* [*Militant League for German Culture*], led by chief ideologist of the NSDAP Alfred Rosenberg. The *Kampfbund* is an organization comprised of extreme right-wing intellectuals and artists who delight in working themselves into hateful tirades against Jews or who are up in arms about alleged "literary works alien to the race" and the "bastardization and negroization of existence." In recent days Johst has dealt with Education Minister Rust multiple times regarding his appointment as First Dramaturg at the Prussian State Theater. With quick reflexes he absorbs into his article the threats against writers in the Prussian Academy that Rust had issued two days prior at the university, and amplifies them: "Thomas Mann, Heinrich Mann, Werfel, Kellermann,

Fulda, Döblin, Unruh, etc. are liberal-reactionary writers who have no business whatsoever coming into contact with the German notion of literature in an official capacity ever again. We propose this utterly antiquated group be dissolved and convened anew in accordance with nationalist, truly poetic viewpoints."

*

Back in his Academy office, Max von Schillings first summons Käthe Kollwitz. In 1919 she was the first woman accepted into the Prussian Academy after more than a hundred years of its existence. Her talent as a graphic artist and sculptor was so apparent, her reputation in Europe and America so great, that the inveterate stag party of the Academy no longer saw any means to omit her from consideration. Unlike Max Liebermann, however, who enjoys playing the princely painter with Berliner gruffness and who resides in two villas on Pariser Platz and the Wannsee, Käthe Kollwitz lives in modest circumstances in one of Berlin's poorest working-class districts, Prenzlauer Berg. Social involvement was always more important to her than financial independence. While she does not belong to a party, she has never left any doubt about her affinity for leftist ideas and organizations.

She is now sixty-five years old and an internationally admired artist, and yet still she literally cannot afford a conflict with Schillings. He informs her of the minister's threats and makes clear to her that upon expulsion from the Academy she would immediately lose all access to her master studio where she has not only taught for years, but also worked – at present on a larger sculptural group in clay that is very important to her. For her that would be a catastrophe because she has no other suitable place she can complete the sculpture. Schillings offers her, in the event of her voluntary resignation from the Academy, permission to remain in her teaching position at full salary until October 1 and to continue using her studio. Her decision is soon made. Käthe Kollwitz never placed value on questions of status, neither on her title as professor nor on her membership in the Academy, and so she yields and declares her resignation.

*

Schillings has had all available members of the Academy – with one exception – convened by telegram for a special meeting. Because Berlin commands an extraordinarily extensive pneumatic mail network, information can be conveyed to almost anyone in the city in virtually no time. The assembly is to begin that same day at 8 p.m., the dramatically short notice indicating just how serious the matters to be discussed are. And so fifty men and one woman – Ina Seidel, a member of the Division for the Art of Poetry – hasten through the rain-soaked winter evening to Pariser Platz, pass through the column-lined side entrance to the Academy, and gather in the large meeting hall.

President Schillings makes a beleaguered impression when he enters. He informs those assembled about his conversation with Minister Rust and his threats against the Academy. Schillings would like to settle the matter with the least amount of fuss possible, which is why the confidentiality of this meeting is especially important to him. Not a word of their discussions is to get out – nor is any mention of his role in it either. Therefore, after his brief introduction, he has a ballot resolution passed obligating all those present to secrecy. Heinrich Mann's and Käthe Kollwitz' signatures on the *Urgent Call for Unity*, he then declares, are incompatible with their membership in the Academy, and Käthe Kollwitz has since realized this, he adds, and declared her resignation this afternoon. Now, a decision must still be made about Heinrich Mann.

What ensues from this terse prologue brings to mind a bizarre tragedy in five acts. The first act shows a president put on the defensive, seeking to equivocate. Gottfried Benn has since looked around the meeting hall, cannot spot Heinrich Mann anywhere, and poses two obvious questions. Has Mann been informed about the topic of this gathering? And why did Minister Rust threaten to disband only the division for literature because of the disputed signatures, but not the one for fine arts, to which Käthe Kollwitz belongs? Schillings hedges by initially offering an answer to the second question only, which nevertheless turns out to be not very persuasive; as president of the literary division, Heinrich Mann simply plays a special role in the Academy.

But the dramatist Ludwig Fulda comes to Benn's aid, probing once more whether Heinrich Mann was informed about the meeting – and Schillings is forced to admit Mann is the only Academy member in Berlin he didn't invite.

This is egregious. Schillings intends to reach a verdict about Heinrich Mann's expulsion without giving him the opportunity to express his views: a sleazy, unacceptable move that under normal circumstances would cost Schillings all confidence within the Academy. In his own defense and to emphasize the severity of the situation as well, he quickly presents the assembled with two alternatives that amount to an ultimatum. Either Heinrich Mann leaves the Academy or he, Schillings, will step down from office.

Even so, Schillings is no longer able to prevent what he would very much like to have avoided; the meeting is suspended, and Oskar Loerke, the secretary of the literary division, takes on the task of summoning Heinrich Mann by phone post factum.

The second act of the tragedy is thus a surprising intermission: waiting on the defendant. Understandably, the agitation in the room will not subside. The small circle of the six writers present gets together to consult about the attack on their chairman. Ludwig Fulda in particular is deeply upset. He has, he says, fought his entire life against every form of censorship. He wants nothing to do with an Academy that expels members because of expressions of political opinion. He wants to resign. Leonhard Frank and Döblin also play with the thought of leaving the Academy. Ina Seidel is palpably tense and wavers in her resolve about what she will do. Benn and Loerke, by contrast, exercise restraint. In the case of Loerke, who conceives of himself as a thoroughly apolitical writer, there are also substantive reasons for this. As the salaried secretary of the division, he would lose a portion of his income by resigning.

But time is of the essence. Among themselves, Fulda, Frank, and Döblin arrange for Frank to intercept Heinrich Mann as soon as he arrives at the Academy building and to implore him not to resign willingly. In this instance Schillings must have him expelled by a vote of those convened. The result of such a referendum cannot be foreseen, however, and if the plenary assembly actually rules against Mann, that will be the inducement for the others to declare their resignation in protest – and in this way publicly to give the expulsion the political red-flag effect and significance it is due.

The now-ensuing third act is the most outlandish and the shortest. Heinrich Mann enters the assembly hall to universal silence. As agreed, Leonhard Frank spoke with him briefly down by the Academy entrance and primed him in advance. But now President Schillings walks directly up to Mann and invites him to have a quick word in his office, together with divisional secretary Loerke, before the debate can begin. More waiting.

Around ten minutes later Schillings returns to the assembly hall quite pale, without Heinrich Mann, and discloses something that makes the convocation a complete farce and ultimately superfluous. Mann is renouncing his office as chairman of the literary division and declaring his resignation so as not to endanger the continued existence of the Academy.

Alfred Döblin is dumbfounded. Heinrich Mann, whom he regarded as a politically astute defender of the Republic, one absolutely firm in his convictions, is shying away from the battle for his republican constitutional rights. Döblin feels downright forsaken. A line by Goethe flashes through his mind: "Heinrich, you horrify me."

Nevertheless, he leaps to his feet, requests to speak, and thereby opens the floor for debate about Schillings' actions – thus beginning act four. He lodges multiple objections at once: against the lack of discussion with Heinrich Mann before the plenary assembly, against Schillings' ploy to broker the resignation behind closed doors, against the striking fact that from among more than fifty members of the Academy not a single voice of protest against Schillings' method has been raised. He demands that the literary division pass its resolutions regarding Mann's resignation at its own meeting.

Schillings, who achieved what he set out to achieve with the voluntary resignation, responds with nary a shrug, however. He merely wanted to spare Heinrich Mann an embarrassing interrogation in front of the assembly, and besides, Mann is still sitting in the president's office and surely willing to talk. At this, Döblin demands Mann be questioned now before the plenum despite his resignation, but his request is summarily denied by the assembly.

Evidently the majority no longer wants to debate, just put the matter to rest quickly and quietly. For the first time, however, it is not a writer requesting the floor, but an architect, City Building Commissioner Martin Wagner. He argues with a decisiveness hitherto unheard. Käthe Kollwitz and Heinrich Mann have been done wrong, Wagner says. There was nothing punishable about the appeal they signed. They were merely making use of their right to freedom of expression. This right is guaranteed them by the constitution upon which even Minister Rust swore his oath of office. Schillings should never have been allowed to offer to arrange the two members' resignations. At most he should have replied to Rust that the plenary assembly of the Academy would vote and decide. By the end of the meeting, he will have to consider, Wagner concludes, whether he still wants to belong to an Academy that tolerates such things.

Wagner is not yet fifty but has long been a high-profile man in town. He belongs to the SPD, worked for the unions, planned the much-celebrated Hufeisensiedlung in Berlin-Britz together with Bruno Taut, and then as City Building Commissioner employed such renowned colleagues as Mies van der Rohe and Walter Gropius. Like almost every sphere of life, however, city planning has also been extremely politicized in the Weimar Republic in recent years. Wagner's projects, particularly his large housing estates for the working class, are attacked as modernist and socialist. Thus it will come as no surprise to anyone if one of his ideological opponents requests the floor just after him, architect Albert Gessner, who joined the NSDAP the year before. Gessner does not respond to Wagner's arguments at all, but launches a personal attack on him. Wagner, he remarks derisively, was not elected by the Academy as a member, but was appointed by SPD Education Minister Grimme, a predecessor of Rust. This sounds as though Wagner were an Academy member of a lesser rank and had no right to take part when the elected members debate.

Naturally, as president, Schillings cannot allow the dispute to descend into such personal squabbling, and so he attempts once more to highlight the central issue of the affair. His only concern, he emphasizes, is whether he may sacrifice the entire Academy for two members. Every member, he is convinced, must draw certain consequences from the fact of his membership with respect to his public demeanor.

It is not entirely clear what Schillings means with these intimations, but apparently it is self-evident for him that upon joining the Academy one refrain from forceful political statements like the *Urgent Call for Unity*. In order to lend a bit more support to this scarcely tenable thesis, Schillings sets politics aside to address questions of style. With their signatures, he claims, Kollwitz and Mann have violated an indispensable sense of tact, for, in the final analysis, Minister Rust must feel publicly branded as a barbarian by the appeal they signed.

He does not salvage the discussion this way, but derails it once and for all. Is it appropriate to fall back on questions of style when one must address a massive political attack that casts doubt on the existence and independence of the Academy? Martin Wagner can hardly contain himself any longer. He first engages in a few rhetorical skirmishes with Gessner and Schillings, then puts forward a motion that has to be understood as a frontal attack against the president. On the contrary, he asks, is it not Schillings who has violated every sense of tact when he suggested Kollwitz and Mann resign, rather than defending them?

This is the open vote of no-confidence in Schillings. A president who does not stand up for Academy members when they are attacked by a politician with dubious reasoning, who himself urges them to resign instead, who does not invite Heinrich Mann to the session in which deliberations about him are to take place, and who in his own defense invokes questionable matters of style – is such a president the right man to lead an Academy?

In this volatile moment during which the situation could suddenly collapse, it is a writer, of all people, who comes to Schillings' defense. Wagner is misconstruing the issue with his motion, Gottfried Benn says. The question is solely about whether Schillings acted correctly to save the Academy, and that he did.

Benn has essentially said nothing new, just repeated Schillings' piously servile argument. But that suffices for Martin Wagner's patience to give out. He no longer has any sympathy for an institution whose members know so little moral courage. He stands up, declares his resignation, turns to the door, and slams it behind him.

And – no one follows him. Wagner remains alone in his demonstrative departure. Not another person gets up to leave. Ludwig Fulda, Alfred Döblin, Leonhard Frank are all roiling, but they are postponing their protest to the meeting of the literary division called for in the next few days. They want to vote with their colleagues who are absent today and keep their powder dry until then.

Another architect gets the last word at the meeting, Vice-President of the Academy Hans Poelzig. In all professional matters Poelzig and Wagner are close to one another. Poelzig is one of the most important exponents of New Objectivity in city planning; he has already completed a number of thrillingly beautiful buildings in Frankfurt, Breslau [present-day Wrocław], and Berlin and taken over the directorship of Berlin's art schools at the beginning of the year. He is definitely no eccentric resident of the ivory tower, but knows exactly the extent to which questions of art have become politicized, in recent years especially. Poelzig nevertheless explicitly thanks President Schillings for sparing the assembly a referendum on Mann's membership, for the Academy, Poelzig attests, is concerned only with art, not politics. That's why a referendum would have been completely impossible, in his view. Obviously, for Poelzig, too, the existence of the Academy appears to be more important than the civil rights of its members.

What still remains for the fifth and final act is a dejected epilogue in the president's office just next to the assembly hall. Naturally those belonging to the literary division want to learn from their abdicated chairman why he gave up the fight before it began. After having explicitly begged him to remain steadfast, Döblin, Frank, and Fulda in particular feel duped. Heinrich Mann stands up to shake everyone's hand, perhaps to comfort them, perhaps to apologize. But the rationales with which he furnishes them are surprisingly meager. There are no legal grounds in the statutes, Mann says, for kicking him out of the Academy. And yet – and now he almost sounds like Schillings referring to questions of tact – he doesn't want the fight for a post in the Academy to be forced upon him by the opposing side. That is not his style. He is not dependent on official positions. For others, though, like Loerke for instance, a disbanding of the Academy would have radical financial consequences. That, too, must be taken into consideration.

Did Schillings manage to achieve an outright victory despite displaying nothing but weakness? On one point at least the president miscalculated. Heinrich Mann was not present when the confidentiality of the session was voted on. Strictly speaking, he did not even participate in the meeting, but was led off straightaway into the president's office by Schillings. He therefore need not feel bound by the general order of secrecy and may inform the press of his resignation from the Academy. Although the meeting did not end until 11 p.m., by the very next day the newspapers contain detailed reports of everything that happened. The liberal papers are sorry for Heinrich Mann's resignation while the nationalist ones exult over it. It becomes clear, however, from all the articles how unscrupulously National Socialist politicians deal with civil rights, sixteen days after Hitler's rise to power.

Of course, the articles promptly alarm those members of the literary division who weren't able to participate in the meeting. The follow-up session Döblin announced is to take place on Monday, February 20. In the meantime, the need for information is great. Loerke most of all, the division's secretary, is besieged with questions. By now, though, he is in bad shape, as one might imagine. The polarization of politics in recent years has unnerved him. He is the sort of person who needs harmony, who simply loves burying himself in aesthetic questions, but who views quotidian problems of any kind, political ones especially, as shameless impositions.

Twenty years earlier, in 1913, he celebrated his greatest literary triumph; he was awarded the Kleist Prize. Other writers and artists hold him in esteem, his poems and discerning essays first and foremost. But he does not meet with success among readers, he earns scant royalties, and living off them is impossible. He therefore seized the opportunity when S. Fischer Verlag offered him a position as editor and at the Academy the post of divisional secretary. The two together provide a good living for him, and a substantial role in the literary business to boot. Only three years ago, together with his life partner and a mutual friend of theirs, he built a house in Frohnau, in the north of Berlin, a lovely location, with a generous yard, small art collection, and a housekeeper. All of this tickles his desire for recognition while also torturing him because he finds less and less time for his writing projects as a result of his bread-and-butter work.

The dispute in the Academy throws him full-on into a panic. He is afraid of losing his position as secretary and feels – he cannot express it drastically enough – pulverized between terrorists of the right and left wings. He despises the National Socialist members like Albert Gessner, but people like Döblin or Leonhard Frank also get on his nerves. To him they seem argumentative, uncooperative, and obsessed with their public. These very two, Döblin and Frank, who are so much more successful with their literature than he, he suspects of having leaked information to the press after the Academy meeting although in some articles Heinrich Mann is explicitly named as the source.

For Loerke it's all getting to be too much. He feels out of his depth in the conflicts he's now being drawn into. To Thomas Mann, who has gotten in touch on his lecture tour for the Wagner anniversary wanting to learn more about his brother's resignation, he writes an incoherent letter. According to Loerke's view it is not Minister Rust undermining freedom of expression, but the *Urgent Call for Unity*, which accuses everyone of cowardice of heart and barbarism who doesn't answer the call. In his eyes that is terrorism. He calls it that verbatim.

Other than that, what primarily turns up for Loerke are skeptical letters from the other division members. What is to be the point of the upcoming writers' meeting requested by Döblin? Is a protest against Rust planned? Wouldn't such a protest once again place the division or the Academy in danger of being disbanded? That would make no sense whatsoever. After all, Heinrich Mann resigned, by his own admission, to avert the threat of dissolution.

Two members only, both absent from the meeting, are intent on uncompromising actions: Alfons Paquet and Ricarda Huch. A colleague of Joseph Roth's, Paquet also writes mostly for the *Frankfurter Zeitung*, having reported as the Stockholm correspondent and written from

Figure 13: Ricarda Huch in 1934

Moscow about the Russian Revolution in 1918. His owes his greatest success to his plays and travelogues. A staunch pacifist, he has been promoting the vision of a conciliated, peaceful Europe since the war, like Harry Graf Kessler and Heinrich Mann. His reasoning in the current dispute is quite simple; the most important purpose of a writers' academy is to defend the freedom of literature and of authors – in political respects, too. If all authors collectively protest Heinrich Mann's compulsory resignation, he will join them, and if no protest comes about, he will resign on his own.

Ricarda Huch sees it from a similar angle, perhaps even more axiomatically. She is convinced that part of an author's labor involves a radical independence that does not comport with membership in state institutions. Only Thomas Mann, with many kind words, was capable of persuading her to join the Academy at the time. She is the undisputed grande dame of German literature and likewise one of the country's most distinguished scholars of literature and history. The sedate, bourgeois impression she makes with her soon-to-be seventy years notwithstanding, she is as ever a headstrong, combative woman. At eighteen she fell in love with her sister's husband – and he with her. She advanced her literary and scholarly career not least to gain distance from her family. The affair with her brother-in-law spanned over twenty-five years – during which time her marriage to a different man failed – before the two could finally marry, and then break up for good three years later.

Ricarda Huch has never bothered a great deal with conventions in matters of literature either. She would write sentimental novellas and novels, comprehensive studies of German history, or a riveting book about the lives and art of the Romantics, but also a detective novel and biographies about the Russian anarchist Mikhail Bakunin or the Italian freedom fighter Garibaldi. She is definitely no stuffy salon authoress.

On the contrary, she admires people who stand up for their convictions, rebels who cannot be intimidated. She will not be dissuaded from that now, after the NSDAP has seized power. She finds it wrong, she writes Loerke, that Heinrich Mann voluntarily resigned. It would have been better to take their chances and see whether Minister Rust would actually have mustered the gumption to disband the writers' division. She will resign from the Academy, she announces, as soon as she knows exactly how Käthe Kollwitz and Heinrich Mann were pushed out – and not because she deems the *Urgent Call for Unity* right, but because for her as a writer the right to freely express one's opinion is inalienable.

*

After the breakup of the premiere of Brecht's *Measures Taken* at Erfurt's Reichshallentheater on January 28, a criminal proceeding is launched in the Reich Court of Justice against those involved. They stand accused of incitement to high treason. This play is concerned with, so it reads again, "a communist-revolutionary depiction of the class struggle for the purpose of bringing about global revolution."

This evening a production of Brecht's *Threepenny Opera* is interrupted at the Stadttheater in Hildesheim. A group of audience members pelts the stage with rotten eggs and apples while a young man leaps onto the balustrade of the orchestra pit and attempts to deliver a speech amid the tumult. The police are called in to assist in the detention of twenty people and remove them from the theater. In the *Hildesheimer Beobachter* the municipal NSDAP demands the play be withdrawn.

*

Hitler gives a speech in Stuttgart's Stadthalle, which Süddeutscher Rundfunk broadcasts. The program is interrupted at 9:17 p.m. and cannot be resumed. Four men have severed the transmission cable in a courtyard driveway with an axe. The police swiftly detain numerous people. The perpetrators are not among them.

Deputy Reich Radio Commissioner Walter Conrad is dismissed. According to rumors, from now on the radio is to be placed under the command of NSDAP propaganda chief Joseph Goebbels.

As part of a big shake-up in Prussia, the superintendents of police belonging to the SPD or the Centre Party in Stettin [present-day Szczecin], Breslau [present-day Wrocław], Dortmund, Frankfurt am Main, Hannover, Halle, Weißenfels, Harburg-Wilhelmsburg, Koblenz, Oberhausen, and Bochum are relieved of command and replaced by officers belonging to or close to the new governing parties. In Berlin, Magnus von Levetzow, Reichstag deputy for the NSDAP, is named police superintendent. Several district presidents and administrators are switched out as well.

Hermann Göring issues a denial of the report by the British *Times* that the Prussian Interior Ministry is planning to arm the right-wing political organizations SA, SS, and *Stahlhelm* and deploy them as auxiliary police forces.

In Dortmund a communist is killed after being stabbed in the back, and an SA man is severely wounded by five gunshots.

During political clashes in Bochum and Leutmannsdorf in Silesia, a total of four National Socialists are killed and three wounded.

The Little Schoolteacher
Thursday, February 16

Inside Anhalter Bahnhof it is loud and lively as always. Margarete Steffin boards her train to Switzerland. There are a good many reasons for her to seek a safe haven from the Nazis. She is only twenty-four but has been performing for a long time with the speaking choir of *Fichte*, an athletic club for the working class, has taken elocution lessons with Helene Weigel at the Marxistische Arbeiterschule [Marxist Workers' School], and has appeared in various agitprop plays as an actor. For just over a year she's been having an affair with Brecht. They met during rehearsals for the premiere of his play *The Mother*. Helene Weigel, Brecht's wife, was playing the eponymous heroine then, she a maidservant. Her role was tiny.

If she is aboard a train to Switzerland now, though, it's not because she is a communist or the lover of a left-wing dramatist persecuted by the Nazis, but because she has tuberculosis. She is a child of the working classes, a genuine proletarian, and ravaged by the disease she acquired from Berlin's grim backstreets and from poor nutrition. Recently she underwent an operation by the Charité's star surgeon, Ferdinand Sauerbruch, who also treated Else Lasker-Schüler's son Paul. Sauerbruch had to remove a section of rib to be able to reach the lungs. Portions of infected pulmonary tissue had already coalesced with the peritoneum, making the procedure especially risky.

Brecht is not a great believer in matrimonial fidelity. He has a running series of romances, mostly brief sexual flings. But the affair with Margarete Steffin is different. He has fallen seriously in love. Helene Weigel has not failed to notice, and for months she has been thinking of splitting up with Brecht, not only because this longstanding affair hurts her, but also for health reasons. Brecht spends a lot of time with Grete, as he likes to call Margarete, and she also lives off and on with him at his place at Hardenbergstrasse 1a, right across from Bahnhof Zoologischer Garten. Brecht has insisted she is not contagious so far, but there is no absolute certainty about that. And that tuberculosis is no laughing matter Helene Weigel knows all too well; her sister Stella has been grappling with the disease for years now.

By this point Grete is more than just a lover for Brecht. Despite being forced to leave school at fourteen to earn money by menial labor, she has read prodigious amounts, has written poems as well as a school play, and speaks Russian. She types out Brecht's manuscripts and lets him rope her in more and more as his secretary, but mostly she gives Brecht – who has never had close contact with what the Marxists call the proletariat – a plausible feeling for the language, thinking, and way of life of the working classes. He dubs this slender young woman his little schoolteacher.

But now her tuberculosis has in fact become contagious. The doctors warn Brecht it has gotten too dangerous for him to continue living with Grete. They will both have to reorganize their daily routines. In actual fact, there was no need for the physicians' warning. Brecht does not intend to wait until the SA is actually standing at his door as the threatening letters foretell. He'll need to vacate his apartment. Getting used to thoughts of fleeing and emigration is not easy for him. He still wavers, but he has already packed manuscripts and materials into boxes and sent a letter to a bookseller friend in Vienna requesting an invitation to a reading so that he can produce an official justification at the border for crossing into Austria.

For Margarete Steffin's convalescence after the operation, Sauerbruch has recommended the *Deutsches Haus*, a sanatorium on Lake Lugano in Ticino. It is a rather luxurious spa hotel perched high up on a mountain slope with a fantastic view of the lake below. Since Grete could never afford a stay there, Brecht and Hanns Eisler bear the expenses. When in astonishment she wonders why, the two characterize it not as welfare among friends, but as an investment; they say they consider Margarete a great acting talent. As one bets on horses, they are banking on Margarete and want to make her the next big star. For that to happen, however, she has to regain her health first.

These days Brecht is also suffering from afflictions, though fortunately much more benign ones than Margarete's. The doctors have diagnosed a hernia, for which he requires surgery, a routine procedure. Brecht has put it off for a while, but now seems to him like the perfect opportunity. He no longer feels safe in his apartment on Hardenbergstrasse. He must face the fact that at any moment a gang of storm troopers might break down his door. He is not especially welcome at Helene's home in Wilmersdorf right now, and a hotel or guesthouse would require its guests to furnish identification papers at check-in, meaning there, too, he would be easy to track down for the police and the SA. Hospitals, on the other hand, have no obligation to register their patients with the police, for which reason alone they are an outstanding hideout with agreeable comprehensive care. And so Brecht reports for his hernia surgery at Dr. Mayer's private practice on Augsburger Strasse – difficult for the authorities to find, easily reachable for his friends in the center of town. Though no longer for Margarete Steffin, who is already aboard her southbound train.

*

Bad news for Else Lasker-Schüler. Only last summer the country's major artistic directors, Max Reinhardt, Leopold Jessner, and Gustav Hartung, were practically on their knees begging her for permission to premiere her *Arthur Aronymus*. Two weeks ago Hartung wrote from Darmstadt that he must delay his production. And now Leopold Jessner, who wanted to produce the play at the Schillertheater, has also postponed the premiere by a month, to a date after the Reichstag election, likely in the hope that by then the civil-war atmosphere will have dissipated and Hitler's government may even have been voted out.

Instead, Else Lasker-Schüler has learned, Jessner wants to stage a different play at the Schauspielhaus on Gendarmenmarkt before Hanns Johst and Franz Ulbrich take the helm there: ironically, a work by Richard Billinger, with whom she already had to share the Kleist Prize and who, with his plays about stolid country life, is riding a wave of success. Such folkloristic subject matter goes down well these days. She has no other recourse but to wait and see whether Hartung and Jessner will make good on their promises after election season.

*

The perpetrators of Stuttgart's "Kabelattentat," the "cable strike" that interrupted the broadcast of Hitler's speech at Süddeutscher Rundfunk yesterday, cannot be ascertained. Three officials with the postal service responsible for the radio's technical operations are suspended.

In the early morning in Berlin-Neukölln, political adversaries surround two National Socialists. One of these two draws a pistol and shoots one of his attackers in the head.

Attacked by National Socialists on February 1 and subsequently arrested by the police, Julius Leber, Reichstag deputy for the SPD from Lübeck, is released from custody this afternoon. He has to visit a hospital because the wounds he sustained during the Nazi attack still need treatment.

I'm Leaving. I'm Staying
Friday, February 17

The telegram arrived yesterday, and right away it seemed like salvation for them both. In the nineteen days Hitler has been in power now, they have been living in growing fear of SA raiding parties. Here in Munich these bands of thugs are not quite as unbridled in their rampages as in Berlin, but by degrees more and more old SPD and KPD friends have vanished. No one knows exactly who has taken them away or what has happened to them, but there are terrible rumors.

Oskar Maria Graf and Mirjam Sachs are no timorous pair. For years they've lived in Schwabing, where they're known in the bohemian bars, theaters, and coffeehouses, but now they hardly dare set foot on the street anymore. Sometimes they'd wake up early in the morning, firmly intent on packing and heading somewhere abroad, but then they would do their calculations, count their money, which is tight as ever, and realize it wouldn't get them far – until, that is, they heard heavy footsteps in the stairwell yesterday, steps that came up to their flat on the fourth floor. And when it was their doorbell that rang, they stood behind their apartment door listening and not making a peep. Any second the door could be smashed in. Again, their buzzer sounded. Outside someone muttered under his breath, beat against the door, and called out: "Herr Graf, Herr Graf – telegram!"

The sender was the Viennese Bildungszentrale [Education Center]. It was inviting Graf to Austria on a long-announced reading tour: "tour guaranteed from February 20 to mid-March." The organizers request Graf leave as soon as possible so that all the tour details can be clarified in advance in Vienna. "Depart for meeting, if possible, February 18."

"Hey now, you could come along!" Graf says to Mirjam Sachs. He breathes a sigh of relief. This could be their chance. Both of them are in danger. Mirjam Sachs is Jewish, and Graf is known about town not just as a writer, but also as an anarchist, a radical pacifist, and not least as a dyed-in-the-wool Bavarian wag. Even now as an adult thirty-six years of age, he loves to wear short lederhosen and traditional Bavarian jackets at his readings, like a kid from the sticks.

Graf is a highly gifted self-promoter. If he weren't a writer, he ought to have become an actor. As a soldier in the war he so convincingly acted the lunatic that he was committed to an asylum and ultimately dismissed as "unusable for service." When he was going to be arrested for having submitted an exposé against the war for publication, he succeeded in making the police officer believe he didn't even know what the text was about.

During the months of the Munich Soviet Republic, he volunteered his services for the revolutionary board of censors, which later earned him a few weeks in prison. But then he wrote himself to literary fame with foolhardy Bavarian calendar stories and with *We Are Prisoners*, a book about his agonizingly tough childhood years on Lake Starnberger, a bit of autobiography that inspired even Thomas Mann to write a hymn of praise in the *Frankfurter Zeitung*.

Graf is well on his way to becoming a folk writer. Unlike Martin Luther's clichéd catchphrase claims, he needs look at no one's mouth. He has grown up with the language and mentality of these people. Yet what emerges from this in his stories is an atmosphere of anarchic humanitarianism and joie de vivre. The heroes of his tales are simple people, crass, uneducated, and with narrow horizons, but predominantly not hard-hearted. They are scamps and self-helpers who let no one rein them in. That is precisely what makes Graf's literature so dangerous for the National Socialists. They view themselves as the sole authority for everything *völkisch*, while understanding that primarily to mean standing at attention and clicking one's heels, as well as spewing hatred at whatever is different or nonconformist.

Graf is an overt provocation for their political brand identity. He urgently needs to disappear before the SA has him disappeared. And the invitation to Austria furnishes them both, Mirjam and him, with what they so desperately need: an official reason to leave and the requisite money to do so.

But now, when the opportunity to flee is here, Mirjam has other plans all of a sudden. She doesn't want to come along. She wants to stay until March 5, until the Reichstag election, to vote against Hitler. If there is any chance of voting him out of office now, then they could use every vote.

"What? Are you crazy?" Graf is horrified. "You want to *vote*? – You think that'll …? Nonsense, you've got to be kidding yourself! Pack up, I say, join me, full stop!" he grouses.

Mirjam is undeterred, though, and in her gentle manner just as obstinate as Graf. She's sticking with her plan of voting against Hitler in the election. To avoid arguing, they set out for a final walk around the city together. For Graf, Munich and Bavaria are more than just his homeland. For him as an author they are his most important topic, the quintessential material on which he subsists. What will he write about if he goes abroad now? How long can a Bavarian raconteur write about a Bavaria he only knows from his memory without his stories growing paler and paler? Writing is the only trade Graf has ever learned. What is he to live off if not writing?

In the end, however, he has no choice. He has to leave and hope that the Hitler nightmare will soon pass because if he does stay and the SA doesn't kill him, then it's the end of the line for his writing; his stories would never be allowed to be published or sold under the Nazis.

Suddenly, out of the blue, two communist friends are standing before them, looking terribly worn out and exhausted. For days they haven't dared return to their apartments. The SA is waiting there, they fear. They urgently need shelter to rest for a few hours. Graf gives them money and his house key but has to warn them. He, too, is on the Nazis' list, and his apartment isn't safe either. They nod they're aware, but they also have no choice.

Even this encounter can't change Mirjam's mind. She will stay in spite of the additional risk the two communists are bringing home to them. The next morning Graf makes one final run at persuading her, to no avail. "You know," she says, "it's just not right that we keep on avoiding and running away whenever something gets uncomfortable or dangerous. – If what we stand for is truly worth anything, and if we firmly believe in it, then we also have to show it. – Don't try to talk me out of it!"

And so, today, Oskar Maria Graf is sitting in the early train to Vienna, alone. Mirjam promised to write him every day or send a telegram in an emergency, but she also said he shouldn't worry right away if he doesn't receive a message. That doesn't come easily to Graf. He's a man who wants to protect his wife, and Mirjam is a woman who makes her own decisions. The train then jolts into motion and pulls out, out of Bavaria, out of Graf's land of literature. Mirjam faces seventeen long days and very long nights until the election, days in which she feels threatened, nights in which rabid fear awaits her. Only after that will she join him in Vienna.

*

Shooting welcome. In his role as provisional Prussian Interior Minister, Hermann Göring issues a circular letter to all Prussian police units over the course of the day. He exhorts the officers to "avoid in all circumstances any appearance of a hostile bearing toward, or even the impression of persecuting, nationalist organizations (SA, SS, and *Stahlhelm*) and nationalist parties." On the contrary, the police authorities are to assist these organizations to the best of their abilities. On the other hand, Göring declares, the police should move against all other organizations hostile to the state with the harshest tactics. And he leaves no doubt about what he means by that: "Police officers who make use of their firearm while carrying out these duties will be given cover by me without regard for the consequences of that firearm use; whoever fails by showing improper forbearance, however, must be prepared to face disciplinary consequences."

A shoot-to-kill order could not be phrased more clearly. According to this decree, whoever does not belong to a nationalist organization is practically an outlaw. The police are to shoot one too many times rather than one too few. Göring personally assumes responsibility. He thereby frees the police from its legal moorings and turns it into a civil war brigade.

*

This afternoon a group of fifteen young men approaches the State Art School on Grunewaldstrasse in Berlin-Schöneberg. Some are wearing SA uniforms, others NSDAP party badges. Whether they are already aware of Göring's shoot-to-kill decree is unclear. The school is where future art teachers for Prussian secondary schools are trained. At the same time, it is regarded as a stepping stone for exceptionally talented students recommended by professors to the municipal art academies. On this day, things are especially quiet at the school; tests are being administered for the state examination.

Around 4:30 p.m. this SA detachment enters the building, making a lot of noise, shouting slogans, and barricading all exits and telephone booths with iron hooks. No one is allowed to leave or enter the school. Several storm troopers infiltrate the examination room and force four of the professors at gunpoint to leave the room, among them the director, Heinrich Kamps, and three of the most artistically high-profile teachers at the school, Philipp Franck, Curt Lahs, and Georg Tappert. Both Kamps and Franck are members of the Prussian Academy of the Arts. Two days earlier they participated in the meeting where Heinrich Mann's expulsion was discussed. They did not speak out. Georg Tappert in particular is the target of severe threats by the intruders until Director Kamps shields him.

All four professors are ultimately led out of the building and thus, as they are told, "put out to pasture." Concurrently, brownshirts nail the doors to their studios shut and smear them with hammer-and-sickle emblems. Other members of the squad climb onto the school's roof and fly a swastika flag. Male students who look Jewish to the SA men are forced to undergo examinations in the bathrooms to see if they are circumcised. Whoever resists or attempts to come to the aid of the four expelled professors is beaten down with truncheons. Before the police can be notified and the riot squad arrives, the occupiers have disappeared.

The organizer and ringleader of the attack, as soon becomes apparent, is an assistant at the art school named Otto Andreas Schreiber. He had written a letter to the new Education Minister, Bernhard Rust, as early as February 11, in which he denounced some of the faculty as cultural Bolsheviks. Subsequently there were discussions at a school consultation about his dismissal, but no decision had yet been taken.

The four professors attacked during the raid now turn to Rust and demand severe punishment for the perpetrators. Rust first announces an investigation of the conditions at the school that prompted the operation by the SA men. Interior Minister Göring meets with the leader of the Nationalsozialistischer Deutscher Studentenbund [National Socialist German Students' League], learns of "the repugnant behavior of certain faculty members at the art school," and likewise announces the start of an investigation: against the teachers, not the brownshirts.

Even Hans Poelzig, who thanked Academy President Max von Schillings for strictly separating art and politics in his course of action against Heinrich Mann two days ago, is drawn into the affair. As the director of all state schools for the liberal and applied arts in Berlin, Poelzig bears responsibility for the school on Grunewaldstrasse also. The ringleader of the attack, Otto Andreas Schreiber, turns to him in this role to demand unhindered freedom of assembly for uniformed storm troopers within all state-run art schools in the future.

*

This evening Hans Sahl heads to the meeting of the *Schutzverband deutscher Schriftsteller* in a bar near Hallesches Tor. Though only thirty years old, Sahl is already a well-known journalist and critic. He writes for numerous desks, mostly for the left-wing liberal *Berliner Börsen-Courier* and for weeklies like *Die Weltbühne*. On the agenda today is a speech by Carl von Ossietzky, which he doesn't want to miss; Sahl holds Ossietzky in high esteem.

Quite a few famous authors have come. Ludwig Marcuse is here, as are Rudolf Olden and Ludwig Renn. Eventually Erich Mühsam bursts into the room, heads straight for the evening speakers' table, and spreads out an evening newspaper, hot off the presses, just purchased on the street. The paper publishes excerpts from the shoot-to-kill order in which Göring pledges to provide cover for any police officer who shoots at alleged enemies of the state: better a bullet too many than one too few.

It is immediately clear to everyone what that means. Police officers are standing in front of the assembly's bar, armed as always. But will they act today as they always have? Is there still a law able to protect the authors from a policeman who takes Göring's decree literally? All at once their points of view change. Isn't the bar much too well lit, aren't too many lamps on, are they not sitting ducks here? A mood takes hold akin to that at a wake, as though the Republic were being borne to its grave.

Ludwig Renn speaks, as do Ludwig Marcuse and Rudolf Olden. But only what Carl von Ossietzky says sticks in Hans Sahl's memory. Although Ossietzky is in fact no great orator – he clutches the table, has a thin voice, and bows his head instead of looking at his audience – he has the courage to turn solemn: "We will probably never see one another again," he says, "but at this hour during which we come together for the last time, let us promise ourselves one thing: namely, to remain true to ourselves and to stand up with our body and our lives for what we have believed in and fought for."

Sahl stares at the door to the meeting room. It is glass, with two policemen standing on the other side. Sahl tries to decipher what is written on the door from behind: ECNARTNE. Right now we're still together, he thinks, but the meeting will end soon. A single pane of glass separates us from policemen who could shoot us whenever it suits them. A single glass door separates us from something as incomprehensible as the word written backwards on it.

It is a cold night. Heavy snow is falling. After the meeting Sahl walks with Ossietzky to Hallesches Tor to reach the subway. Ossietzky has flipped up the collar of his coat; he is coughing, and he is ill. Sahl steals a glimpse of him in profile. His angular face with that prominent chin has always reminded him of a nutcracker.

"You have to flee," Sahl says. "Why are you still here? You are one of the first they'll take away. We need you, but not as a martyr."

By now they have arrived at Hallesches Tor. Ossietzky pauses to say goodbye. "I'm staying," he tells Sahl, who imagines he hears a nut cracking. "Let them come and take me away. I have thought about it for a long while. I'm staying."

*

At an election event for the German State Party in Oberndorf am Neckar, the evening's speaker, Württemberg's Economics Minister Reinhold Maier, must defend himself with his own fists against an assault by National Socialists and comes away with minor injuries.

Around forty communists attack two National Socialists on Wallstrasse in Berlin-Charlottenburg, the place where Hans Maikowski and Josef Zauritz were killed on January 30. During a chase down Wilmersdorferstrasse to Schillerstrasse three shots are fired from the ranks of communists, and one of the National Socialists is fatally wounded by a bullet to the neck.

No Treasure in the Silver Lake
Saturday, February 18

Harry Graf Kessler is invited to afternoon tea at the home of Helene von Nostitz. Everything seems to be the same as always with her. The wife of a diplomat and relative of Paul von Hindenburg, she hosts an old-school salon where politicians, artists, and wealthy aristocrats enjoy one another's company. Today at tea a Russian choir Kessler likes a great deal is scheduled to sing. Helene von Nostitz, like Kessler, grew up in various European countries, speaks several languages, counts Rilke, Rodin, and Hofmannsthal among her friends, and several years ago wrote a touching, mildly nostalgic book about so-called high society life in Europe before the First World War.

Thereafter, Kessler will move to the soirée thrown by Gottfried Bermann Fischer, son-in-law of the publisher Samuel Fischer. Because Kessler is currently negotiating with them both about whether his memoirs will appear with S. Fischer Verlag, he would like if nothing else to underscore with his visit his interest in signing a contract. Bermann Fischer's house is full, the atmosphere extremely tense. Many of the publisher's authors have come. Almost all of them are conversing about their desire to leave town within the next few days. Kessler meets Alfred Döblin for the first time, as well as former theater impresario Theodor Tagger, who now writes plays under the pseudonym Ferdinand Bruckner. Also infected by the fraught atmosphere, they have a long conversation about the political situation. Bruckner even speaks of a Conciergerie mood, an allusion to the Paris Conciergerie where hundreds of prisoners awaited their execution by guillotine during the French Revolution.

*

Carl Zuckmayer also senses the growing danger. More and more friends, acquaintances, and theater folk are leaving the country, often without saying goodbye or leaving an address. They are just gone. Alice, his wife,

121

is unable to sleep at night, frightened that policemen could suddenly bang on the door to arrest him.

Zuckmayer has thus decided this year to vacate his Berlin city apartment and move to his country home near Salzburg earlier than planned. He doesn't view this as fleeing, nor indeed as the beginning of an exile. Perhaps he will return to Germany by early March, just after the election. For the time being, however, he feels better knowing the Austrian border lies between him and Hitler.

Before setting off, he returns a set of keys to Heinrich George that George had left with him. Zuckmayer has known him for years, from the period just after the war when both were still virtual nobodies in the theater world. In 1920 he was invited to a party at George's apartment in Frankfurt and, as soon as he entered, witnessed the man of the house standing on a table buck naked, drunkenly playing the violin. He was caterwauling, demonizing all so-called bourgeois art, and celebrating ecstasy as the only honest, true, unvarnished form of expression in acting. George is a berserker of the stage with the body of a bull who can shift on a dime from explosive rage to the most delicate, lyrical tones. Initially it was mostly directors of Expressionist theater who made him their star, but by now there is hardly anyone in the German film or theater business who can resist George's charisma.

Zuckmayer also admires his abilities, of course. George's lack of restraint and ego-centrism, however, give him the creeps. Even when he spends alcohol-soaked evenings with him from time to time, he always keeps a little distance. In the past George often collaborated with avowed left-wing directors, having performed in plays by Brecht and Ernst Toller, and is at home in the leftist milieu of actors. Last summer, however, he unexpectedly took over the lead role in a *völkisch* propaganda play in Kolberg, Pomerania, on the Baltic Sea [present-day Kołobrzeg] and shortly afterward accepted a gig as voice actor for the radio play version of a First World War drama written by SA poet Eberhard Wolfgang Möller – which at the very least is irritating. Could it be that George's passion for frenzied, ecstatic outbursts and an un-bourgeois art has found a new home with the Nazis?

*

Georg Kaiser's new play *Silver Lake* is being premiered in three cities simultaneously: in Leipzig, Erfurt, and Magdeburg. The theaters virtually clambered for the honor of being the first to stage it. Max Reinhardt would like to produce it in Berlin soon. Strictly speaking, Kaiser's text isn't a play, but a libretto. The music was written by Kurt Weill who, since the international success of Brecht's *Threepenny Opera*, numbers among the A-list of stage composers in Germany.

The critics are not exuberant but are favorable. Naturally Kaiser remained true to himself in this play as well and concocted a somewhat abstract fable in which philosophical questions of justice and injustice, revenge and forgiveness are debated. It has little to nothing to do with politics.

The Leipzig performance in particular boasts big names: Gustav Brecher, one of the country's most celebrated conductors, is musical director, general manager Detlef Sierck has taken on the role of director, and the stage design is by Caspar Neher, one of Brecht's oldest friends and closest collaborators.

The three premieres have remained largely unmolested, but the National Socialists are already planning protests against the play. Kurt Weill is Jewish, and Kaiser is regarded as a leftist author if only because his books appear with the left-wing liberal house Kiepenheuer. In Erfurt a few initial expressions of displeasure by nationalist groups are enough to cause the play to vanish from the stage after only its second performance.

In Magdeburg it's not solely the various NSDAP organizations up in arms about the play, but the *Stahlhelm*, the *Landbund* [*Rural League*], the local group of the German Nationalists, the *Nationalverband Deutscher Offiziere* [*National Federation of German Officers*], and the monarchist women's *Bund Königin Luise* [*Queen Louise League*]. Together they accuse artistic director Hellmuth Götze of making the theater "into an instrument of wholly unartistic attempts at Bolshevization" and the play of containing "countless overt and covert invitations to class struggle and violence." The *Madgeburger Tageszeitung* proclaims it will cease publishing theatrical reviews until the play is stricken from the repertoire. It is subsequently dropped six days after its premiere.

In Leipzig *Silver Lake* is able to hang on for a week longer. Although Kaiser is not Jewish, the *Leipziger Tageszeitung* refers to him as a "literary Hebrew" and the Altes Theater as a "hotbed of Jewish literati," and is appalled Kurt Weill was "allowed as a Jew to use a German operatic stage to his sleazy ends." Eventually, on March 4, brownshirts disrupt the performance with shouting and vulgar behavior until Gustav Brecher, subject to especially brutal attacks for being a Jew, is forced to quit the conductor's podium and end the show.

The artistic directors of all three theaters are dismissed over the following weeks. Georg Kaiser's literary career is abruptly cut short. Until his death in 1945, no other plays by him will be performed on German stages. Kurt Weill is forced to flee to Paris. Detlef Sierck will leave for the United States with his wife, where he earns acclaim under the name Douglas Sirk as a director of mostly melodramas. Gustav Brecher takes a circuitous route in emigrating to the Netherlands. Fearing the German troops, he along with his wife take their own lives in May 1940.

*

Influenza is on the decline. In Berlin only 300 to 400 new infections are reported each day.

In Doberan (near Rostock), SA troops attack an event hosted by the loyal republicans of the *Reichsbanner*. One member of the *Reichsbanner* is killed. Nine others from this organization and two National Socialists are seriously wounded.

In Duisburg-Hamborn, members of the KPD are ambushed in a boathouse. One of the men is killed by two bullets to the head and one to the chest. Three others suffer serious gunshot wounds.

During a brawl in Chemnitz-Erfenschlag between Nazis and men of the *Reichsbanner*, one man is so gravely injured in a stabbing that he dies en route to the hospital.

What's the Point of Writing?

Sunday, February 19

When Klaus Mann wakes up in his parents' house this morning, he feels nothing but the desire to die. Aside from the staff, the house is almost empty. His parents are in Paris, his siblings scattered across the country, and only Erika is with him in Munich. Sometimes they go for walks together, but Erika has so much else on her mind, mostly the work for her cabaret and of course Therese Giehse, her new love. There's not much room left for him.

As soberly as he can, he takes stock of what he would lose if he gave in to his wish to die right now, at this very moment. He is only twenty-six, but he suspects his chances of a truly happy union are slim. He is too fickle, too seducible, too easily bored by other people for a steady partnership to make him happy in the long run. The only person with whom he gets along implicitly and with whom he could imagine a life together is his sister Erika. Whenever he finds an opportunity to have a brief chat with her despite all the day's bustle, perhaps even just a few words, he notes it down that evening in his diary like a success story.

And now the chance at literary fame for someone like him is lost. As long as Hitler is in power – he's under no illusions about this – there is no place for him any longer in the German book market. He hasn't been able to do any focused work for days, so great is his political and personal nervousness. That makes everything even worse. Otherwise he is consistently at his desk every morning, like his father. Working steadies him a bit mentally, grants him some stability. But what's the point of writing now?

If he had poison, he wouldn't hesitate – if it weren't for Erika and his mother. He doesn't wish to cause them any pain. Through them he is bound to life. It becomes clearer and clearer to him, however, that he wouldn't survive it if Erica were to die; her death would directly entail his own. Not even working could stop him then. He harbors no fear of death. Death can only be a release.

*

Figure 14: Klaus and Erika Mann

Adolf Grimme, former Prussian Education Minister, has organized a rally at Berlin's Volksbühne with the *Sozialistischer Kulturbund* [*Socialist Cultural Association*] of the SPD. Days ago it was registered and approved as required by the regulations. When Grimme sets out for the theater an hour beforehand, however, he discovers that all access roads and paths of ingress have been completed cordoned off. The SA, he is told, is mounting an open-air concert next to the Volksbühne at 12 p.m., which is why all the neighborhood streets have been closed to traffic "for security reasons." Berlin's new superintendent of police, Magnus von Levetzow – installed four days earlier by Göring – is supervising the measures personally.

The *Kulturbund*'s rally has to be canceled because attendees cannot get to the theater, plain and simple. Grimme is indignant, of course. The *Kulturbund* will seek redress from the Prussian state. But beyond that, the matter is extremely embarrassing for Grimme. After all, Thomas Mann entrusted him with a lengthy letter, an *Avowal of Socialism*, that Grimme was to read at the event. It would be inexcusable not to share such a declaration from a Nobel Prize winner with the public now, just before the election. For Grimme that is out of the question. He must come up with an idea.

*

Surprising news awaits Harry Graf Kessler when he arrives at the Krolloper this morning for the conference of *Das freie Wort*. The prior evening the conference's organizing committee elected him to the event's steering committee without telling him. Kessler is flabbergasted but takes it in his stride. He knows all arrangements had to be made in a mad rush. It was only two weeks ago that Kurt Grossmann and Willi Münzenberg came up with the idea for the election event-in-disguise at the café on Kurfürstendamm. Now almost a thousand people are sitting in the hall, among them around a hundred journalists.

Münzenberg financed a large portion of the costs in advance from his communist publishing coffers and is mindful that neither his name nor his party appear mentioned. Until now the KPD was not even willing to cooperate with the Social Democrats in a popular front. If Münzenberg is now covertly supporting an event on the classically liberal topic of freedom of expression, that shows how big his heart has gotten in resisting Hitler – and the extent of the left's powerlessness. For weeks communist demonstrations, rallies, and assemblies have been disrupted, attacked, or violently disbanded by the Nazis, or just banned by the police in advance.

From the outset Grossmann, co-organizer of the congress with Rudolf Olden, tried to flaunt big names while assembling the program. He wanted to give the event a certain luster and attract public attention. Then came the cancellations from Albert Einstein, Ricarda Huch, and Heinrich Mann. The advertised opening remarks by Thomas Mann didn't pan out either. Now, instead, a bevy of venerable but not exactly electrifying professors are to deliver well-meaning addresses. The only prominent guest in the audience is Käthe Kollwitz. Grossmann has raised high expectations with his billings; it is all the more certain now that the audience will be disappointed.

In late morning he is called out of the hall to the telephone. Adolf Grimme is on the line, briefly reports how the police and SA have managed to torpedo the *Sozialistischer Kulturbund* rally at the Volksbühne, and asks whether he might present Thomas Mann's message of greeting – an *Avowal of Socialism*! – at the congress. Grossmann is thrilled.

From the start, a police lieutenant and a detective inspector monitor the event and threaten to disperse it without delay should even a single phrase be uttered that might be construed as subversive according to the emergency decrees from February 4. Grossmann offers them a place at the table on stage so that their importance will be immediately apparent to everyone, including the audience in the ballroom, but they prefer to remain in the background.

Naturally Grossmann and Olden have reckoned with surveillance. As a precaution, therefore, they adopt the congress's resolution, together with the demand to restore the freedom of expression without restrictions, at the very beginning, before there is any reason to break off the proceedings. Only then come the addresses, which are quite erudite but dreadfully dull and ponderous. There are few listeners in the hall who can follow them. Nor can the two police surveillants; the detective inspector has been leaving the ballroom from time to time, people whisper to Grossmann, to telephone headquarters and request assistance. How is he supposed to prohibit what he doesn't even understand?

As soon as Adolf Grimme enters the hall, Olden and Grossmann interrupt the program sequence and send him up to the rostrum. The mood changes in a flash. Grimme is a well-known man, and boos resound when he relates the dirty trick the Nazis used to obstruct the event at the Volksbühne. And now, finally, Thomas Mann's message, which Grimme is reading aloud, serves the listeners some phrases that can galvanize them. In essence Mann repeats what he has often said before; nationalism is an idea of the past, the nineteenth century, the future belongs to the cooperation among nations. "Every human being of feeling and sense, even every better politician, knows that the peoples of Europe are nowadays no longer capable of living and thriving on their own, isolated and apart, but that they rely on one another and together form a community of fate. To oppose such a vital necessity with some such *völkisch* nature-romanticism as one's argument is nothing but obstructionism."

Grimme has scarcely left the stage when the next professorial lecture puts the audience back to sleep. The first listeners get up to make their way home. But Grossmann and Olden have made provisions for that. The final speaker is Wolfgang Heine, an SPD man and highly talented polemicist. He roasts the new government with so much fury and wit that the hall bursts into liberated laughter – and the new overseer sent by police headquarters leaps up and vociferously declares the event terminated. Chanting choruses arise at once – "Keep on talking! Keep on talking!" – with shouts of "freedom!" and "Red Front!" In the end, while clearing the room, a large proportion of the audience sings the *Internationale* and *Brüder, zur Sonne, zur Freiheit* [*Brothers, to the Sun, to Freedom*]. That lends the exodus from the opera house an intense, rousing pathos. Grossmann and Olden can be satisfied with their programming.

On his way home Harry Graf Kessler senses that this was the last opportunity for a long while to publicly champion freedom of expression and opinion in Berlin. When he arrives at home, the news of the congress's breakup has already made the rounds. From his apartment window he can see the porter's wife, whose husband is in the SA, menacingly shaking her raised fist up at his floor from the courtyard and screaming hysterically: "That serves them right. That bunch of thugs up there is going to need a very different sort of medicine."

The city's heated atmosphere intrigues Kessler. He leaves the house again to participate in a *Reichsbanner* protest gathering in the Lustgarten in front of the Berlin Cathedral. The park is full to bursting, thirty to forty thousand people, Kessler estimates, most of them waving the black-red-gold flag. The sequence of the rally shows how dangerous any attempt to stand up for the Weimar Republic has become. Beforehand, the demonstrators gathered in groups in the different boroughs and only ever walked together for mutual protection on their way to the Lustgarten. One of the convoys of marchers came under fire by the Nazis. Two people were wounded. Both were patched up with makeshift bandages but are at the assembly all the same. Even if they had wanted to, it would have been too risky to return home alone. After the usual speeches the demonstrators then walk together through Französische Strasse to Gendarmenmarkt. Only after gathering once more on the steps of the Schauspielhaus do they divide up into groups and band together to process back to their boroughs.

*

This evening Georg Bernhard, former editor-in-chief of the *Vossische Zeitung*, is hosting a large party with a house concert at his villa. Harry Graf Kessler and Heinrich Mann are also among the guests. Like Kessler and Mann, Bernhard ranks among the tenacious standard bearers for reconciliation with France. That is why the nationalists in the country oppose him – and because he is Jewish. He turned the *Vossische Zeitung* into one of the nation's most influential and important papers, but in 1930 he fell out with his publishers, the Ullstein brothers, and had to leave the newspaper. Since then, he's been working as a lobbyist for a trade association while still maintaining sterling political connections. A soirée at his home is always a hub of news.

Heinrich attends a reception like this alone, without Nelly Kröger. Bernhard has invited foreign diplomats as well as some liberal politicians who have since been ousted by the Nazis. The mood is appallingly dismal. Only three weeks ago many of the guests met at the Press Ball in the Zoo Ballrooms, chatting with and toasting one another. Naturally they gave some thought then to Schleicher's resignation. Such a change in government could have professional consequences for them, which is part of the rules of the game for democracy – sometimes you hold a government office, sometimes you're in the opposition – but in the end it wouldn't change much. They felt secure and confident. After all, they were among the state's policymakers.

Now all that is in the past. The ground has begun crumbling away beneath their feet. For some of those present, Bernhard's reception will be the last party in Berlin for the foreseeable future. Their bags are packed and tickets purchased. They anticipate having to remain abroad for only a short while. It cannot be long before Hitler is ruined. For now the situation is too uncertain; it's better to steer clear.

The main topic of conversation is the speed with which the National Socialists are bringing the administration and police to heel and replacing executive staff. The most recent decisions leave many speechless. Göring's shoot-to-kill order, they try to reassure themselves, is likely directed first and foremost at the communists, not the bourgeois parties. But there is no legal basis for it, the decree is unquestionably illegal – a fact which, frighteningly, bears no consequences.

Also among the guests is Wilhelm Abegg, former State Secretary in the Prussian Ministry of the Interior. Just over two years ago, Heinrich Mann and Wilhelm Herzog were in his office importuning him to take more decisive action against Hitler and the SA's street terror. Abegg has since been removed from office, his so outstandingly trained and equipped police force now under Göring's command. But Abegg of course still has confidants in the ministry who secretly pass him information, and the intelligence is startling, even unbelievable. The National Socialists are planning a blood bath, he tells Harry Graf Kessler and Heinrich Mann. The blacklists, according to which arrests and systematic murders are to take place, are said to have already been compiled and distributed. It was disclosed to Abegg that the Nazis will probably strike shortly before or after the elections on March 5. Abegg takes these leads very seriously. He himself switches apartments every night to avoid an arrest and will soon go to Switzerland. It makes no sense to submit to being butchered here in Berlin, he says. Graf Kessler should tread carefully. He also issues Heinrich Mann an insistent warning.

A few guests broach the subject of the dramatic Academy meeting last Wednesday with Heinrich Mann. The newspapers printed extensive commentary on Mann's resignation. The affair is the talk of the town.

Heinrich Mann can tell them little they don't already know since he didn't actually take part in the meeting at all. Even the French ambassador, André François-Poncet, is listening to him. His official residence is located on Pariser Platz, directly opposite the Academy building. Although Mann attempts to downplay his resignation from the Academy, François-Poncet responds very seriously: "If you cross Pariser Platz," he says to Mann, "my house is open to you." The implication is unambiguous. François-Poncet regards Heinrich Mann as so jeopardized that he offers him the extraterritorial soil of his embassy as safe harbor in case of emergency.

*

In Erfurt at around midnight, two storm troopers come to blows with two communists and start shooting. One of the communists dies at the scene, while the other is taken to hospital with serious injuries.

In Osthofen (near Worms), around 250 Nazis attack a group of twelve to fifteen members of the *Reichsbanner*. Five men are gravely injured, and one child is shot and wounded.

Pay up!
Monday, February 20

Publisher Wieland Herzfelde begs Harry Graf Kessler for a word. The two have known each other since the war, when Herzfelde was still a very young soldier. He has never left any doubt about his being a communist, and that has never particularly bothered the count. Since the day Hitler was appointed Reich Chancellor, Herzfelde hasn't spent a night in his flat. He is one of the few who realized straightaway what the Nazis were capable of as soon as they held power, and the SA raid on the apartment and studio of George Grosz, one of the most important artists with Herzfelde's press, just after Hitler's seizure of power, confirmed his fears.

Herzfelde has information that matches only too well what Count Kessler learned yesterday from ex-State Secretary Abegg. An informant from the SA has reported to him that the Nazis are planning a bogus attempt on Hitler's life. The attack – which Hitler will of course survive unscathed – is to be both signal and justification for a blood bath the National Socialists then intend to unleash among their adversaries. A conversation between SA chief Röhm and Hitler confirming this information has supposedly been overheard, too. The plot, Herzfelde thinks, must be made public as quickly as possible, in the foreign press as well. In his view those are the best means of thwarting their agenda. Count Kessler must assist with his international connections. If what the Nazis intend is public knowledge in the first place, it makes no sense for them to stick to their plan.

*

Oskar Loerke is at the end of his tether. All day yesterday he was uneasy and tried to distract himself with work. Today at the Academy, the writers' debate about Heinrich Mann's resignation – put more truthfully: about his expulsion – is on the agenda. Loerke hates political controversies like these. They render him helpless, and he doesn't have the energy to contend with such things. One thing is clear to him, however;

the discordant writers' division is still in danger. A Nazi minister like Rust will have little patience with them. Should the debate end with a declaration of loyalty to Heinrich Mann or even with overt criticism of Rust's actions, he will shut down the division or at least radically reconfigure it – and Loerke will lose his post as Academy secretary in short order, or even sooner.

A mood more oppressive than Loerke has ever experienced spreads even before the meeting. Leonhard Frank paces menacingly. Döblin is eerily reserved. Expectations are sky high, but despite all section members having been invited to the debate, only a pathetically small circle of seven authors has gathered by early evening around 6 p.m. Thomas Mann has remained in Paris after concluding his Wagner lecture tour. Ricarda Huch, deputy chairperson of the division, was unable to travel from Heidelberg. Ina Seidel, who was present for Heinrich Mann's resignation on Wednesday, has reported sick. The usual out-of-towners have sent their regrets in writing. Only Rudolf Binding has traveled in from Hesse. He is among the most conservative – some would say the most reactionary – authors in the Academy. He writes expressive, well-constructed stories that are read by many, but his war diaries form something like the ideological opposite of Remarque's *All Quiet on the Western Front*. They celebrate military combat as the most important test in a man's life, through which his character is forged to the requisite toughness in the fire of battle. Binding is that sort of stuffed shirt who likes to spout off about lofty ideals but at bottom cultivates an elitist arrogance.

While the prior session sprouted into a drama in five acts, today's develops into a kind of duel with seconds, into single combat between authors who have much in common but are still radically different: Gottfried Benn and Alfred Döblin. Both are trained physicians, both obsessed with literature, both passionate avant-gardists. Before the First World War both belonged to Berlin's bohemian scene around Else Lasker-Schüler, who offered herself up for the amazed gaze of tourists in the *Café des Westens* on Kurfürstendamm. And both published their first texts in *Sturm*, the magazine of the Expressionists edited by Herwarth Walden, then Lasker-Schüler's husband.

Döblin, however, is a novelist and epic poet to the core, a prolific writer whose tremendous torrents of language never seem to run dry,

Figure 15: Alfred Döblin in 1929

who publishes book after book at a rapid pace. Three years ago he achieved enormous success with *Berlin Alexanderplatz*: the story of Franz Biberkopf, a simple man who tries to stay afloat amid the maelstrom of metropolitan life. It is a masterpiece, the rare example of a successful, monumental big-city novel, written with a daring montage technique, but at the same time so exciting, so touching and alive, that it thrilled critics and the public alike. And then, to top it off, when Heinrich George, superstar of German cinema, slipped into Biberkopf's skin for the film adaptation, the character grew into a modern Berlin myth. All that has made Döblin if not a rich man, then still a wealthy one able to move his medical practice from the city's poor East to Kaiserdamm in Charlottenburg.

Benn, by contrast, is a lyric poet who fights for every single word, every syllable, every sound. His few books are often vanishingly slender and only reach a vanishingly small readership. For some critics, however, his poems are among the best and most significant written in recent years. He is an author for connoisseurs; they sing hymns of praise about him and reinforce his perception of belonging to the nation's intellectual aristocracy. Poetry is for Benn the sphere of the very highest sophistication, which, if it is to earn attention, must reach far beyond the fashions and vicissitudes of the present. Unlike Döblin, who sees himself as a politically thoughtful, socially engaged writer who carefully studies the present, Benn views himself as a poet who wants to leave all political and time-bound elements behind him in order to press forward to a lasting, indeed eternal, legitimacy with his poetry. He loves an aphorism he once found in Nietzsche: Thereafter, the true geniuses stand solitary in their epoch and are as giants calling out their messages to giants of other epochs, across chasms of millennia, unbothered by the wantonly clamorous homunculi skulking away beneath them.

Benn's life nevertheless contrasts drastically with his haughty self-image. His clinic for dermatological and venereal diseases is located on the second floor of a bleak Kreuzberg corner building and earns so little that its four rooms must also simultaneously serve as his residence, which he has furnished with used, indifferently cobbled-together household items. An atmosphere of melancholy squalor, which doesn't exactly help entice financially solvent patients, permeates the whole place. Benn treats predominantly prostitutes who ply their trade in the side streets. If the opportunity arises, he also enjoys tending to writer colleagues: Carl Sternheim, for instance, the oft-staged dramatist who suffers from syphilis, though who turns out to be a reluctant, nearly unimpressionable patient. Or even Oskar Loerke, on whom he made house calls to assist when he was lying in bed once years ago with tonsillitis and a high fever.

Although Benn is a rather short, somewhat pudgy man missing half his hair, he has astonishing success with women. Mostly they are writers, artists, or actors. Yet he is no romantic, but a lover with a fairly cool heart. He writes masterful love letters while almost always keeping his girlfriends at a distance and occasionally maintains two or more relationships at once. Not every one of the women deals well with that. Mopsa Sternheim, Carl Sternheim's daughter, is only twenty-one and thus almost twenty years Benn's junior when she falls in love with him and attempts suicide because of him. Three years later the actor Lili Breda calls Benn up to say goodbye to him. Right after hanging up the phone, she throws herself from the window of her sixth-floor apartment. Even now there are two actors with whom Benn is having a relationship: Tilly Wedekind, Frank Wedekind's widow, and Elinor Büller. Both run into one another from time to time in Berlin's theater world, and Benn is quite eager to maintain discretion. If at all possible the women are not to learn a thing about his liaison with the other.

The contrast between his claim to literary greatness and his meager material existence nags at Benn. He is a proud man, easy to offend. The fanciest magazines and presses publish his poems and essays, but they pay poorly. That outrages him so much that he once calculated he earns on average only 4.50 marks a month with his literary endeavors. Because his microscopically tiny, distasteful practice, as he calls it, also generates so little, now at age fifty he hardly sees any chance of ever leading a tolerably adequate existence. When he invites Tilly Wedekind into his flat for the first time after a visit to the theater and leads her through its four shabby rooms, she ends up standing in his consulting room with

Figure 16: Gottfried Benn in 1934

the gynecological examination chair and the shiny steel instruments in the glass cabinet, wearing an evening gown. Because he feels most at home in it, Benn even slips on his white coat. Well, Tilly thinks, now he's going to slaughter you. With his remote look he appears sinister to her. Then, however, he leads her into his living quarters, the walls of which are practically covered with bookshelves, fetches bread rolls, fruit, and sparkling wine, and the situation relaxes.

When he was so low on money several years ago that he was unable to pay his taxes on time, the tax office swiftly threatened him with seizure of property, and he was beside himself with rage at this humiliation. This washed-up and worn-out state, he raved then, needs to be smashed to pieces.

The Academy is all the more important to Benn. A year ago Oskar Loerke called him up one evening unexpectedly and informed him the literature division had elected him its newest member. "Please don't joke around with this old man," he replied. He was tremendously happy. Now, finally, he was getting the official recognition he sorely lacked. Finally, he was being accorded his place among the nation's literary elite. No longer was he a poor doctor to prostitutes who hardly earned more than a handful of good reviews for his poems. Now he was taking his seat at the round table of the most prominent German-language authors of the age.

Internally, his appointment to the Academy was no simple matter. Thomas and Heinrich Mann made the case for Benn's induction because in him they saw a wordsmith of the highest order, but also an intellectual who views history and culture from a brutally cold-hearted, almost scientific perspective. That jibed well with the smart objectivity that had characterized the fashion of the time for several years. Oskar Loerke, a friend of Benn's, advocated for him, too. But Ricarda Huch, the deputy chairperson of the division after all, viewed Benn's emphatically nihilistic tone as cheap posturing and not as the result of a lifestyle disenchanted to the core: "I find Gottfried Benn outrageous. There are many disgusting aspects to life, but one is not a poet because one strings together one repugnance after the other; it is also true that our language is shopworn, but one does not overcome this barrier by using nothing but unusual, esoteric, showy words."

A measure of the Academy's importance for Benn can be gleaned from the fact that he almost never misses a meeting. Today President

Schillings has come to the writers' division because, as he makes plain right away, he wants to prevent any public protest in the Heinrich Mann affair. The situation, he says, continues to be difficult, and he explicitly asks the writers, in the interest of the future of the Academy, to come to a conciliatory agreement.

At once Döblin butts in and flusters the president with a simple question Schillings by rights had to see coming. Why does he consider the situation still to be difficult?

Schillings' answer comes off, as it so often has, as vague. He likes to play it close to the vest. The difficulties, he says, are expressed in the numerous newspaper opinion articles.

That is odd reasoning, plucked out of the air, because of course everyone present knows that it is not the newspapers that decide on the Academy's continued existence, but the new government. As Schillings must admit, however, the latter has not been in touch again after Käthe Kollwitz and Heinrich Mann took their leave on Wednesday. If Schillings still presses the division not to arouse any new dangers with a declaration of protest, he will thereby indirectly reveal one thing above all; any public criticism of government, which an independent Academy should obviously have the right to issue, could lead to closure at this time.

Does Minister Rust even have the right to disband the Academy? Is there a statutory basis for doing so? If so, what does it look like? All of a sudden, legal questions are the sole focus of the discussion. But no one is debating the question about whether it is even worth fighting for the continued existence of an Academy with a muzzle imposed on it.

Benn has little interest in formal legal questions, however, shoves them aside, and would rather learn from Döblin what today's meeting actually aims to accomplish. On Wednesday Döblin had announced a protest by the section for poetry. Now Benn would love to know whom this protest ought to be directed against, since Kollwitz and Mann resigned voluntarily after all. The division can hardly lodge a protest against that.

Thus begins the clash between him and Döblin, wherein the other meeting participants do occasionally speak up, but essentially have little to contribute. Döblin is primarily concerned with showing that Rust had no right to pressure the Academy and Heinrich Mann with his ultimatum because the Academy, by statute, is independent and need brook no political demands or interference. As Döblin summarizes the situation, Schillings did secure the Academy's existence with his obsequiousness toward the minister, but squandered its dignity and independence.

Benn finds this argumentation altogether wrong. As he understands the Academy's statutes, Heinrich Mann accepted an office as chairman of the literature division for which he receives a yearly allowance for expenses and is consequently indentured to the minister as a kind of expert on literary matters. And it is this very minister Mann accused of barbarism on an election poster and whose party he issued the call to oppose through a collaboration between the KPD and SPD. Heinrich Mann thus began waging a war against a legally and constitutionally formed government. Only thereafter, Benn emphasizes sharply, did the government mount its defense. It isn't the Academy that was attacked; Heinrich Mann attacked the government.

For that reason, Benn argues, a protest is completely out of the question, too. His zeal increases more and more. There are members of this Academy, he inveighs, who incessantly waive the interests of the Academy. Everything else is more important to them: the Weimar constitution, the coalition of the workers' parties, unbridled political agitation. And yet with its grand tradition the Academy, he insists, is a glorious institution – and the only one that can elevate artistically representative writers and honor them before all others.

The core of the conflict between Döblin and Benn thus becomes obvious. By publicly denouncing the Nazi's dealings with the Academy, Döblin ultimately wants to defend the constitution and civil rights. On the other hand, for Benn, who was never a friend of the Republic, its constitution is secondary. His concern is preserving the Academy – not least because it has great significance for him personally.

The positions are irreconcilable. What's more, Döblin foresees himself and his two allies Frank and Fulda being in the minority in case of a vote. Meaning only two options remain for them: either they can lend visibility to their protest by resigning demonstratively, albeit thereby relinquishing any influence over the Academy and handing Benn and his people the opportunity to paint themselves as the winners of the conflict. Or, in spite of it all, they attempt to smuggle into the heralded declaration a convoluted formulation of their criticism and hope it is understood by the public as a sign of resistance.

Wrestling with this brief declaration takes a very long time, almost two hours. Schillings doesn't have that kind of time, needs to attend a different meeting, and takes his leave though not without reminding those present that he as president must give his blessing to any Academy statement before it may be published. There is no doubt he wants to retain absolute control in this matter. Furthermore, because consent from members not present likely needs to be obtained in the event of such a crucial response, the situation becomes even more unclear. A rapid, decisive reaction of the kind Döblin envisioned last Wednesday after Martin Wagner's resignation in solidarity is probably not possible at all.

In the end, agreement is reached on a sentence of thanks to Heinrich Mann – banal enough – and two cumbersome sentences that are supposed to register self-assurance but instead sound like a faint-hearted formula of compromise: "The Division for the Art of Poetry deeply regrets the resignation of the great artist Heinrich Mann from its ranks and thanks him for lending the Division his name and energy as its chairman for many years. The Division is determined, even in impassioned times, not to be deterred in the slightest from its duty to protect the freedom of artistic creation. It feels itself compelled to this declaration because it is distinctly aware that the richness of German art has at all times sprung from the diversity of worldviews."

*

Just two to three hundred meters away at 6 p.m., the very same time the members of the section for poetry are convening in the Academy, another meeting is beginning that will have a considerable impact on the nation's future. In the Palace of the Reich President, the site of Hermann Göring's office since 1932, twenty-six influential economic leaders are arriving. Among them are the chairman of the *Reichsverband der deutschen Industrie* [*Reich Association of German Industry*], Gustav Krupp von Bohlen und Halbach, and Georg von Schnitzler, board member of I. G. Farben, but also businessmen like Fritz Springorum, Friedrich Flick, and Günther Quandt. Hitler gives a half-hour speech for the gentlemen in which he rhapsodizes about the advantages of dictatorship over democracy, swears to the inviolability of private property, and touts the NSDAP as the sole savior in the face of the communist peril in the nation. After that he leaves the meeting, and Göring takes the floor. He doesn't have much to say. He only briefly mentions that the party's campaign chests and those of the SA and SS are fully depleted and that the upcoming election on March 5 is of key importance for the country's destiny. Then he, too, leaves the room. At that point, Reichsbank president Hjalmar Schlacht, organizer of the meeting, rises from his seat with the words: "And now, gentlemen, pay up!" and demands from the assembled business leaders donor pledges to the tune of three million Reichsmarks. The very next day Göring delivers the happy news to the campaign manager, Goebbels, that as of now three million are available for the NSDAP and the German Nationalists. Goebbels is delighted and immediately musters his propaganda division: "Now we'll crank up a campaign."

*

The replacement of leadership staff in administrative offices by the Nazis continues. At Berlin's police headquarters four officers and a woman councilor are furloughed. One of these officers was charged with monitoring right-wing radical activities in the division of the Political Police.

In Kaiserslautern, former Reich Chancellor Heinrich Brüning speaks at a joint campaign event for the Centre Party and Bavarian People's Party. After the rally ends, Brüning must be led out of town under police protection because serious clashes with Nazis ensue in the streets. Shots are fired, and thirteen people are injured.

After a confrontation between communists and National Socialists in Frankfurt-Bockenheim, one of the communists dies in hospital from a shot to the abdomen. A second is critically injured.

Pretty Good Cover
Tuesday, February 21

"If you cross Pariser Platz, my house is open to you." Heinrich Mann cannot get the French ambassador's comment at last Sunday's reception out of his head. Politically competent people are already offering him sanctuary in Berlin as though he might soon need to run for his life in his own city. As a matter of fact, he notices that his and Nelly's apartment on Fasanenstrasse is being surveilled of late. On top of this, rumor has it his passport is to be rescinded in the next few days to prevent him from fleeing abroad. He does not want to let it get to that point.

Yesterday he had a long conversation with Nelly and explained his plan to her. He intends to flee; she is to stay. Or at least for the time being. He needs her in Berlin to sell the housewares and furniture, terminate the rental contract for the apartment, cancel the life insurance policy, withdraw the money from his accounts, and get it to him in France. And Rudi Carius, whom the police are still hunting for because of the murders on Wallstrasse, needs her in Berlin, too, after all. That is Heinrich Mann's plan. Then he went through the most important documents with Nelly and explained to her precisely what she needs to accomplish in the next few days. Finally, they packed a suitcase for him, small and not very heavy, with only the bare necessities.

In the morning, right after breakfast, they both leave the apartment separately. Nelly first: she takes the suitcase and hurries off to the train station. Heinrich follows a few minutes later. He avoids any haste and any semblance of a getaway. He is carrying only an umbrella and, instead of hailing a taxi, walks to the nearest streetcar stop. At the train station he buys a ticket to Frankfurt am Main, an inconspicuous destination, not a border town. In the meantime, Nelly has deposited the suitcase on the train, which is already readied for departure. She places it in the luggage rack of an empty compartment and then exits the train again. When Heinrich arrives, they stroll back and forth along the platform as though calmly passing the final minutes of waiting. Anxious and emotional, Nelly sobs a bit. Heinrich comforts her. Finally, he boards the train, opens the compartment window, exchanges a few words with her on the platform, and then the train departs. And Nelly returns to Fasanenstrasse at her leisure.

What person tailing him would surmise that Heinrich Mann is on the run, on his way into exile? It all looks like a brief day trip, as if he had out-of-town business to attend to while his companion awaited his return at their shared apartment. And if someone should inquire at the ticket counter after the destination of the ticket he bought, then the answer will be Frankfurt. Pretty good cover.

*

The Nazi *Kampfbund für deutsche Kultur* prevents a reading by satirist and cabaret artist Alexander Roda Roda in Königsberg [present-day Kaliningrad]. Roda Roda has been invited by the city's *Goethebund* [*Goethe League*], but the *Kampfbund* protests against his performance because Roda Roda is Jewish and allegedly contributes "to the decline of German culture." He numbers among the most successful comic authors of recent years. As a former Austrian officer, he delights in making fun of military bigotry in his short texts. The *Goethebund* has tried to defend Roda Roda against the attacks with the arguments that he was baptized a Catholic and was an ultimately unpolitical author, but after Königsberg police headquarters advised the *Goethebund* to withdraw the event on its own because they can count on trouble, the performance was canceled. Threatening trouble proves more and more to be the Nazis' preferred means of eliminating political opponents from public life.

*

Now that their parents are traveling, Erika and Klaus seize the opportunity: a *Pfeffermühle* Carnival party for around forty people. After the end of the show, around midnight, the first guests arrive on Poschingerstrasse, naturally in costume. A couple of authors, otherwise mostly actors. Things quickly get out of hand. Erika gets very drunk early on, falling over and unable to keep anything else down. Klaus has to fetch her from the children's bathroom and put her to bed. One of the actresses has a hysterical fit, though it is unclear why. A jacket is lost, though unclear where or when. Two guys begin fighting, unclear why.

Klaus plays the host and steps in to smooth things over. Therese Giehse is dressed as a soldier and made up as a clown, which comes across as creepy: a horror clown. Toward morning the atmosphere turns very gay, campy. Klaus feels repulsed and grumpy. He lays his head in the lap of Marita, Magnus Henning's wife. At 7 a.m. almost all the guests are gone. Herbert Franz, who acted in the *Pfeffermühle*'s February lineup, is still here. They go upstairs, where Elisabeth and Michael, the two youngest siblings, are just sitting down to breakfast. Then they collapse into bed, exhausted, and revel in their morning melancholy and affection.

*

An SPD rally in Hannover is disrupted by Nazis. During the ensuing scuffle four people are seriously injured. The rally's speaker, Reichstag deputy Richard Partzsch, suffers head injuries. At a second SPD gathering in Hannover, a shootout erupts between men of the *Reichsbanner* and brownshirts: one dead, seven gravely injured.

In Krefeld, Münster, and Trier, campaign events for the Centre Party are ambushed by SA squads. There are several casualties. At the fight in the hall at Krefeld, the event's speaker, former Labor Minister Adam Stegerwald, is also attacked and wounded. In response to a Centre Party complaint to the Prussian Ministry of the Interior, Minister Göring answers that Stegerwald's mugging was perpetrated by provocateurs wearing SA uniforms.

In Hamburg's Schanzenstrasse, twenty communists attack a bar frequented by Nazis. During the shootout an innocent woman bystander and a publican are shot and killed. Another woman and a storm trooper sustain injuries. In Stendal, Nazis shoot dead one of their adversaries in a clash with men from the *Reichsbanner*.

The *Weltbühne* takes stock and publishes a retrospective "List of Losses" from the prior week: "At the behest of the provisional Prussian Minister of the Interior, the following high-level officials were removed from office or suspended: 9 district presidents, 13 superintendents of police, 4 under-secretaries, 1 assistant secretary, 3 police colonels, 2 police lieutenant colonels, 1 technical director of the police force, 1 *Landjäger* major, 1 police major, 1 police vice president, 1 district chief executive; those affected are in part without party affiliation, in part members of the State Party, the Centre Party, or the SPD; the positions were filled with persons from the faction of the National Socialists and the German Nationalists or with those close to one of these two parties."

Surviving the Coming Weeks
Wednesday, February 22

Yesterday Heinrich Mann arrived in Frankfurt late. He took a hotel, but only a fleeting night was left for him. This morning he is already back on the train to Karlsruhe, where he will transfer to the train bound for Kehl am Rhein, a sleepy border town in which presumably only a few are apprised of him and his most recent conflicts with the new government. After arriving at Kehl station, he makes his way on foot, carrying both suitcase and umbrella, to the bridge leading across the Rhine to Strasbourg. Its wide stone archway with the low towers on either side is already visible from afar – it almost resembles an old city gate – and behind it the massive steel construction leading straight as an arrow into the freedom of France. The border guards exit the shallow wooden building to the right of the street. Fortunately, the visa he obtained before his last trip to France is still valid until September. He produces his passport, which the men scrutinize thoroughly before waving him through. A moment later the same procedure again with the French border guards. When he sets foot on the left bank of the Rhine, he can breathe a sigh of relief. He has reached safety. His feet will never touch German soil again.

In Strasbourg, too, he goes to the train station. During the stopover in Karlsruhe he already changed a bit of money. At the counter he purchases a ticket to Toulon, and at the post office he sends a telegram to his friend Wilhelm Herzog in Sanary-sur-Mer, requesting he meet him at Toulon station this evening.

Ultimately, the telegram is his tacit acknowledgment of having made a false appraisal of his situation. A week earlier in Berlin, Herzog had urged Mann to join him on the night train to France immediately after his lecture on *The Generals of the Republic* in order to put their watchdogs in black, who were writing down everything, behind them once and for all. Mann found Herzog's misgivings overblown and put him off. That was seven days ago now, just seven days. Today he was forced to sneak out of the country by clandestine means. He, one of the nation's most important writers, may be glad if no one recognizes him. He's traveling on foot, carrying a small suitcase and an umbrella, and nothing else.

*

Wilhelm Abegg is having breakfast at Harry Graf Kessler's. As ever, he feels splendidly informed about everything happening in political Berlin and is not shy about bringing Kessler up to speed.

But of course he is still convinced the Nazis will cause a blood bath either before or after the election, a massacre like St. Bartholomew's Day from the sixteenth century when the French killed thousands of Huguenots in a single night. Abegg is certain even Hitler can't halt the plan anymore because he has nothing else to offer his people otherwise. Hitler is like an animal tamer sitting together in the same cage as ten ravenous lions; if he doesn't give them blood, he himself will be mauled. Hitler, Abegg relates, doesn't go anywhere without twelve tough guys as his bodyguards. Göring and von Levetzow, Berlin's new superintendent of police, belong to the extremist wing of the party and would not support Hitler in the event of a palace coup. Levetzow, Abegg has learned, even wants to have Reich President Hindenburg arrested if he opposes him. Papen and Hugenberg are deeply afraid of this extremist wing. They have procured an invitation from the Bavarian People's Party for Hindenburg to go to Bavaria for the election days because he is no longer safe in Berlin. And, yes, Abegg can confirm that the Nazis intend to fake an attempted assassination of Hitler. Former President of the Reichstag Paul Löbe, an upstanding SPD man, means to reveal this conspiracy in a speech shortly. Even that probably won't be of any use, though. Luckily the horror can't last very long. The Nazis will inevitably clash with their coalition partners, Papen and Hugenberg. In six weeks, but by July at the latest, Abegg estimates, the government will collapse, and then scores will be settled with these people.

At length Abegg issues the count another insistent warning as he did on Sunday at Georg Bernhard's reception. Kessler must by all means remove himself to safety before the election. The only concern now is surviving the next few weeks.

Once Abegg has taken his leave, Count Kessler's servant Friedrich indirectly and unintentionally confirms the warning. Friedrich, still a very young man, was in Pankow yesterday visiting his father, a retired official and ardent Nazi. His father expressly commanded him to resign his position in the count's home; "unpleasantness" is to be expected there in the near future, and his father doesn't want his son to be embroiled in it. Friedrich is white as a sheet when he reports this to Count Kessler. Kessler leaves the choice to him whether he goes, not wanting to endanger anyone. But, Kessler says, Friedrich may one day come to regret having abandoned him at a crucial moment.

*

On the train to Toulon, the landscape of southern France passes Heinrich Mann by. He has no desire to spin his escape into a tragedy or play the victim. In the end, he is a world-famous author and has always felt at home in France. The Prussian Academy isn't that important then after all, and Hitler's power will soon come to an end, about that he has no doubt. And so when he arrives this evening in Toulon, his mood is effusively cheerful. His loyal friend Herzog does indeed fetch him from the train station, but it has gotten late so they visit a small hotel, sit out on the terrace, and enjoy the mild weather (for mid-February), and Mann first tells of the events of recent days. He does so with wit, parodying Schillings' accusations, which were meant to induce him to resign from the Academy, telling about Gottfried Benn, who thwarted the declaration of protest against Minister Rust, and interrupting himself all the while repeatedly because he is forced to laugh at these people's hidebound zeal and philistine intrigues.

Herzog is a bit surprised at Mann's risibilities, but he joins him in laughter and extends his friend an offer to live with him in Sanary in the days to come, in the little house he has leased there. Heinrich Mann, however, does not see himself as an emigrant in need of support, and instead intends to get on with his life as always. He has already telegraphed Félix Bertaux from Strasbourg, the Germanist with whom he and his brother are friends. Bertaux is the steward of a French bank account for him, and Mann has asked him to wire him money from it. He wouldn't want to live in a fishing village like Sanary. He longs for the brightness of a big city; he shall go to Nice and do as he usually does and live in the *Hôtel de Nice*. As soon as Nelly has liquidated the apartment and the accounts, she is to join him there. He therefore does not need to change very much about his habits at all. In a mixture of defiance and pride, he, one of Germany's writers of highest renown, does not mean to grant this Nazi riffraff the power to steer his life from its usual course.

It is not he who experiences the actual magnitude of the Nazis' power on this day, but Nelly. The flat on Fasanenstrasse is ransacked by the SA, and Nelly is taken away to a police precinct. Heinrich Mann fled not a day too soon.

*

The swapping of personnel in the Prussian Interior Ministry continues. As the *Frankfurter Zeitung* reports, today alone over a dozen leading officials, district presidents, and district chief executives are assigned to non-active status by Hermann Göring and replaced by successors of his choice.

Göring deputizes by decree 40,000 SA and SS men and 10,000 members of the *Stahlhelm* as auxiliary police officers. On February 15 he was still issuing denials of this plan. Now the men are being armed and possess the same authority as regular police officers or *Landjäger* for the duration of their service. As recently as April 1932, Hindenburg had ordered the disbandment of the SA and SS by emergency decree. With over half a million men, the NSDAP's two private armies were regarded as a serious adversary for the Reichswehr in the event of a domestic conflict. Although there could never be any doubt about the organizations' anti-republican intentions, the ban was lifted again two months later. In the first month thereafter ninety-nine people died amid the street terror in Prussia alone, and around a thousand were injured.

In Großbeeren (outside Teltow), National Socialists storm the city's former poorhouse to attack a *Reichbanner* supporter living there. The door to the man's apartment is blasted open with hand grenades, he himself seriously injured by clubbing. The building, home to a total of nine families, is completely gutted by fire.

A confrontation between ballot distributors in Berlin-Pankow erupts into a gun battle. A local resident, following the exchange of fire from a window, is fatally wounded.

A Minister in the Audience
Friday, February 24

Klaus Mann writes a brief note to Erich Ebermayer. He would like to complete work on the dramatization of Saint-Exupéry's *Night Flight* fast. Who knows how long he'll still be in Germany? He thinks it best if they sit down together as soon as possible to bring it all to a close. But where should they meet? Klaus doesn't think Leipzig, where Ebermayer lives, all that compelling. "Of course," he writes, "we could also lock ourselves in a little room in Berlin; but I could be murdered there, which, on the other hand, I might also find titillating for a change." Certainly, Klaus Mann's coquetry is running wild here again, but the comment isn't quite coming out of thin air either, of that Ebermayer is aware. Perhaps it helps drive home for Ebermayer how little time they have left. And, besides, the line is a cry for help packaged in a great deal of irony, too.

*

On the Berlin airwaves this evening, Hanns Johst's drama *Schlageter* is broadcast in a radio play version. To underscore the author's importance, a talk about Johst's literary oeuvre is programmed beforehand, written by Hans Hinkel, one of the NSDAP's leading cultural policymakers.

The drama's title character, Albert Leo Schlageter, is an idol and martyr for nationalists. For ten years he's been the object of virtually cultic reverence. As a nineteen-year-old he volunteered for the military at the outbreak of the First World War, fought for years in battles of attrition as Ernst Toller had done at Verdun and on the Somme, and was wounded multiple times. After the war ended, he had no work qualifications and found no path back into civilian life. Discharged by the army, he joined various *Freikorps* units, battled Soviet troops in Latvia and Polish insurgents in Upper Silesia, and in 1920 supported the Kapp Putsch, which attempted to eradicate the Weimar Republic. He was also active in politics, participating in the founding assembly of the *Großdeutsche Arbeiterpartei* [*Greater German Workers' Party*], a front organization for the transiently banned NSDAP. When Germany fell behind on its reparations payments to the world war's victorious powers in 1923, French and Belgian troops occupied the Ruhr region in a punitive action. In response Schlageter mounted several attacks of sabotage there, was arrested, tried before a French court martial, and executed.

In his play Hanns Johst glorifies Schlageter as the "first soldier of the Third Reich." In his telling Schlageter is no mercenary brutalized by war and lacking in clear military discipline in times of peace, but an educated, ethically sensitive patriot who is unable to bear Germany's humiliations by the Treaty of Versailles. The propagandistic intentions are unmistakable: Johst reinterprets Schlageter as a knight without fault or blame, his life as a great pious sacrifice for the nation, and the "archenemy" France as an existential threat to Germany. In the heavily symbolic final scene, Schlageter is ushered to his execution and tied to a post with his back to the audience. From the rear of the stage, the firing squad trains its rifles on him and thus also at the viewers in the theater.

Johst worked on his agitative passion play for around three years and dedicated it "to Adolf Hitler in loving adoration and unwavering loyalty." The broadcast of the radio play version is only an initial dry run. The political circumstances couldn't be better for launching the play in the theater. As co-artistic director of the Schauspielhaus on Gendarmenmarkt, Johst adds it to the repertory personally. Not only his theater, but nearly all the country's stages are currently revamping their programming. After the Nazis' takeover the risk from performing plays by leftist or Jewish authors has become incalculable. And so they have to disappear from the repertoire and be replaced by plays amenable to the new rulers. Like *Schlageter*, for example.

The Berlin premiere on April 20, Hitler's birthday, is a triumph for Johst. It is a nationalist High Mass, a *völkisch* evening of consecration with which the new regime commemorates itself. An especially martial line from the play creates a furor, and the store of Nazi quotations is no longer imaginable without it: "When I hear the word culture [...] I release the safety on my Browning!" Quite a few celebrities in the audience: while Hitler himself may not be present, those who are include Vice-Chancellor Franz von Papen, Reichswehr Minister Werner von Blomberg, Joseph Goebbels, and Berlin's superintendent of police, Magnus von Levetzow, along with Prince August Wilhelm of Prussia, conductor Wilhelm Furtwängler, Academy president Max von Schillings, and many more. After the final curtain, the audience rises to its feet – not to leave the theater, but to sing the German anthem and, with raised right arms, the Horst Wessel Song.

The play thereby received the highest blessing of national politics. Other stages around the country scramble to reenact it, and in the following months alone it is staged at over one hundred theaters. In this way Johst establishes himself as the representative writer for the new era, and nothing more stands in the way of his impending ascent to the very highest offices. His positions will include, among others, head of the *Reichsschrifttumskammer* [*Reich Chamber of Literature*], president of the German PEN-Club, and, with special support from his friend Heinrich Himmler, *Gruppenführer* of the SS.

*

Therese Giehse is the star of Erika Mann's cabaret *Die Pfeffermühle*. She acts, she sings, she directs. The bits in which she appears get the most laughs as well as notable plaudits from critics in the newspapers. Even so, she is also employed by the Munich Kammerspiele, where she evolved into a star in her early thirties. Directors entrust her with their most important roles. She does not want to content herself with this, nor can she; she is restive, driven, always eager for something new. The *Pfeffermühle* opens up the chance for her to perfect her comic talent, finally direct, and bring political topics to the stage. Aside from that, she finds collaborating with the Mann siblings stimulating. At first glance she and Erika form an idiosyncratic couple. Erika is thin, athletic, very androgynous; Therese voluptuous, stout, brawny. And with Klaus she shares a perpetual restlessness and inner tension.

When the *Pfeffermühle* presented its first program in January, Therese Giehse had to juggle two commitments at once. She often performed twice a day, here by afternoon and there by night. On some days she would be on stage at the Kammerspiele in Gerhart Hauptmann's *The Rats*, run out of the theater during intermission, down Maximilianstrasse, then left to Neuturmstrasse 5, into the little cabaret stage *Bonbonniere*, change her costume, sing a couplet, act in a sketch, then burst into the dressing room, change, and run back to the Kammerspiele to finish

Figure 17: Therese
Giehse in 1933

Hauptmann's drama. An extreme hazard, but she can depend unquestioningly on her almost eerie versatility.

On February 1, the *Pfeffermühle* launched a new program, and once again all performances are jam-packed. The new troupe's success has outgrown the *Bonbonniere*, and Erika Mann is already hunting for a new, larger theater where they intend to perform as of April. Once more, all the tables are occupied today, but the little ensemble is more nervous than usual. Just three buildings down the street, in the Hofbräuhaus, Hitler is giving a speech in front of 2,000 old party comrades. Thirteen years ago to the day, on February 24, 1920, he founded the NSDAP in the Hofbräuhaus and declared his party platform. Now he returns as Reich Chancellor to be feted and to implement his platform point by point. A neighborhood could hardly be more discomforting.

Or could it be even worse? While delivering the transitions between sketches as master of ceremonies, Erika recognizes a surprising guest in the half-dark of the theater. Sitting at one of the tables is Wilhelm Frick, Reich Minister of the Interior, a Nazi of the first order, supreme head of police for the entire country. Apparently he is skipping his Führer's speech in the Hofbräuhaus and prefers to observe the evening at the *Pfeffermühle* personally. What's more: as Erika Mann can see, he is even actively writing, taking notes, likely so as not to miss any of the troupe's punch lines, impertinences, or allusions. Or could that be a blacklist Frick is compiling here?

*

Oberregierungsrat Rudolf Diels, whom Göring promoted to chief of the Prussian Political Police after his own swearing-in, is now also appointed director of Berlin's Political Police, which grants him extraordinarily wide-reaching authority.

In Leipzig, two major clashes between National Socialists and men of the *Reichsbanner* take place. In a brawl in the western part of the city, a thirty-year-old chauffeur suffers a fatal stab wound. During a shootout in Zeitzer Strasse, over twenty shots are exchanged and numerous people are injured.

In Berlin, several gunfights break out: three men are injured in front of a KPD bar in Pankow, and three more in Kreuzberg. On Skalitzer Strasse, an SA man succumbs to a gunshot wound to the chest. On Bergmannstrasse, a KPD man suffers a shot to the calf. In Siemensstadt, Nazis on their way home at 4 a.m. are shot at by communists, with one casualty among them. After yesterday's shootout in Gesundbrunnen, the police report four injured in the hospitals today.

In Breslau [present-day Wrocław], a bomb attack is carried out at the office of the Social Democratic *Volksblatt*. The explosion is so powerful that even buildings on the opposite side of the street suffer damage. No one is injured.

Civil War Tribunal and Police Protection
Saturday, February 25

Gabriele Tergit is a short, energetic woman in her late thirties. She prefers wearing her dark hair up and glasses with strikingly round lenses. She works as a court reporter for several of Berlin's best newspapers, the *Berliner Tageblatt*, the *Berliner Börsen-Courier*, and *Die Weltbühne*. Almost every day she goes in and out of Berlin's criminal court in Moabit, a "place for men," as she puts it. It's no site for the squeamish. There the hate, misery, and tragedies of an era rent asunder are heard in court. Taken together, all these trials paint for Tergit a more exact picture of society than any sociology seminar could.

Her articles are witty, sharp-tongued, and read a lot. She has also written a novel already, *Käsebier Takes Berlin*, a dynamic portrait of Berlin, a tour de force through the city's various milieus, and above all a profession of love for newspaper publishers.

Since the butchery between Nazis and their adversaries in Berlin's streets has become part of daily life, she writes more and more frequently about political proceedings as well. By now she refers to the Criminal Court as a "war tribunal," a "civil-war tribunal" with all too many nationalist-minded judges – and is forced to endure being publicly insulted for this by Goebbels as a "contemptible Jewess."

Today she is en route to Kantstrasse. A communist holds out his collection plate – he's collecting for the unemployed – and a Nazi shakes his for the Hitler Youth. The pavement is littered with tiny paper swastikas, the confetti of the civil war. A street vendor hopes to sell violets, but no one has money for flowers these days.

Housed at number 152 are the modest editorial offices of the *Weltbühne*. Tergit has come to hand in an article for the next issue. The editor-in-chief, Carl von Ossietzky, reads it at once, and while the text is being set and Tergit waits for the galley proofs, they chat about the many colleagues, journalists, and authors who have already crossed the border to safety. Ossietzky thinks it better to stay.

"I'm definitely staying," says Gabriele Tergit. "We've got to watch history unfold."

"That's what I would like, too," says Ossietzky, while making a face that telegraphs doubts about whether watching history while working is actually possible.

Then the galleys arrive. Gabriele Tergit stands up to say goodbye: "See you later."

But she will never see Ossietzky again.

*

The trouble in Darmstadt has not lessened for artistic director Gustav Hartung. Since the city council banned the premiere of Brecht's *Saint Joan of the Stockyards*, the Nazi attacks against him, his programming, and especially his Jewish employees have not ceased. The municipal theater committee has been instructed to scrutinize Hartung's personal

Figure 18: Gustav Hartung in 1930

politics. The NSDAP and the national liberal DVP demand he dismiss the Jews from his ensemble. But Hartung is obstinate and refuses to do so.

Furthermore, he has scheduled for this evening the premiere of Ferdinand Bruckner's most recent play, an adaptation of Kleist's novella *The Marquise of O....* The play is no harmless retelling of the old subject matter, but rather modifies certain aspects of it that certainly do not fit into the Nazis' philosophy. First and foremost, however: Bruckner, too, has Jewish heritage. He was born Theodor Tagger in Sofia. His father was a wealthy bank clerk, his mother a Frenchwoman. He grew up in Vienna, Paris, and Berlin, worked as a journalist, wrote poems and his first plays at a young age, and in 1922 founded the Renaissance-Theater in Berlin with private investors. In short, he is a highly educated, worldly intellectual and cultural entrepreneur and thus represents much of what the Nazis profoundly hate. It requires all the more courage on Hartung's part to keep to the planned premiere. A great deal is at risk for him.

And yet he and Bruckner are linked by a special past. In 1926 the Renaissance-Theater, which Bruckner was still running under his birthname Theodor Tagger, was just about to go bankrupt. Although it was a private venture, meaning it had to be financed by revenues, Tagger didn't show any operettas or light comedies. Instead, he had turned his theater into an experimental stage for young dramatists critical of contemporary issues – and often enough played to a half-empty house. It wasn't long before he couldn't pay the rent anymore and had to take special care not to cross paths with a court officer.

At that point Hartung took over the theater but was initially very short of cash as well – until he stumbled upon the play *Youth Is a Sickness* by an almost entirely unknown author named Ferdinand Bruckner. Hartung pounced, and his production became a sensational success with a months-long run. Immediately the whole world wanted to meet the new author, but he was apparently publicity-shy, never showed himself anywhere, and only let it be known that he was a doctor living in Reims where he tended to a rich patient. Even Hartung had no idea who was behind the pseudonym. When three years later a lawsuit was filed regarding the performance rights to other Bruckner plays, Tagger's wife blabbed before the court, and Tagger was forced to admit his authorship. With regrettable consequences to the present day: since his bankruptcy with the Renaissance-Theater, he still has considerable debts he must repay with the royalties he earns under the name Ferdinand Bruckner.

His biggest success, *Youth Is a Sickness*, evinces a few similarities with Klaus Mann's scandalous play *Anja and Esther*, with which Klaus and his sister Erika, together with Pamela Wedekind and Gustaf Gründgens, stoked their audience's erotic fantasies and their critics' fits of rage in the mid-1920s. After the war, the collapse of the monarchy, and inflation, Bruckner's characters are lacking direction, too, in both moral and political respects as well as in erotic ones. Young medical student Marie loses her beloved to her best friend and seeks solace in a lesbian affair. When her lover is obliged to realize, however, that Marie is unable, in spite of everything, to extricate herself from her former boyfriend, she kills herself with sleeping pills, and Marie resolves to provoke and torment a narcissistic, cynical fellow student to the point that he murders her.

Bruckner's adaptation of *The Marquise of O...* has the potential for similar scandal. In Kleist it is a Russian nobleman who avails himself of the Marquise's unconsciousness and rapes her, then falls in love with and marries her. Bruckner, on the other hand, makes the Russian into a Prussian cavalry officer and the Marquise into an emancipated young woman who, despite her pregnancy, is not prepared, under any circumstances, to marry the man who assaulted her while she was unconscious.

Only yesterday the *Hessische Landeszeitung* printed a fresh denunciation of the theater, and also of the premiere of *The Marquise of O...*, even though no one has yet been able to see the finished performance. A few hours later Bruckner arrived in Darmstadt on the train from Berlin to watch the dress rehearsal together with Hartung. Bruckner is satisfied neither with his play, nor with Hartung's production. Until 1:30 in the morning they both huddle with the actors and abridge the text in order to streamline and amend individual scenes.

Hartung knows he has to reckon with disruptions during this premiere, so he puts his theater under police protection for this evening as a precautionary measure. That doesn't much worry Bruckner. During the day he sightsees in town, visits the theater's photographer, has pictures of himself taken, and most notably buys a ticket to Vienna where the Austrian premiere of *The Marquise of O...* will take place in four days. Alas, the train connections are poor; he has to follow a very circuitous route via Frankfurt, Würzburg, and Passau, so it will be a long night journey. But he wants to leave hostile Darmstadt again tomorrow by any means possible.

Fortunately, the evening's disruptions are limited. Several SA squads march outside the theater and line up in formation, but the police, under the command of Hessian Interior Minister Wilhelm Leuschner of the SPD, deters them from infiltrating the foyer or the auditorium. Instead, they remain on the street in front of the theater where they endlessly chant their slur "drop dead, Judah!" – bad enough.

After the performance Bruckner and Hartung remain with the actors until five in the morning. This is no boisterous premiere party, but rather hours upon hours of speculation about the future prospects for Germany. Then the morning newspapers arrive. The reviews are reserved, but better than Bruckner expected. Around midday he boards the train for Vienna. He is traveling light, with no intention of staying in Austria for long, just seeing the premiere and then back to Berlin. Nevertheless, it will take him twenty years to return to Germany.

*

In Wuppertal, a demonstration march by the NSDAP comes under fire at two different locations. Two SA men are grazed. After the march disperses, policemen search the buildings where the shots are said to have been fired. When KPD members resist, the policemen use their weapons, shooting and killing two men and injuring two others.

In Harrisleefeld (by Flensburg), clashes erupt between members of the *Reichsbanner* and National Socialists. A *Reichsbanner* man is shot. In the city Neiße in Upper Silesia [present-day Nysa], three members of the *Reichsbanner* are shot at by night. One of them dies.

In Lindenfels in the Odenwald, a melee breaks out between residents of a workers' estate and SA troopers. One brownshirt is stabbed to death, another seriously wounded.

Following an SPD rally in Dresden, *Reichsbanner* people begin arguing with policemen who want to arrest a participant in the gathering. An officer then draws his weapon and shoots dead one of the SPD men.

While standing watch at the Volksbühne over the KPD's Karl-Liebknecht-Haus, which has been closed by police order, two policemen shoot and kill a man who allegedly physically attacked them.

Travel Advice

Monday, February 27

At around midday, Walter Mehring visits the editorial office of the *Weltbühne* on Kantstrasse. He's been writing short features for the newspaper for years, but this time he's not coming as a contributor, but as the bearer of bad news for Ossietzky. A friend working in the Ministry of Foreign Affairs paid Mehring's mother a Sunday visit yesterday and, unsolicited, gave her urgent travel advice for her son: "Your son feels most at home in Paris. He should go back to Paris." His mother understood right away and asked how long the trip should last. The visitor hesitated briefly. "I would say fifteen years." The thoughtful man isn't solely concerned about Mehring, however, but about other authors as well. In the days to come, he predicts, there will be a lot of arrests.

Ossietzky smiles, listening intently and silently. The information does not surprise him. Mehring implores him to leave the country immediately. Ossietzky demurs, neither agreeing nor disagreeing, but does not object when someone from the editorial team books him a ticket by telephone to the next available foreign country. At that moment Hellmut von Gerlach enters the room, sixty-seven years old, chairman of the *Liga für Menschenrechte*, and for decades one of the major guiding figures of Germany's left-wing liberal peace movement. Ossietzky admires him a great deal and entrusted him with the editorship of the *Weltbühne* while he was incarcerated last year.

"Mehring thinks," Ossietzky tells him, "we all need to get out now."

Gerlach flares up while fiddling with his umbrella: "Enough with the panicking already! Anyway, I for my part am staying regardless."

"Then I'll stay, too …!" Ossietzky replies.

As Mehring turns to go, Gerlach wishes him well: "Godspeed."

*

Brecht's hernia operation went off without a hitch, and he came through everything without any complications. For the time being, however, he is still in Dr. Mayer's private clinic where he is well provided-for. It's unlikely he could find a more pleasant place in Berlin at the moment.

What comes next is still uncertain. Brecht has of course discussed emigration with other authors now and again, especially the idea of sticking together as a group in exile. But this plan has a critical disadvantage; he and Helene still do not have a passport for their young daughter Barbara, now more than two years old, so they could not legally leave the country with her. For this reason, they've often debated whether it might suffice to hide out somewhere in the countryside, maybe in Bavaria, for a few weeks until Hitler is forced to resign. Heinrich Held, the head of the Bavarian People's Party, seems to hold the reins firmly in hand there as Minister-President and to be keeping the Nazis in check to some degree.

Then, however, as requested, Brecht's invitation to a reading in Vienna arrived, where his play *The Mother* is to be premiered, a production he would like to see. For now, he will travel to Austria. But when? And how long will he stay there?

One thing is certain. He has to get out of Berlin. He's had the boxes with his manuscripts and other materials hauled out of his apartment and safeguarded with friends. The children are a difficult matter. Brecht has asked his father in Augsburg to shelter Barbara at his home, for the time being, but how can he ever get her across the border? For now, he and Helene have put up Stefan, now nine, with Elisabeth Hauptmann, one of Brecht's many former lovers and today one of his most important assistants. After Brecht and Weigel's marriage in 1929, she attempted suicide, but was saved. Fortunately, Brecht was able to mollify somewhat those then-tempestuous surges of emotion and include Elisabeth again as an integral part of his theater family. He absolutely needs her for his work, but also for the organization of his life.

At around noon the phone in Brecht's clinic room rings. Calling from Vienna, Hanns Eisler conveys good news. He monitored the dress rehearsal of *The Mother* at the Konzerthaus and saw the premiere yesterday. Two thousand spectators were there, enormous applause, a huge success! Eisler is pleased, though at the moment can't yet anticipate when he'll return to Germany. For now, his plans are also unclear. He's still of two minds.

Then come two pieces of bad news, two pieces of very bad news, one by mail. Brecht receives a letter from Fritz Wreede, owner of the theatrical publishing house Felix Bloch Erben. In 1929 Brecht signed a general contract with Wreede for future years that contains many exclusion clauses, but which ultimately ends up giving the theatrical publisher the sole right of representation for Brecht's new full-length plays and in return paying Brecht one thousand inflation-proof gold marks per month as an advance – regular proceeds that Brecht has firmly budgeted for. In his letter Wreede is now complaining that Brecht delivered *Saint Joan of the Stockyards* too late and did not uphold certain agreements in his adaptation of Shakespeare's *Measure for Measure*. Some of the letter's formulations have disconcerting, juridical undertones as though Wreede were concocting arguments for a legal dispute. Ultimately, he writes, in light of the new political circumstances, there are no performance prospects for either of the two plays. Wreede therefore considers it unacceptable to continue making the monthly payments.

On top of his perilous political problems, Brecht thus now has to add serious financial worries. And the next piece of bad news comes from Walter Mehring. It is a message of the kind one prefers not to discuss by telephone these days, but delivers in person. Mehring and Brecht have known one another for years. They both belonged to the *Gruppe 1925*, a loose amalgamation of leftist authors who met a few times until the late twenties.

Like Brecht, Mehring is a slight man, short, with a large head and a wan face. He has a cool, biting wit. His chanson lyrics and satires have made him one of the city's most coveted cabaret authors. Once when Brecht was still quite young and unknown, Mehring introduced him to Trude Hesterberg. Brecht wanted to perform in her cabaret as a balladeer with his own poems and ballads. He auditioned for her, and she liked him, finding the sound of his voice eerie, almost demonic. But Brecht's appearance on stage turned out to be a fiasco. Brecht wasn't off book with his own poems, repeatedly got stuck, and then stood helplessly on stage, looking for crib sheets. Aside from that, the audience had no appetite whatsoever for Brecht's thin, croaking voice.

Now Mehring is conveying the same warning to him that he delivered to Ossietzky, while also reporting that Ossietzky does not under any circumstances intend to leave the country. Brecht thinks little of so much demonstratively unbending martyr's mettle. Mehring's message alarms him. Obviously it is about time for him to end this so very agreeable stay in his recovery room.

*

Three days ago, Katia and Thomas Mann traveled onward from Paris, the final station of his Wagner tour, to Arosa in Switzerland. It is one of their most favorite places to vacation. Katia Mann was here for treatment twice before because doctors diagnosed an apical catarrh that they feared could portend tuberculosis. Thomas and Katia are so fond of the landscape and the *Neues Waldhotel* that they enjoy traveling back here even without medical need. This time it is Thomas Mann who would like to relax for a few days after the strains of his work on the essay about Wagner. Afterward he wants to return to Munich, back to his desk, where the manuscript for *Joseph in Egypt* awaits him. That is the plan.

The seven-story, castle-like hotel offers an imposing vista of the Grison Alps. The view may not be quite as spectacular as the one from the *Deutsches Haus* in Ticino where Margarete Steffin is currently trying to cure her tuberculosis, but it is impressive nonetheless. During a stay here in 1912, Thomas Mann developed his initial ideas for *The Magic Mountain*, and later employed quite a few details of the locale and the hotel in his novel. What enamored him above all was the elongated dining hall, with the full splendor of the mountain panorama unfolding outside its windows. It is furnished in the style of New Objectivity, with vivid hues, its walls clad to half height in wooden paneling, above which are wallpaper with colorful stripes and the solid-brass chandelier hanging from the ceiling.

Mann has had his mail forwarded here from Munich, and with it the quarrels involving the writers' division of the Academy in Berlin have caught up with him. Alfred Döblin described to him the pair of most recent meetings in a lengthy letter: the first in which his brother Heinrich was pressured to resign, and the one in which Döblin attempted to push through a statement of protest, but to no avail. The letter's summary has an air of resignation; Döblin expects the section will soon be disbanded, possibly just after the elections. Perhaps it would be better to preempt such a move and resign of their own accord, most preferably as a group. Yet Leonhard Frank, Döblin writes, does not wish to leave the battlefield voluntarily, but to continue fighting. What about the Academy are they defending, though? In any case Döblin feels awful because in public it now looks like they had all accepted Heinrich Mann's mandated resignation virtually in silence and without resistance.

René Schickele, born in the Alsace and having labored for decades in essays and novels toward a reconciliation between France and Germany, has also been in touch. Shouldn't they establish a private writers' academy, he proposes in his letter, in case the Nazis disband their division?

Yesterday Thomas Mann first sent an extensive reply to Döblin, resorting in it to pugnacious vocabulary. By no means must they do the new potentates the favor, he says, of dissolving their division by themselves. Naturally he wanted to quit as well when he heard of his brother's resignation, but now he thinks it better to wait for the time being and leave it to the new occupation authorities – as he refers to the Nazis – to abolish the section by force. That, he believes, would be a far more visible event for which the National Socialists would then have to bear responsibility in public. Furthermore, it is impossible to predict, he points out, how things will turn out with Germany. He cannot deny faint hope for the elections next Sunday.

Today he writes to Schickele in roughly the same tenor. In his view the best strategy at the moment is to do nothing. If the Nazis break up the Academy, they once again reveal their intolerance and caprice for all to see. If, however, they leave the liberal authors in their writers' division, they admit publicly that there is a small group of honest men offering them resistance. For them, both options would necessarily be politically irksome indeed, wouldn't they?

*

Gottfried Benn is also busy with correspondence today. He is writing a letter to an old friend, Egmont Seyerlen. The pair have known one another for over twenty years. At the time, still prior to the First World War, they were young authors trying to make a name for themselves on Berlin's literary scene. To a certain extent Seyerlen caught the better start. In 1913, the posh S. Fischer Verlag released his debut *Die schmerzliche Scham* [*Painful Shame*], a novel about a schoolboy and puberty that suited the times well. By contrast, Benn's first cycle of poems, *Morgue*, was published in 1912 by a one-man press in Wilmersdorf, not in hardcover, as a lyrical pamphlet of sorts. A booklet like that, with only nine poems for fifty pfennigs, could easily have been overlooked, but the opposite was the case. Benn's debut evolved into a literary scandal of sizable magnitude. With their mercilessly cold regard for illness, death, and decay, his poems stirred indignation, even horror, among timorous readers used to the sentimental tone of the *Jugendstil*. For them, Benn was a monster, a barbarian of language who shocked them – but in so doing opened a new door to modernist literature.

Seyerlen soon ceased his literary activity and worked for a time as a wholesaler, manager, and business consultant. Now he is about to make it big as a much sought-after economic expert. While living in close proximity in Berlin's Bavarian Quarter, he and Benn had rather intimate dealings with one another, exchanging views not least about love affairs or sexual questions. Now Seyerlen is living in Bavaria and has requested advice in medical matters by letter.

Benn's response is brief. In his view Seyerlen's troubles cannot be more than neurosis. He suggests he undergo a thorough checkup at a sanatorium for a week and otherwise proposes – in an amicably teasing tone – self-improvement and eroticism in torrents.

Benn provides a much more detailed report on the current brouhaha in Berlin's literary world. Fear and terror hold sway, he writes. The presses are sending their politically unpopular books to field warehouses in Austria so that the Nazis cannot confiscate them. Many writers, too, have since fled to Prague or Vienna where they intend to wait things out until Hitler's government has gone belly up. Benn can only scoff at such hopes: "What children! How deaf! The revolution is here and *history speaks*. Whoever doesn't see that is an imbecile. Never again will the individualism of old, never again will the honest socialism of old return. This is a new epoch of historical being, talking about its worthiness or unworthiness is foolish, *it is here*. And if after two decades it is gone, it will have left behind a different humanity, a different *Volk*. I've been talking about this until I'm blue in the face, but the leftist folks refuse to believe it. See above: children and deaf people."

Aside from poems, in recent years Benn has written more and more essays and radio lectures. The radio stations pay good fees, and Benn is always short of money. These essays are not just bread-and-butter work for him, however. Although by his own admission he wants nothing to do with current affairs as a poet, he has embroiled himself in political debates about literature.

It started harmlessly at first, like one of the usual kerfuffles in the feuilleton. With his brash self-image as a lyric poet who accepts only the timeless autonomy of art as his guiding principle, Benn is brilliantly suited to be a counterforce to the aesthetics of social commitment, which sees in literature a weapon for political combat. Critic and poet Max Hermann-Neiße thus celebrated Benn in 1929 as a brave avant-gardist who cannot be ideologically coopted by anyone, and played him off against innovators of popular, but often simplistically crafted, agitprop art. Authors such as Johannes R. Becher and Egon Erwin Kisch subsequently felt attacked by Hermann-Neiße and in turn made Benn out to be the epitome of an escapist, ivory-towered, ultimately asocial poet-snob, whereupon Benn – who is much too concerned with recognition to be able to ignore such recriminations – threw himself headlong into the journalistic conflict of opinion.

Yet this conflict has its own momentum. Benn argues, polemicizes, intensifies, and escalates his way into extreme positions. If leftist writers claim rationality and enlightenment as the highest measure of their literature, he can only shake his head. Have not myth, frenzy, and the irrational in art been the far more powerful forces since time immemorial? In his eyes the battle for progress and social justice degradingly reduces literature to trite propaganda, and what's more, the conflict itself ultimately bespeaks naïveté. As a reader of Nietzsche, Benn is firmly convinced that history at its core knows no progress, no morality, no hope. It ruthlessly brushes aside the fate of millions. The only law it follows is the law of living and survival. For that reason, too, terms like "breeding," "race," or "*Volk*" become more and more important for Benn the physician and scientist. The years of the Weimar Republic and democracy are, to his mind, years of social disintegration, decadence, and downfall. If the *Volk* is now turning away from this form of government, if it wants to grant itself a stricter regime again under the reign of National Socialism in order to breed itself into a sovereign race, then that is for Benn a thoroughly comprehensible, historically necessary reaction. For him it becomes ever more irrefutable that the bourgeois values of the Republic, that liberalism, pluralism, and the rule of law, are antiquated and finished. Sometimes he is downright amazed at his own views. One time, while standing at the window of his practice with Tilly Wedekind, watching the marching columns of young Nazis on Belle-Alliance-Strasse moving toward Tempelhof Field, he suddenly says to her: "Now even the brown uniforms appeal to me."

All of this converges in his letter to Seyerlen. For Benn, a new episode of history began four weeks ago with Hitler's takeover, an epoch in which archaic values, which he always considers the more powerful ones anyway, are restored to their rights once more. Individualism is superseded by a willingness to make sacrifices and surrender the self to the bigger picture. Democracy with its arduously negotiated compromises is supplanted by an organically formed *Volksgemeinschaft*. The socialist collective is replaced by the mythic collective and communities of fate as embodied by nations.

There are no questions of justice or injustice here. Historical upheavals of such magnitude as Benn now sees coming always take place by force. That is regrettable, to be sure, but in the end not important. All that is important is the new regime that is established and will produce a different humanity, a different *Volk*. Every revolution claims victims – they are unavoidable – and to a certain degree Benn numbers among these victims, too. After all, at forty-six he is no longer a young man. "A new race is rising," he writes Seyerlen, "one very alien to us. May it cultivate and shape a happier history, a more joyful age, a more civilized *Volk* than we had. [...] I radically bid farewell to myself and everything we sprang from and that seemed to us beautiful and worthy of life."

Benn regards himself not just as a poet, but also as a thinker, which fits his notion of the intellectually elite he counts himself part of. And an elite of this kind views and adjudges historical processes from a dizzyingly lofty perch. Benn has little sympathy for the everyday minutiae of politics. He does not wonder whether he, like many writers before and after him, might be confusing the very large-scale conceptions of world and history in his literature with political realities. With sweeping talk of a revolution-as-juggernaut that need make no allowances for moral justification, he opens the door for despotism without so much as glancing at the grim figures who are leading this alleged revolution. Benn speaks of an epochal turning point with such assurance of victory not least because he does not at all apprehend the social, economic, and technical preconditions of a modern industrial society. He sees only his ideas about the philosophy of history, and should reality not correspond to these ideas, then that is all the more unfortunate for reality.

*

After Walter Mehring said goodbye to Brecht at the clinic, he trudges through the increasing chill to a café where the SDS, the *Schutzverband deutscher Schriftsteller*, has scheduled its afternoon meeting. There Mehring is expected to read from his texts, and of course he will relay the warning that came to him from his friend in the Foreign Affairs Ministry. Before he can enter the café, however, a beauty with dark, untamed locks approaches him on the street: Mascha Kaléko. She is twenty-five, a clever, witty woman already considered one of the country's important new poets with her sober, ironic verse. Many newspapers print her poems, and several weeks ago her first small volume appeared with Rowohlt Verlag with the pretty title à la New Objectivity *Das lyrische Stenogrammheft* [*The Lyrical Booklet of Shorthand*]. At this very moment Mascha Kaléko's mind is not on literature, though. "Mehring," she whispers to him under her breath, "You need to make yourself scarce right now! The auxiliary swastika police is up ahead with a warrant for your arrest!"

Mehring wheels around at once. He doesn't want to stand out so he walks slowly, glad for every meter he puts between himself and the café. Step by step he slinks to safety. Then he decides to put into action this very moment the advice that friend gave him via his mother. He walks to the train station and boards the next train to the border.

*

Brecht isn't leaving just yet. He has found a shelter for himself and Helene Weigel where they can safely spend the night. He has known Peter Suhrkamp for a very long time; they met in 1920, of all places at the home of Hanns Johst on Lake Starnberg. They were both visiting him at the time to discuss his play *Der König* [*The King*], which had so impressed Thomas Mann that he avowed his collegial love to Johst in a letter. At the time Suhrkamp was still working as a teacher, but was already securing connections to find traction as a literary critic, editor, or reader for a publisher. Since then Brecht, the savvy networker, has stayed in touch with him. For a while Suhrkamp worked at Darmstadt's theater for Gustav Hartung as dramaturg, then later in Berlin as editor of the monthly *Uhu*, where he regularly printed poems by Brecht. These days, at S. Fischer Verlag, he edits the *Neue Rundschau*, a conservative literary journal for the educated middle class that no one has ever suspected of harboring any sort of pretentions to leftist politics, or Marxism for that matter. In short, Suhrkamp is for sure not on any police arrest list, and he is prepared to quarter Brecht and Helene Weigel in his apartment. Then tomorrow the couple can decide on their next steps.

*

The SPD has organized a large Karl Marx rally at the Sportpalast for the evening. The fiftieth anniversary of Marx's death is not until March 14, but of course the party hopes that moving up the event will have propagandistic repercussions for their campaign. After several initial declamations, the police break up the gathering on account of some

Figure 19: Mascha Kaléko in 1930

such alleged remarks critical of the government. The hall must be vacated.

That sort of thing has been happening for weeks. There's hardly an SPD event that isn't canceled or disrupted by the SA. When the attendees emerge outside the Sportpalast, they are met with an ember-red glow in the night sky: firelight. The news flits through the crowd with frenzied speed: the Reichstag is burning!

*

It is after 9 p.m. that the fire in the Reichstag building is reported. The fire department responds with fifteen fire engines and is able to contain one fire in the parliamentary restaurant. Yet the firemen are powerless against the over twenty other blazes flaring up throughout the building. In the plenary chamber with the cupola above it, the fire grows as in a chimney and quickly reaches temperatures of almost 1,000°C (1,800°F). Rudolf Diels, chief of the Political Police, arrives on the scene soon after the fire brigades. Within the burning building, a half-naked, obviously mentally disturbed Dutchman is apprehended babbling "Protest! Protest!"

On this day Hitler is dining with Joseph and Magda Goebbels on Reichskanzlerplatz. Goebbels ignores the first phone call reporting the fire, regarding the news as a joke. Only when the report is confirmed by a second call does he inform Hitler. They race by car down arrow-straight Charlottenburger Chaussee through the Tiergarten to the government district.

Hermann Göring has reached the site of the conflagration before them. He climbs over the fire hoses lying about higgledy-piggledy. Water from the engines freezes in gigantic puddles. When Hitler and Goebbels arrive, and Franz von Papen shortly thereafter, Göring, howling, accuses the communists of having set the blaze as the signal for a countrywide coup attempt. He orders the entire police force to be on highest alert. In view of the burning building, Hitler whips himself into a fit of apoplectic agitation. Diels hears him screaming hotheadedly: "There will be no more mercy; whoever gets in our way will be mowed down ... Every communist functionary will be shot where he stands. The communist deputies must be hanged this very night. Everything and everyone in league with the communists is to be arrested. There will be no more quarter now for Social Democrats and the *Reichsbanner* either."

At around 1 a.m. the fire is largely under control. Diels and his officers, as well as SA and SS squads, begin detaining communist officials and other Nazi adversaries according to the lists compiled weeks earlier. That same night the police chief reports to Goebbels that the arrests are proceeding according to plan. Together with his vice-chancellor, Papen, Hitler makes his first decisions; the newspapers of the SPD and KPD are to be banned. A short while later Hitler gathers his most important people at the Hotel *Kaiserhof.* The mood is ebullient, everyone is beaming. The Dutchman arrested in the building has labeled himself a communist. "That's just what we needed," Goebbels rejoices. "We've gotten off completely scot-free."

*

Ernst Rowohlt and Rudolf Ditzen are sitting with their wives in the restaurant *Schlichter* and can be roundly pleased with themselves, Rowohlt first and foremost. As a publisher he has done everything right by Ditzen. He recognized this mentally so vulnerable writer's astonishing talent and was undeterred from his faith in him. Although the first two novels flopped and Ditzen ended up in jail twice for embezzlement and fraud, Rowohlt held unshakably firm to him. After his incarceration Rowohlt even hired him at the press part-time so that he'd enjoy at least provisional financial security and be able to continue working on his third novel, which would go on to earn a little money at any rate.

Early last summer the time had finally come. Ditzen, who writes under the pen name Hans Fallada, completed a new manuscript, his fourth novel. The *Vossische Zeitung* is serializing it, bookstores, readers, and critics are rapturous, and the title, *Little Man – What Now?*, has immediately become a popular saying, a cipher for the perplexity of the age. It is the story of an average office clerk who tumbles with his wife and child through the chaos of the global economic crisis, loses his job, home, and any confidence in the future, but finds a last redemptive foothold in his love for his little family: a rather sentimental novel of the times that could hardly be more topical or more touching. The book becomes a veritable bestseller, other countries' publishers line up at Rowohlt to buy the translation rights, and film producers promptly pounce on the text – even now, just a couple of months after the book launch, the film has begun shooting.

That's all the more reason for Ernst Rowohlt to invite the Falladas to *Schlichter* today, a fancy restaurant beloved by many writers and artists. The painter Rudolf Schlichter is the owner's brother; new paintings or drawings by him are always hanging on the walls as though it were a permanent sales exhibition. His friends George Grosz and Wieland Herzfelde number among the regulars, Brecht and Kurt Weill met here, and in 1928 Brecht offered the young director of the Theater am Schiffbauerdamm the first half-finished draft of *The Threepenny Opera*, which then went on to be the greatest success in each of their lives.

Rowohlt wants to keep Fallada happy, by hook or by crook. They enjoyed excellent food, drank a great deal of *Steinwein*, and rinsed it down now and again with a spot of raspberry brandy. Rowohlt pampers his new star author because Fallada is as unnerved as he is indignant by work on the film. He spends entire days at the studios, ever afraid the director and screenwriters could pare down his novel into a cheap humdrum tale.

As his publisher, Rowohlt worries, with justification, that Fallada could imperil the whole film project even though it is the best publicity for the book he could hope for. But this author is sometimes unreachable with reasoned arguments. Since his childhood, Fallada has been mentally extremely unstable and is still hard to predict. As a schoolboy he wanted to end his life together with a classmate. The two teenagers worked themselves into nihilistic revulsion at the world and tried to stage their suicide as a duel. Fallada actually shot and killed his friend while himself surviving, despite being critically injured with two bullets to the chest. A court subsequently declared him of unsound mind and sent him to a mental institution for a time.

No sooner was he free, he became involved in a hapless love affair. He met Anne Marie Seyerlen, very cultivated, eight years his senior, and the wife of Gottfried Benn's friend Egmont Seyerlen. Still, the relationship of this unequal pair shattered, and Fallada slipped into life-threatening drug and alcohol binges. Only after several stays in rehab clinics and in prison was he able to overcome his morphine addiction, despite remaining a drinker. While he tries to keep his alcohol consumption moderate, sometimes he loses all control over himself in his inebriation.

For that reason alone, it was not a good idea for Rowohlt to order such generous quantities of wine and schnapps with the meal, but Rowohlt does not worry about these things. He is a man of virtually boundless energy and initiative, a raucous strongman and self-promoter who seems to fear just one thing in life: boredom. He loves when anecdotes about him are spread and is always prepared to create opportunities for that to happen; at celebrations and parties he enjoys biting into champagne flutes, chewing and swallowing the glass, to the amazement of the other guests. Or he rolls manuscripts authors have offered his press into paper tubes, thumps himself on the back of the head with them, and claims to be able to judge the quality of the text by the sound of their impact.

His publishing house's parties are correspondingly popular and infamous. Without distinct political convictions of his own, Rowohlt invites not only leftist and liberal authors, but also right-wing and extreme right-wing writers, delighting in the highly explosive atmosphere that arises from the confrontation between the two factions. Some of his best authors and closest associates are Jews, but that doesn't keep Rowohlt from signing a man like Ernst von Salomon, who fought in the *Freikorps* after the war and was sentenced in 1922 to five years in the penitentiary for his involvement in the anti-Semitic assassination of Walther Rathenau.

This evening, by comparison, proceeds calmly. Rowohlt wants to reassure Fallada, to allay his concerns about the film. All four are already sipping their mocha, which is prepared table-side with mini coffee machines here at *Schlichter*. Rowohlt and Fallada are merry from their wine, but placid. Their wives care little for what their husbands are discussing, but are instead chatting among themselves, when suddenly a waiter bursts into the place and yells: "The Reichstag is burning! The Reichstag is burning! The communists torched it!"

Fallada and Rowohlt leap to their feet, looking around, electrified. They shout for the bill, shout that they need a taxi cab: "We wanna go to the Reichstag! We wanna help Göring play with fire!"

The two women blanch. This is pure madness. Screaming at the top of one's voice to blame the Nazis in such a volatile situation – pure madness. They jabber at their drunk husbands in soothing words, escort them out of the restaurant in the hope that snow and wintry air will cool their tempers, and steer them into the nearest taxi – not to take them to the Reichstag, however, but first to drop off Rowohlt and his wife at their flat. Then Fallada and his wife Anne, whom he likes to call Suse, ride home. Their route leads them past the Reichstag at not too great a distance. Fallada sees the flames shooting up from the cupola above the building: a lurid, menacing portent against the black winter sky.

*

The satirist Alexander Roda Roda is invited to one of the popular soirées hosted by Georg Bernhard, the former editor-in-chief of the *Vossische Zeitung*. The guests do not sit down at table until late. During the meal one of them, the Dutch envoy, is called to the telephone. Presently, the others wonder what is taking the diplomat so long. As it turns out, he left the house immediately after the call without a parting word. Not until the following day does it become clear why. A Dutchman by the name of Marinus van der Lubbe claims to have set the German parliament building on fire. A diplomatic disaster: the envoy was needed forthwith.

*

Willi Münzenberg is not only a successful communist publisher, but also a Reichstag deputy for the KPD. His district is located near Frankfurt am Main, so at the moment, six days before the election, he is out campaigning. Today he is giving a speech in Langenselbold, east of Frankfurt. He is in fine fettle; his listeners are enthusiastic, and even the police officer tasked with monitoring the event and breaking it up if in doubt, shakes his hand, spellbound. Ten minutes after Münzenberg has left the assembly with his father, a unit of storm troopers arrives to arrest him. Münzenberg is unaware of this and is taken in his limousine to Frankfurt, to the apartment of a friend with whom he is staying.

*

When the report of the fire arrives, all hell breaks loose at the news desk and in typesetting. Theodor Wolff has been editor-in-chief for long enough to know what he's now facing: a torrent of news, conjectures, leads, rumors, calls from his reporters, first communiqués from the police and fire department, first photos, first reactions from politicians. Infinite amounts of information, most of it unimportant, but always presented as a sensation. How much of it is printable? How much of it is hysteria or a complete fabrication? His task, and that of his best people, is now to differentiate between what is reliable and what are exaggerations and propaganda, between real and fake news, and to strike the right tone in the paper for the historic gravity of this day.

In the corridors there's running, cursing, shouting. Wolff is sixty-four years old, has been editor-in-chief of the *Berliner Tageblatt* for twenty-seven years, and is a sturdy man with a pince-nez and a large mustache who can be seen only rarely without a cigarette between his lips. He started out at nineteen with his cousin Rudolf Mosse, legendary head of the Mosse-Verlag, and learned the newspaper trade from the ground up. Under his direction the *Tageblatt* has grown into one of the country's leading liberal newspapers. He nabbed Rudolf Olden, one of the smartest commentators on German domestic politics, for the editorial team, he gave Alfred Kerr, the pope of the theater, every liberty with the feuilleton in order to tie this difficult, proud man to the editorial desk, and he discovered many young up-and-coming talents like Gabriele Tergit, who has been writing her extraordinary literary court reportages for him since 1924.

Figure 20: Theodor Wolff and Albert Einstein in Switzerland in 1927

Or, like young Wolfgang Bretholz, that bustling Austrian he made head of department for domestic politics when he was not yet even thirty years old and who now comes clomping into his office in a panic, disturbing him on the job. He has seen, he blurts out, one of the Nazis' arrest lists his colleagues obtained. The name Theodor Wolff was way up at the top! The police or the SA could be here any minute. They know where to find him. He needs to get out of the editorial office at once, out of this building, out of Berlin.

Wolff hesitates. He is a respectable citizen. Must he fear the police? As editor-in-chief and with this news situation he can't just … Bretholz grabs Wolff's coat and hat, paying no heed to his boss's protests, and drives him away from his desk, out of the room, and onto the street to his car. It isn't far to Anhalter Bahnhof. Hopefully the platforms aren't yet being watched. By the time they arrive, Wolff has accepted his fate. Maybe Bretholz is right? Perhaps it is better if he left Berlin for a few

Figure 21: The Mossehaus, home of the *Berliner Tageblatt*

177

days. He looks around inside the station. Informers are nowhere to be seen – but would he even recognize them? He catches the night train to Munich.

*

Klaus Mann is enjoying the days of Carnival. Usually he'll pick up Herbert Franz from the *Bonbonniere* after his performance in the *Pfeffermühle* and head out with him, and sometimes with Erika, too, to balls or private parties. Tonight the two are also out. Klaus is perfectly in love with Herbert as never before since they've known each other. Toward the morning he accompanies him to the train station, and they have a wonderful moment together in the streetcar. On the return ride the tram runs out of gas. For a half hour they sit on Prinzregentenstrasse. He finally makes it home by 6:30 a.m.

*

In an armed attack on a Nazi pub in Hamburg, an eighteen-year-old schoolboy is shot dead.

After a shootout in Wuppertal, a KPD man succumbs to his severe gunshot wounds.

At around 4 a.m. in Frankfurt-Höchst, an SS leader is attacked and fatally wounded by gunfire.

Communists fire upon a National Socialist demonstration in Berlin-Friedrichshain. Four men are critically injured, one of whom dies.

In Berlin-Kreuzberg, around 500 meters from Gottfried Benn's practice, a heavy gun battle erupts. A twenty-four-year-old Nazi student suffers fatal injuries.

Dictatorship Is Here
Tuesday, February 28

Yesterday evening Carl von Ossietzky left the editorial offices of the *Weltbühne* with friends to go to the home of Gusti Hecht, his mistress. She is a young, somewhat tomboyish, and very talented colleague. Strictly speaking, she studied architecture and earned her engineering degree in Vienna. A few years ago, one of her designs won the competition for the construction of a new synagogue in Berlin-Tiergarten, but it was never realized. Disappointed, she got hired shortly after that as a photo editor for the *Welt-Spiegel*, the Sunday supplement of the *Berliner Tageblatt*, and just three months later Theodor Wolff promoted her to head of department, responsible for the entire section.

Fearful she is not. The day before yesterday, the last Sunday before the election, she put the picture of a mass rally against Hitler by the SPD on the front page of the *Welt-Spiegel* and filled a two-page spread inside with photos of other demonstrations under the title "The March of the German People against Fascism."

Maud, Ossietzky's wife, does not know about her. When at some point after 9 p.m. yesterday news came over the radio that the Reichstag was in flames, his friends and Gusti Hecht hounded him again to leave the country right away. But Ossietzky can't be persuaded. He always finds new reasons to stay. He wants to wait for the election next Sunday. He doesn't know how he'll make his living abroad. He has debts; furnishing the new apartment was expensive. No, he has made up his mind he will stay. And besides, he thus reassures his friends, after the move to the new flat he neglected to install a nameplate on the door, so raiding parties ought to find it hard to locate him.

When he returns home, Maud also presses him to flee, but she fails like all the rest, too. Ossietzky wants to stay. Around 3:30 a.m. the doorbell rings. Two detectives arrest him. They allow him first to wash and get dressed, then take him away. "Chin up," he says to Maud in parting, "I'll be back soon."

*

The danger for Erich Mühsam is great, that he knows. As one of the former ringleaders of the Munich Soviet Republic, he, like Toller, is high up on the list of people the Nazis are after. Yet Mühsam has a second problem; he has no money. For days he has been trying to scrape some together to be able to abscond abroad. Yesterday he finally rounded up enough for a ticket to Prague and for the first few days there. He aims to depart early this morning, his suitcase is packed, and his wife is to follow him later. The couple are still sleeping when the buzzer rings at 5 a.m. Two detectives take him into custody. He has experience with arrests, having been in prison twice since the war. "It will be even crueler this time," he says to his wife. Then, as always, he says a calm goodbye to her and also to Nicky and Morly, the couple's dog and cat.

*

Egon Erwin Kisch is arrested in his apartment on Motzstrasse. As with Erich Mühsam, it is five in the morning when he hears the buzzer, followed by the footsteps of his landlady heading to open the door. Then she knocks at the door to his room: "Herr Kisch, please open the door." When he unlocks it, two surprisingly polite detectives arrest him. He is permitted to wash and get dressed, they ask him whether he has a weapon or intends to flee, and since he answers no to both, they forgo handcuffs.

The three of them head to police headquarters at Alexanderplatz not in a patrol car, but by subway. Kisch squeezes between the other passengers, early risers on their usual way to work, but an uncertain future awaits him. At headquarters the two officers hand him off to colleagues on office duty and obtain a receipt for him. The corridor leading to the department of the Political Police is packed: a gray multitude of pallid men torn from their morning slumber. Kisch recognizes the lawyer Alfred Apfel first, in-house counsel for the *Weltbühne*, who has defended many leftist activists already. Great, he thinks, perhaps he can get me out of here, and calls out: "Hey, Dr. Apfel, I've been arrested."

"Me too," he replies.

180

Then Kisch recognizes the others: Carl von Ossietzky is here plus several other writers, scientists, doctors, as well as Reichstag deputies for the KPD who technically have immunity. Prominent company. Nervous young auxiliary policemen with swastikas stand watch over them until they are led in groups into the basement to the police jail. As they empty their pockets to surrender keys, matches, pencils, and shoelaces, the new police superintendent Magnus von Levetzow pushes his way through the crowd, snarling about. He calls them "lowlifes," orders one of them who does not immediately stand at attention before him into a darkened cell – and disappears again. After that the others are crammed into a communal cell, forty-seven in one room. Pallets line the walls. A bucket sits in the middle. One for everybody. Then nothing else happens. The waiting begins.

*

Figure 22: Helene Weigel and Bertolt Brecht, Denmark 1936

Early this morning Brecht and Helene Weigel set out from Peter Suhrkamp's apartment. An old school friend of Brecht's now working in Berlin as a physician takes them to Anhalter Bahnhof in his car. Nobody recognizes them on the platform. They board the next train to Prague and are relieved when the coaches finally start rolling and gaining speed. During the journey, however, they suddenly realize they made a mistake. Three valuable rings belonging to Weigel have been left behind in Brecht's apartment. Given their financial straits, it is a bitter loss. At the border they meet with no difficulties, their passports are in order, and Brecht can show his invitation to a reading in Vienna as the reason for the trip.

As soon as they arrive in Prague, they call the young pianist Georg Knepler in Berlin. He recently accompanied Helene Weigel in her performance of the *Wiegenlieder einer proletarischen Mutter* after which they were detained for a time. The two describe to Knepler the trunk containing the rings and ask him to get them. A dangerous mission: Knepler is a communist and a Jew. To encounter SA troopers monitoring or searching Brecht's apartment near Bahnhof Zoo could prove disastrous for him. But Knepler is lucky. He finds the forgotten rings, leaves the apartment again right away – which still looks unmolested – and dispatches the three pieces of jewelry to their owner.

*

The cabinet convenes midmorning. Hitler is preparing his circle of ministers primarily for two emergency decrees he would like to have Hindenburg sign. In his view the psychologically opportune moment has arrived for the final reckoning with the KPD, and as he says explicitly, he does not want to make that conditional on legal considerations. No objections to this are raised by the ministers.

After the meeting concludes, he presents Hindenburg with the *Verordnung des Reichspräsidenten zum Schutz von Volk und Staat* [*Decree of the Reich President for the Defense of People and State*] and the *Verordnung gegen Verrat am Deutschen Volke und hochverräterische Umtriebe* [*Decree Against Betrayal of the German People and High Treasonous Machinations*]. Hindenburg affixes his signature without hesitation. The second decree serves mostly to institute the death penalty for certain political offenses. The first is much more comprehensive: all important fundamental rights are abolished by it. As of today, there are no more limits on state-sanctioned abuses. The freedoms of speech, press, association, and assembly, confidentiality of mail and telephone, and the inviolability of home and property are abrogated. Add to these the rights of personal freedom: from this point forward the police can arrest anyone at its discretion, extend prison terms without restrictions, and prohibit detainees' contact with their families or attorneys. In other words, anyone within Germany's borders is at the mercy of the government's and public authorities' whims. The floodgates are open for terror.

While the suspension of constitutional rights is nominally in effect only "until further notice," today's two decrees will not be rescinded before the end of the Nazi regime. The constitutional state is abolished. Furthermore, paragraph two of the *Verordnung zum Schutz von Volk und Staat* grants the Reich government the right to absorb the powers of all the states in the Reich. Federalism is thereby also eliminated.

Only thirty days after his swearing-in as Reich Chancellor, Hitler has created the fundamental statutory basis for his absolute control. He now only requires the Enabling Act, passed a few weeks later, to permanently dispense with parliament altogether. In an interview with the English *Daily Express*, Hitler is asked what truth there is to the rumors that the SA and SS were planning a massacre among their political enemies. He answers, amused: "I need no St. Bartholomew's Night. By means of the *Emergency Decree for the Defense of People and State* we have established tribunals that will charge enemies of the state and deal with them in a way that will put an end to these conspiracies once and for all." Dictatorship is here.

*

The morning newspaper headlines drive home for Willi Münzenberg the position he is in. The Reichstag in Flames! Arsonists Are Communists! Arrest Warrants for All KPD Functionaries! His girlfriend Babette Gross calls his Berlin apartment. Münzenberg's secretary relays to her that the police had already been there in the night bearing an arrest warrant with an ancient photograph of Münzenberg.

Together with Münzenberg's chauffeur, the three consider their remaining options. Profiles for prominent wanted communists are printed in the midday newspapers, Münzenberg's among them. He had

Figure 23: Babette Gross and Willi Münzenberg

better not be seen on the streets anymore. And all border crossings likely have wanted bulletins for him, making an escape abroad highly risky.

Then Babette Gross remembers that her sister Margarete's father-in-law lives in a small village near Darmstadt: the Jewish philosopher of religion, Martin Buber. She only knows him in passing, to be sure, but hopes for advice from him on how Münzenberg might flee. The latter's driver parks near Buber's house, and Babette leaves the two men behind in the car. Buber is startled she came but does in fact have an idea. To the outrage of German politicians, and especially the Nazis, the Saarland has been under international administration by the League of Nations since the First World War – and still is. Since Germans believe the border to the Saarland does not lead to a foreign country, but from Germany to Germany, the checks on the German side there are decidedly lax. A friend of Buber's lives in Saarbrücken as a university instructor. Buber hands Babette a letter of introduction in which he asks his friend to offer Münzenberg shelter for a few days.

All they need now are serviceable identification papers for Münzenberg with a fake name. Back in Frankfurt, amid the hubbub of Hessian Carnival, Babette Gross contacts a young KPD comrade who relinquishes his passport to her without any fuss. The photo in it looks nothing even remotely like Münzenberg, but he has no other option. Fortunately, it is already dark when they reach the Saarland border by car. The customs official shines a cursory light into the vehicle and scarcely pays any attention to the passports. They may continue onward. Münzenberg is saved.

He never returns to Germany. In subsequent years he tries to organize the resistance of leftist emigrants against Hitler's Germany from Paris. Because in so doing he abides by his own ideas without toeing the KPD line prescribed by Stalin, he is expelled from his party in 1938. In 1940 he attempts to flee to Switzerland from the advancing German military. Weeks later he is found dead west of Grenoble in a wooded area. His corpse has a rope around its neck. It remains unclear whether he killed himself or communists loyal to Stalin murdered him.

*

Alfred Döblin turns on the radio around 9 a.m. and only now hears of the fire in the Reichstag. It is, the announcer says, a communist attack. Döblin turns it right off again. The claim that communists are the arsonists he doesn't believe for a second. The key question in his eye is "cui bono," who benefits from the fire? To him the answer is obvious.

Then the telephone begins to ring and never stops. Caller after caller beseeches him to save himself. In his view this is completely overblown, even ridiculous. This afternoon visitors arrive who also urge him to flee. He still resists, but at some point he finally gives in and plans to go away for three or four months, until the country has gotten rid of the Nazis.

At around 8 p.m. he departs his flat on Kaiserdamm with a small suitcase. Standing before the building's entrance is a man wearing a civilian coat over his SA uniform on account of the cold. He scrutinizes Döblin and follows him to the subway station. On the platform he waits to see which train Döblin takes and then boards the same car. He also follows him when Döblin exits the train at Gleisdreieck station. By now Döblin is aware how grave the situation is; he can be arrested at any moment. All of a sudden a throng of people pours out of a newly arrived train. Döblin leaps down a flight of stairs and from the next best platform into whatever train is departing.

He has given his pursuer the slip. He changes trains again immediately, this time toward Potsdamer Platz, and from there to Anhalter Bahnhof. A train leaves for Stuttgart around 10 p.m., and in a stroke of luck he manages to nab a ticket for the sleeper car. After departing he gazes out the hallway window at the city lights passing him by. He loves them a great deal. How often has he pulled into Anhalter Bahnhof here, seen the same lights, and sighed with relief at being back home? Berlin is the city of his life. Now he is leaving without knowing whether he will ever return.

*

Yesterday Harry Graf Kessler dined at the restaurant *Lauer* on Kurfürstendamm with his friend and associate Max Goertz. People know them there; they are almost regulars of a sort. At around 10 p.m. the proprietor of the restaurant came to their table and informed them of the fire at the Reichstag. Kessler ended his meal, returned home, and noted down in his diary that the assassination attempt the Nazis had planned had in fact taken place, though not on Hitler's life, but on the Reichstag building.

Today he summarizes what the newspapers report about the attack. A Dutch communist by the name of Marinus van der Ludde has been arrested and "promptly confessed to having been put up to the deed by communist members of parliament; he was allegedly also connected to the SPD. This twenty-something-year-old vagabond is purported to have distributed and ignited flammable material around more than thirty sites inside the Reichstag without his presence or actions or procurement of these piles of material having been noticed by anyone. In the end he ran straight into the policeman's arms, after having doffed all of his clothes except his trousers and deposited them in the Reichstag as a precautionary measure so that no oversight of any kind might prevent his identification. He is even said to have waved out the window with a torch."

*

Klaus Mann must come to Berlin absolutely at once. His theatrical agent has sent him a telegram. The great Victor Barnowsky, actor, successful director, and lord over at least three stages in Berlin, is keenly interested in *Athen* [*Athens*], his most recent play.

Klaus Mann wrote it last autumn and published it under the pseudonym Vincenz Hofer. No one knows that *Athen* was written by him, so perhaps the play has actual chances of being performed. It suits the political situation perfectly; he has made the Greek field commander Alcibiades a dictator preparing for war, the Athenians a people now tired of democracy, and Socrates into a big-city intellectual whose appeals to reason no one wants to listen to. Klaus Mann is excited. Should he travel to Berlin now, straightaway? Or is it in fact too dangerous? For now, he sits down at his desk and writes to Barnowsky.

Toward noon Therese Giehse comes to have lunch with him and Erika. Naturally they chat the whole time about the Reichstag fire, which arrives at such an eerily opportune moment for the Nazis. Suddenly, news comes over the radio that Ossietzky, Mühsam, and Kisch have been arrested in Berlin. And that's where Klaus is supposed to go now? A production of *Athen* under Barnowsky would be a huge success, perhaps a breakthrough for him. But as things stand now, Klaus realizes soberly, nothing will come of it either.

As though this stroke of misfortune weren't enough, Hans Feist stops by for an afternoon visit. They go for a walk and drink hot chocolate at the Chinese Tower. In between, Klaus calls Herbert Franz with whom he is very much in love. Feist, who was already getting on his nerves in Berlin with his obtrusive devotion, overhears in conversation that he and Erika are setting out to Lenzerheide in Switzerland for a ski vacation the day after tomorrow. A long, pointless, and torturous discussion unravels about why Klaus does not want Feist along for the brief trip. Back on Poschingerstrasse, Klaus treats himself to some relaxation with morphine. After the *Pfeffermühle* show Erika and Therese join him, and Erika also enjoys a little morphine snack. At 3:30 a.m. he finally goes to bed.

*

According to initial newspaper reports, 130 communists are taken into so-called protective custody by police and SA the night after the Reichstag fire. On this and on subsequent nights, however, it soon becomes clear that thousands were arrested. In no time, all the penitentiaries are utterly overcrowded. The SA proceeds not to turn over detainees to the police, but to keep them in its own cellars, lockup rooms, or improvised concentration camps.

From Hamburg, Worms, and Duisburg-Meiderich come reports of a total of five dead following political clashes – and, like every day, countless injured throughout the country.

Fading from the World
Wednesday, March 1

At three in the morning, the door to Kisch's prison cell is torn open and the light turned on. Kisch wakes with a start, blinking, as an officer approaches and hands him a single piece of paper: the arrest warrant. It is backdated to February 28.

Yesterday, late in the evening, all the men were called out of the communal cell, one after the other, and transferred to individual cells. Kisch is now sitting on his bunk, reading what he's been accused of: "You are under strong suspicion of having committed an act punishable pursuant to §§ 81 to 86 of the Criminal Code."

Paragraphs 81 to 86 of the Criminal Code deal with offenses like high and petty treason. These are the paragraphs that since yesterday can carry the death penalty according to the new emergency decrees. The arrest warrant is a poorly duplicated form. Kisch's name was entered by hand into the corresponding blank. A hectographed death-threat. The cell door is slammed shut. The light goes out. Kisch is on his own, holding the paper.

*

Alfred Döblin only remains in Stuttgart for a few hours. The journey from Berlin in the sleeper car was quiet, without any disturbances. Stuttgart seems pleasant and peaceful, the gutted ruin of the Reichstag far away. Suddenly Döblin feels silly. Was it not hyperbolic to run away? And from what? Will he one day be ashamed of his fear? Then he continues onward to Überlingen on Lake Constance, where he finds a seat in the train station tavern and writes to a medical colleague, Professor Ludwig Binswanger, in Kreuzlingen.

Kreuzlingen is quite close by, a small town on the southern coast of Lake Constance, on the Swiss side. Döblin prefers not to telephone – the lines abroad may be wiretapped – and he takes care not to mention a word of his escape from Berlin in his letter to Binswanger. Instead, he gives suggestive hints. Because of the enormous unrest in Berlin lately, he writes, he has been unable to work and wonders whether he might stay in Binswanger's sanatorium for eight to ten days.

Binswanger is a psychiatrist and enjoys an excellent reputation among German writers. He is a man with a broad education and is a good, but not uncritical friend of Sigmund Freud. From a combination of psychoanalysis, phenomenology, and existential philosophy, he is developing new therapeutic approaches he calls Daseinsanalysis. His sanatorium *Bellevue* is located in an expansive park difficult to access from outside. It is not a single building but a campus of more than a dozen villas in which well-heeled patients receive the very best care, both medical and gastronomic. The cuisine is outstanding, plus there is a tennis court, a billiard room, a bowling alley, as well as multiple swimming pools. Many celebrities and artists have been guests or patients at *Bellevue*: Wilhelm Furtwängler, Martin Buber, Aby Warburg, and Gustaf Gründgens, for instance. Leonhard Frank, a pacifist during the First World War who had to fight for a long time to obtain an exit permit to enter Switzerland, spent over three months here. And three years ago, Binswanger treated a syphilitic Carl Sternheim for his psychotic episodes.

Döblin already paid his colleague a visit with his wife last year, as a tourist, but also out of scientific curiosity. And of course Binswanger now willingly accepts him as a refugee at his institution. Döblin arranges a car to take him there. There are no difficulties at the border. He is safe.

*

At the same time Fritz Landshoff is traveling in the opposite direction. A few days ago, he took a vacation from Kiepenheuer Verlag to visit his ex-wife and their daughters as they skied in the hamlet Zuoz in Graubünden. This was an opportunity Ernst Toller, with whom Landshoff shares a flat in Berlin, did not want to pass up either, so he has also come to Zuoz. His reading tour of Switzerland took place over a month ago now, but out of an abundance of caution he did not return to Germany after Hitler's takeover. That was certainly a wise decision, but in Switzerland he now feels like he is fading from the world and cut off from everything important to him – from Berlin's literary scene, from the political resistance to the Nazis, and of course also from Christiane Grautoff, his forbidden fling. In short, a first exile tantrum is plaguing him. It is the typical exasperation of the suddenly isolated émigré. The temptation to throw caution to the wind and travel back to Germany is getting more and more intense. In long conversations Landshoff has used all his powers of persuasion to spell out for Toller the magnitude of the danger and to discourage him from making irrational decisions.

Now Landshoff is on the return trip from Switzerland. Yesterday afternoon he briefly interrupted the journey in Frankfurt to meet his friend Heinrich Simon, the managing director and editor-in-chief of the *Frankfurt Zeitung*. Of course, they were virtually electrified the entire evening by the news of the Reichstag fire and discussed the anticipated consequences. Simon was firmly convinced the Nazis have no chance of ever gaining a foothold in southern Germany, in Württemberg, Baden, and Bavaria. The "Main River Line" will hold, he said, of that he is certain.

Later Landshoff takes the night train from Frankfurt to Berlin. He arrives at Anhalter Bahnhof in the morning and heads straight to his and Toller's apartment on Sächsische Strasse to freshen up and change clothes after the uncomfortable night. No sooner is he in the bathroom, there is a knock at the door. He slips on his bathrobe and answers it. Standing before him is an older woman, his neighbor who lives a floor below them. "I would like to warn you," she says in a hushed voice, "last night there were several men from the SA here who asked me about you and Herr Toller after they found no one home in your flat. I urge you to leave your apartment immediately and never come back."

Luckily, Landshoff's suitcase is still packed. He sheds his bathrobe, dresses hastily, and leaves the building not ten minutes later. He is a Jew, he is a socialist, he published books as an editor that are on all the Nazis' Indexes – it is quite possible that his brief holiday in Switzerland saved his life last night. From this point forward he stays overnight only at alternating addresses.

*

In her room at the Sächsischer Hof, not far from Landshoff's and Toller's flat in Wilmersdorf, Else Lasker-Schüler receives disheartening news. Gustav Hartung writes her from Darmstadt that he must relinquish his hope of bringing *Arthur Aronymus* to the stage for the foreseeable future. He is quite fond of the play, but the mood in the city is so charged that calm rehearsals are no longer possible – especially none involving children, without whom the play cannot be performed. He would never, he writes, obtain "permission from parents for their children's involvement" because his theater is now the target of constant public slander and SA raids cannot be ruled out: "We will have to wait for a time when we are dependent on literary quality once more and not on political fanaticism."

*

This evening Kisch is transported out of the police prison at Alexanderplatz. The jailers grab him and a good twenty other captives initially imprisoned with Kisch from their private cells.

"Where are we being taken?" one of them asks.

"You'll see very soon," the officer snaps.

They are forced to line up two by two. Carl von Ossietzky is here again, as are Dr. Apfel the attorney and others Kisch saw yesterday. They are marched as a column through hallways and up staircases, past the row of SA auxiliary police who abuse them today not just with insults, but with kicks: "Now you'll see what's going to happen to you, you red swine. Now you'll all get a bullet through the skull ..." – not a pleasant greeting for people just handed an arrest warrant with the threat of death.

A transport vehicle is waiting in the courtyard. The whole group of prisoners is squeezed into it. One after the other they are forced to climb inside, the men clumping together into a solid ball of bodies. No one can move an inch. Breathing is difficult. The van door is pressed shut behind the last of them, and as soon as it closes, there is total darkness. Only after more than an hour does the vehicle stop. The door is wrenched open. They squint into a different prison yard. All the walls are red brick, five meters tall or more, watchtowers above them, also brick. Officers in uniform encircle them as they painstakingly peel themselves out of the transport van. They are inside the fortress of Spandau Prison.

*

Wanting to continue on to Vienna, Brecht and Weigel stay in Prague only briefly. They've heard, however, that Wieland Herzfelde, who fled from Germany a few days earlier, has begun rebuilding his Malik Verlag here in Prague. And so they visit him. Publishers in Germany had become unapproachable for Brecht, so new contacts in exile couldn't hurt. Afterward he and Weigel fetch from the airport their son Stefan, whom Elisabeth Hauptmann had put on a plane in Berlin. Little Barbara, their daughter, remains out of reach for the time being. The situation is a mess.

*

Officially, the number of people arrested in Berlin is now listed at 150. In actual fact it is much higher. By comparison, according to official sources, in the Rhineland 1,200 and in Westphalia 850 people have been arrested. It is estimated that by mid-March in Prussia alone 10,000 people will disappear in prisons or camps. The police advise, moreover, that those detained may not receive visitors until further notice; neither their attorneys nor their relatives may meet with them, speak with them, or advocate for them. The prisoners are under the sole authority of the police. Because no further implementation provisions were stipulated in the *Notverordnung zum Schutz von Volk und Staat*, there are no legal remedies against the arrests. And imprisonment is indefinite.

During politically motivated street fights in Berlin, Hamburg, and Bochum, a total of five men are killed. At countless other clashes throughout the country, quite a few people are badly or even critically injured.

The Fake Mother
Friday, March 3

Helene Weigel was born in Vienna, where her family lives. No wonder she urges Brecht to travel there initially, even if he doesn't like Austrian intellectuals. They are too passive for him, their thinking too inconsequential for his taste.

First, they are put up in Helene's mother's flat, at Berggasse 30, not a two-minute walk from Berggasse 19, where Sigmund Freud sees patients at his practice. That same evening the concert performance of Brecht's and Eisler's *The Mother* takes place at the *Österreichischer Bund der Freunde der Sowjetunion* [*Austrian League of Friends of the Soviet Union*].

Yet what's most important right now is the fate of little Barbara. The situation is escalating. When Helene Weigel calls Brecht's father in Augsburg, he comes across so very distracted and oddly dismissive that Helene assumes the SA is in the process of ransacking his house. Indeed, brownshirts have inquired with Brecht's father by telephone whether one of Brecht's children is visiting at his home. That's why he now fears someone could be listening in on his telephone and why he replies so evasively. At once Weigel and Brecht are in a frenzy. What will happen to the child if she falls into Nazi hands? Will they use her as a bargaining chip to force her parents' return to Germany?

Immediately after the SA phone call to Brecht's father, the nanny left the house with Barbara. She has gone into hiding with her at her own parents' home for the time being. Weigel is now using every conceivable contact in her old home town to find a way to get her daughter to Austria. Through friends she's gotten to know an English Quaker couple, Donald and Irene Grant, who live in Vienna with three children. Irene Grant has a passport with her four-year-old son entered into it as well and agrees to risk the attempt to get Barbara out of Germany. Brecht and Weigel have so little money, however, that Irene must ride third-class to Augsburg. There she collects the child from the nanny and promptly sets off on the return trip with her to Austria. It is not a long journey, but it is a precarious one. Barbara is not a boy and is only two and a half years old, and she doesn't know Irene at all. She must not display any conspicuous unfamiliarity with her fake mother whatsoever in the presence of border officers, nor behave as a girl. Fortunately, Irene has a great deal of experience dealing with children and gets along with Barbara without any trouble. In the end Weigel and Brecht are able to embrace their daughter once more in Vienna.

*

Ernst Thälmann, Chairman of the KPD, is arrested at a safe house in Berlin. He led a meeting of his party's Politburo on February 27 and went to ground at once after news of the Reichstag fire and early mass arrests reached him. Since then he hasn't left his quarters once, but following a denunciation, the police are able to track him down.

At an election rally Hermann Göring, the Prussian Minister of the Interior, announces how he will deal with the options the new emergency decrees grant him: "The measures I take will not be enfeebled by any sort of legal scruples. The measures I take will not be enfeebled by any sort of bureaucracy. I need not exercise justice here; here I need only obliterate and exterminate, and nothing else!"

At the former airport in Nohra (outside Weimar), the first official concentration camp is set up. On the premises there are two buildings connected by a flat-roofed structure. One of the floors with three halls is now used as a concentration camp for up to 220 detainees. The rooms are furnished not with beds, but with straw and blankets.

Reports of fatalities from politically motivated brawls come in from Hamburg, Höchst im Odenwald, and Bernburg an der Saale. In Oldenburg, a KPD *Landtag* deputy is lured from his home, beaten up, and then gravely injured with five shots from a revolver as he lies on the ground. In Berlin alone, 140 people are arrested for political offenses.

Don't Open the Door!
Saturday, March 4

It's five in the morning when the door to Gabriele Tergit's and her husband Heinrich Reifenberg's apartment is jolted by banging and kicking, along with the constant, piercing ringing of the buzzer. The couple's nanny rushes to the door to open it, but Reifenberg shouts "Don't open the door!" and Gabriele Tergit races to the telephone.

Reifenberg is an architect and a circumspect man. His wife's colleagues, Rudolf Olden, for instance, have been cracking sardonic jokes for some time that they will all find themselves in the Nazis' concentration camps together with many other liberal or leftist journalists sooner or later. Reifenberg, however, has not contented himself with joking, but has had their apartment door reinforced with iron hinges, a safety lock, and a steel security chain to the extent that it is now withstanding the attack from outside.

He walks over and carefully opens the door with the security chain engaged. An SA man puts his foot into the gap at once: "Arrest warrant for your wife."

"From whom?"

"Straight from Reich Minister Göring."

Reifenberg throws himself against the reinforced door leaf with all his might until the storm trooper withdraws his foot and the door slams shut once more. By now Gabriele Tergit has reached a colleague by telephone who works for Berlin's Nazi newspaper *Angriff*. He is flabbergasted, having heard nothing about Tergit's being on any arrest list, and implores her: "Call Mittelbach right away. He's omnipotent. He was made head of Police Division 1A."

Tergit knows Hans Mittelbach from her court visits. He is a state attorney and works with Rudolf Diels, head of the Political Police. She gets him on the line. He is a Nazi as well but as a jurist does not approve of the SA's intruding into private homes without authorization: "Call a riot squad!"

Minutes later the police have arrived. The kicks against the door and the buzzing cease. State prosecutor Mittelbach calls back and asks Tergit to put him on with the director of the riot squad. Mittelbach's directive is that only the leader of the SA troop may enter the apartment under police supervision and conduct a home search.

The brownshirt who now enters the flat has strikingly red hair and is well known about town. It is Fritz Hahn, aka "the Red Cock," commander of *Sturm 33*. Suddenly it becomes clear which SA division is standing on the other side of the apartment door and was bested by its iron hinges. Tergit owes her life to her husband's circumspection.

The house search is a charade. A policeman examines the couple's collection of cacti, the birds in the cage, and Reifenberg's architecture office and arrives at the conclusion: "These people here are no communists." When the men enter the nursery, Tergit's four-year-old son commands them from his bed "You get out!" and the police leave the room.

As the SA moves to depart empty-handed, Tergit cannot help herself. "Do you think," she says to Hahn, "that I'm going to put up with the fact that you wanted to drag me off? I'm going to report you for trespassing, attempted assault, and intimidation." Hahn is wearing a shabby, torn brown uniform. For years he has made his living from street terror, has beaten men to a pulp, likely killing more than one of them, and orchestrated his comrade Maikowski's murder for Goebbels. He stares at her for a while, looking askance over his tin pince-nez right at her face and saying nothing. Then he leaves.

After the riot squad has also departed, Tergit says to her husband: "I'm not staying."

"There is still good snow," Reifenberg agrees. "Go to Spindlermühle." A ski resort in the Giant Mountains, just 300 kilometers from Berlin, but in Czechoslovakia and thus safe. Gabriele Tergit also considers this a good idea and leaves the country the same day with her son. It is her thirty-ninth birthday.

*

In heavy gunfights between various political organizations in Düsseldorf, Cologne, Essen, Duisburg, Hamborn, and Bremen, a total of seven people are killed and several critically wounded.

Figure 24: Gabriele Tergit and Heinrich Reifenberg

The Reich cabinet resolves to act against foreign newspaper corre-spondents accused of maliciously agitating against the German government. Camille Loutre, correspondent for the *Petit Parisien*, is the first to be deported because he portrayed the Reichstag fire in a manner not in accordance with "the official statement."

Casting a Ballot
Sunday, March 5

Max Goertz, Harry Graf Kessler's associate, heard on the radio the speech that Hitler gave in Königsberg [present-day Kaliningrad] yesterday for the conclusion of the election campaign. This morning he is at Kessler's with his wife for breakfast and still upset. The speech was crude political deception. With a quavering voice Hitler espoused propositions that diametrically controvert his previously articulated convictions, probably to dupe gullible voters. The SPD was needed, pacifism was essential, Germany wanted to live in peace with all peoples, he rejected militarism. How many layers of sheep's clothing must Hitler have donned to bring himself to make such assertions?

The crowd at the polling station is large. Kessler has to wait in line for fifteen minutes before he can cast his ballot. A hint of spring is in the air: swathes of blue sky, sparse clouds, mild temperatures. Outside the polling place only the posters of the NSDAP are on view, as are those of the German Nationalists who consolidated onto one ticket with Franz von Papen and the *Stahlhelm*. Not a single tiny flag or posting of the SPD, KPD, or the republican State Party is in sight. Wachhorst de Wente, member of parliament for the State Party, hung the black-red-gold flag of democratic Germany from a window of his flat to celebrate election day, but the SA auxiliary police took it down right away, Kessler has heard.

The city otherwise makes a calm, expectant impression on him. It is not a long way to the train station. There Kessler buys himself a *Völkischer Beobachter*, intending to read about Hitler's Königsberg speech. The Nazi paper does not mention a word about it for its readers, however, just the usual slogans. Obviously Hitler fears being bound to his cheap lies if he allows them to be printed. Everything therefore remains in the vague sphere of the spoken word. Max Goertz and his wife say goodbye to Kessler on the platform. At 3 p.m. he boards the express train to Frankfurt am Main, a journey of six hours.

When he arrives, there will be no mistaking how Germany will look in the future.

*

In Lenzerheide, the weather has so far been bleak: rain turning to wet snow. Klaus and Erika have made their way down to the village from their chalet on foot and watched the usual little ski race in spite of the rain.

They are spending quiet days here in the mountains. They set out from Munich on Thursday, traveling by train to Chur and then by car up to their cabin, the same one as last year. Klaus has hardly gotten around to skiing yet. He has spent most of his time in his room sitting and typing because the weather was simply too disagreeable. He and Erika have discussed the planned April program for the *Pfeffermühle* a few times, and of course they have spoken by phone with their parents who are right over in the neighboring valley, just a mountain ridge away, in Arosa.

While on winter holiday here in Switzerland, none of them is able to go to the polls. Of course the suspense is acute. After dinner Klaus drives down into town. In the spa's entertainment hall, there is a small party where they're demonstrating some sort of stupid dance, after which prizes are awarded to the winners of the ski race. Now and again Klaus goes over to the radio to hear the election results. They are disastrous enough. But it could have been even worse, he records in his diary tonight. It even looks bad in Bavaria. Terrible changes are afoot.

*

Mirjam has kept her promise; a letter has arrived from her every day for seventeen days, until today's election: a period of sheer fright that stretched on as though it would never end. Today, finally, Oskar Maria Graf is waiting at Vienna's Westbahnhof, for today Mirjam cast her ballot against Hitler in Munich, as she had planned, and was then able to board the train to Austria.

When Graf was traveling to Vienna just over two weeks ago, happy about the invitation from the Bildungszentrale, he ran into an acquaintance aboard the train who was unable to bear it in Germany anymore. She leaned against him and wept uncontrollably in despair at what the Nazis were doing to her country. In Vienna the friend who

Figure 25: Mirjam Sachs and Oskar Maria Graf

had procured his invitation to Austria asked him about Mirjam right away. After all, she is Jewish and for that reason alone in danger. Graf recounted for him how he had tried to change Mirjam's mind, but that there was nothing that could dissuade her from remaining in Munich until the election. "My respect for your wife," the friend said. "Courage is so rare ... Let's hope for the best."

It has all gone well. Mirjam was not arrested, not accosted, was able to tick the box against Hitler on the ballot, and then hotfoot it to the train station to leave the country. Now the train is pulling into Westbahnhof, but Mirjam does not alight. She can't do it; it's too much. Mirjam is so terribly scared and exhausted that Graf has to board the train to retrieve her. The seventeen days and the seventeen long nights in Munich have left their mark. She has no more strength. Fear has taken hold within her, and she will never again get rid of it.

*

Harry Graf Kessler arrives in Frankfurt am Main shortly after 10 p.m. He is promptly on the lookout for a bar, for any sort of venue, in order to inquire about the election results. He is told the Nazis, together with the German Nationalists, have won around 51 percent. The majority.

*

The official end results read: 43.9 percent for the NSDAP and eight percent for the German Nationalist Kampffront Schwarz-Weiss-Rot [Black-White-Red Combat Front], a clear victory for the governing parties. They receive 340 seats in the Reichstag, with 324 having sufficed for a majority. In spite of all the obstructions during the campaign, the SPD wins 18.3 percent, and the KPD secures 12.3 percent. Only then come the more liberal powers like the Centre, BVP, or German State Party, which do not even earn a hundred seats altogether.

At Reich President Hindenburg's intervention, the Prussian state parliament is dissolved. The rightful Prussian minister president, Otto Braun, who has been deprived of his powers de facto since the "Preußenschlag" of July 1932, flees to Switzerland.

In election-day political clashes in Offenbach, Trier, Oberhausen, Oldenburg, Peine (outside Hannover), Wiesenau (close to Frankfurt an der Oder), Breslau [present-day Wrocław], and Bankau in Upper Silesia [now Bąków], a total of nine people are killed.

The Emigrant's Solitude
Monday, March 6

"Do you deem it possible," Heinrich Mann writes to Pierre Bertaux, son of his friend Félix Bertaux, "to establish a French-German publication in order to prepare the future influence of both democracies?" The sentence is indeed a bit perplexing coming today, one day after the election that Hitler, enemy of democracy, has won. But Mann leaves it in his letter regardless.

As he declared he would to Wilhelm Herzog the evening after his getaway, he has continued on to Nice and put up at the *Hôtel de Nice*. The hotel is not one of those chic palaces hugging the coast, but a dignified old establishment in the heart of the city, amid a stylish park. This is where Mann has always preferred to stay whenever he was in Nice, and he sees no reason why he should change anything about that – even less because of the Nazis. Sure, life would be more economical in a fishing village like Sanary-sur-Mer, but he has reserves and life insurance policies in Berlin, the money from which has only to be transferred to France. Besides – and of this he is firmly convinced – Hitler will soon be out of the political picture once more. At Georg Bernhard's soirée in Berlin, he was saying the Nazis would stay in power for at most six months; now he gives them two years.

Ultimately it is not so surprising after all when he writes in his letter today about the influence of democracies in Germany and France. Heinrich Mann does not wish to look backward, but into the future. And he insists on quick decision-making. If something is to come of this project of a French-German periodical, it must happen immediately, for in a journalistic undertaking such as this, one can bank on measurable successes only in the long term. After Hitler, who will soon fail, so Heinrich Mann believes, the communists will want to seize power for themselves. Whoever means to help reason and democracy to victory must therefore act now – and a transnational publication seems to him the appropriate instrument of propaganda to do so.

Yet for Pierre Bertaux, however, the letter might still be a bit perplexing given that he is but twenty-five years old and possesses little journalistic experience. But Heinrich Mann got to know Pierre well when the latter studied in Berlin in 1927 and 1928. He is a highly gifted young man with clear political views and a notable talent for organization. With his charm and sparkling intelligence, he wins almost everyone over in no time at all. Even Heinrich's difficult nephew Golo made friends with him. Pierre would be exactly the right person to attract supporters to the idea of a new journal like this, which would ally their peoples. It could be the project of a lifetime for him.

If Heinrich Mann is honest with himself, however, he must admit that the idea was born somewhat out of loneliness. It is the typical daydream of an emigrant who no longer clearly bears in mind his country's political realities and overestimates his own reflections. Heinrich Mann does not like living alone, and Nelly is still in Germany. Liquidating the apartment on Fasanenstrasse has proved more difficult than anticipated. Heinrich feels so lonesome that he even wrote to ask Wilhelm Herzog in Sanary whether he might want to keep him company for a few weeks in Nice. Herzog is not opposed, but cannot come until mid-month.

With Nelly, Mann agreed that she should pose in Berlin as his secretary who must settle her boss's affairs after his sudden departure – no easy task and, as becomes quickly apparent, one Nelly is not at all equal to. She lacks experience in dealing with matters of business and law and with surly Prussian authorities. "I'm sitting right in the middle of this whole mess," she writes to France, "am forced to take the blame for everything, to explain myself everywhere, am persecuted, and you are there and see and hear nothing of it."

In short, things unfold differently than Heinrich Mann expected upon arriving in Nice. Even if he began his stay in France as a kind of unanticipated holiday with confidence and good cheer, within a few weeks he becomes acquainted with the hardships of exile.

The journal project with Pierre Bertaux fails, and he earns much less than he'd anticipated for his articles for French newspapers. Soon his assets in Germany are beyond his reach, and since he fears the Nazis will take his daughter Leonie into protective custody to force his return to Germany, he has no other choice but to persuade his ex-wife Mimi to leave the country with their daughter, too. As Mimi has no income, that will be a costly proposition for him.

To be sure, Nelly does not remain much longer in Berlin, but it takes months before she arrives in the south of France with him. The custodian of the building on Fasanenstrasse reports her for theft, burglary, and misappropriation because she, in consultation with Heinrich, tried to sell the furniture to pay the outstanding rent. The police detain her for three days until Nelly calls her half-brother Walter to her aid. He is *Scharführer* of an SS cavalry division but has no qualms vouching for his sister, although she has always had affinities for communists. No sooner does she leave the jail, she sets off to her parents' home in Niendorf on the Baltic Sea.

At first, she attempts to salvage portions of Heinrich Mann's fortune and transfer money to him in France, but almost all her efforts fail. In the end she decides to follow Mann to France, yet she lacks the necessary visa in her passport that would permit her to travel abroad. Fortunately, her eldest half-brother August Hermann is a fisherman, owns his own boat, and can smuggle her out of the country without major problems. Once she arrives in Denmark, Heinrich Mann wires 900 francs to her in

Figure 26: Nelly Kröger and Heinrich Mann in 1936

Copenhagen, and from there she makes her way to him, reaching him in the summer.

Since the deaths of Hans Maikowski and Josef Zauritz on January 30, she has remained in touch with the KPD man-in-hiding, Rudi Carius. The Berlin police have since arrested several dozen suspects for the double murder, almost all of them communists they make responsible for the two homicides. Initially they seek Carius only as a witness, then as an accomplice. Fifty-two men are ultimately tried and sentenced to long prison terms. Carius, however, is able to elude the investigators and travels to Nice to Nelly and Heinrich Mann. After the brief drama of their flight, the protracted tragedy of emigration now begins for all three. Nelly and Heinrich Mann will never see Germany again.

*

On the basis of the *Notverordnung zum Schutz von Volk und Staat*, Reich Minister of the Interior Frick assumes police command in Hesse and in Bremen, assigning it then to Hessian NSDAP deputy Heinrich Müller and Bremer NSDAP member Richard Markert, respectively. Armed SA sentries take up position outside the homes of the Social Democratic head of government in Hesse, Bernhard Adelung, and the Hessian Interior Minister, Wilhelm Leuschner.

Johannes Gerdes, the KPD deputy from Oldenburg who was lured from his home and shot at by a squad of storm troopers on March 3, succumbs to his injuries.

Eight men are killed in political clashes in Altona, Hamburg-Billstedt, Quickborn, Schönebeck on the Elbe, Düsseldorf, Wuppertal, Berlin-Friedrichshain, and Selb in Upper Franconia.

Courage, Fear, and Fire
Tuesday, March 7

An NSDAP delegation consisting of two *Landtag* deputies and two theater employees approaches Gustav Hartung at Darmstadt's Landestheater. They present the artistic director with an offer that is difficult to distinguish from an ultimatum. Hartung, they propose, may remain in office if he dismisses seven either Jewish or politically undesirable artists from the ensemble and hands over repertory programming to the party. Failing that, they give him the opportunity to step down now voluntarily. Hartung listens to what the men have to say and replies to their proposals with a simple no. He has a contract as artistic director and general manager and does not intend to brook interference in his work. Before they take their leave empty-handed, his visitors issue threats; they had "other means yet" of forcing his resignation.

Scheduled for this evening is the premiere of George Bernard Shaw's comedy *Too Good to Be True*. While Hartung is reviewing the final dress rehearsal in the afternoon, several SA divisions invade the theater plaza, making clear they intend to prevent the evening's performance. After the rehearsal concludes, Hartung climbs on stage and gives a short speech: "We will no longer be able to bring out this play, which is a tragedy, not just for the play, for us all and for Germany. I am firmly convinced it won't be long now before we perform the play in freedom and democracy."

*

Oskar Loerke's fear for his position as Academy secretary continues to grow. In the literary section right now, a series of conflicts has erupted, one after the other. The servile declaration of protest at Heinrich Mann's coerced resignation – which the members were only able to agree to after a lengthy dispute – was ultimately not allowed to be published. President Schillings would not approve it. He had admonished all the meetings' participants upfront to maintain strict confidentiality since Academy communiqués may only be publicized with his consent, and yet by the morning after the meeting, the *Vossische Zeitung* and the *Berliner Tageblatt* had the full scoop on the final statement. Schillings made this into a huge scandal internally, phoning all participants, and then stubbornly insisting Alfred Döblin and Leonhard Frank were the traitors.

Both of course deny it. Nevertheless, they have disappeared from Berlin, as has Heinrich Mann. Döblin sent a letter from Switzerland, writing that he left Berlin for a short while due to the bad weather and solemnly declaring that the newspapers' information did not come from him.

But that is now yesterday's news. Loerke must arrange the next meeting, where a new division president is to be elected. Time is of the essence. Given his imperiled position as secretary, Loerke does not want to take any chances, and just when he would like to coordinate closely with Schillings, the president has taken ill and has travel plans, besides.

So Loerke writes him a letter. First, he mentions Ricarda Huch, whom Schillings has not yet met. As deputy chairperson of the literary division, she would now have to assume temporary control, following Heinrich Mann's resignation. Loerke writes of her in very high terms. She is, he notes, a candidate to Schillings' liking: a level-headed, independent figure with a national profile. But she left Berlin last year and now, at almost seventy years of age, is living with a childhood friend in Heidelberg. According to the statutes, without residency in Berlin she is ineligible for a leadership role in the Prussian Academy, and Loerke suspects that for this reason she will likely relinquish her office of her own accord.

Presumably, then, a new deputy will have to be found at the next meeting, in addition to a new chairperson. To be able to bring off these watershed decisions with minimal friction, Loerke points out, an administrative matter could play an important role; in short, experience dictates that many out-of-town members will only travel in for the session if they can count on being reimbursed for their travel costs. And these members, he writes, are those who may prove more obstructive than beneficial in the coming ballot – whereas members who will be especially helpful to Schillings at the meeting are prepared to come at their own expense.

Loerke informs his president at the closing of his letter, moreover, that a decision will not be made on the question of reimbursing travel costs until next week, at the ministry. Schillings can therefore exert his influence in this matter as he sees fit. It is a carefully worded letter with which Loerke can be pleased. All key elements are alluded to with utmost delicacy, and yet the document provides the president with an easily decipherable set of instructions for what he can do to secure a majority in the upcoming votes in the literary division. And of course Loerke may trust the letter will also show Schillings in passing how useful Loerke can be for him if he retains his position as Academy secretary.

*

A group of brownshirts roves through Dresden's Innere Neustadt district. Lining both sides of the gentle curve traced here by Grosse Meissner Strasse are four- and five-story bourgeois houses with beautifully subdivided façades and small businesses on the ground floor. The SA troopers veer off in front of the Social Democratic *Volksbuchhandlung* and scramble into the store, tearing books from shelves and carrying them over the narrow sidewalk onto the street. There they throw their plunder into a pile and set it aflame. The bookseller was warned just before the raid and was able to rescue portions of his stock in coal sacks. But most of his books are transformed into a dirty gray clump of ash outside his business. It is the first book burning by the Nazis.

Figure 27: Book burning under police protection after the storming of the *Dresdner Volkszeitung* by SA troops, March 8, 1933

Others follow. The next day, on March 8 at around 4 p.m., storm troopers occupy the SPD-allied *Dresdner Volkszeitung* on Wettiner Platz, fly swastika flags, haul newspapers, books, and other documents out of the building and out of its bookstore, and burn them in the street. The same thing happens on the same day in Zwickau at the bookstore of the *Sächsisches Volksblatt*, on March 9 at the *Volksbuchhandlung* in Pirna, and on March 12 at the bookstore of the Social Democratic *Volksblatt* in Bochum. But it isn't always just about books. In around a dozen cities, union buildings or SPD party offices are stormed, their files and archival material carried out in front of the buildings and set on fire.

Two months later, on May 10, the *Deutsche Studentenschaft* [*German Student Union*] organizes the huge book burning in Berlin and twenty-one other German university towns. The students are not obligated to do so by the NSDAP, but carry out the action on their own initiative. For a number of years, a markedly nationalistic, *völkisch* climate has predominated at most German universities; those without employment or education are by no means the only ones enamored of the Nazis. Since Summer 1931, the *Nationalsozialistischer Deutscher Studentenbund*, a subdivision of the NSDAP, has dominated the *Deutsche Studentenschaft*.

Starting April 26, in preparation for the burning, books by proscribed authors are removed from private collections – and later from university holdings and other public libraries, bookstores, and lending libraries – according to hastily compiled lists and taken to collection points. Then, on the evening of May 10, after fomenting demonstrations in university lecture halls, torchlight processions march to the book pyres. Part of the production involves criers who toss the books by persecuted and condemned authors into the flames after pronouncing predetermined "fire verdicts": "Against literary betrayal of soldiers in the Great War, for training the *Volk* in the spirit of defensibility! I consign to the flames the writings of Erich Maria Remarque. Against the conceited denigration of the German language, for fostering the most precious asset of our *Volk*! I consign to the flames the writings of Alfred Kerr. Against impudence and pretension, for respect and reverence in the face of the undying German spirit! Consume, flames, the writings of Tucholsky and Ossietzky as well!"

*

As he did in Hamburg, Hesse, and Bremen, Reich Interior Minister Frick now assumes command of the police in Baden, Württemberg, and Saxony and assigns the pertinent duties to commissioners belonging to the NSDAP.

In politically motivated clashes in Düsseldorf, Wuppertal, Duisburg-Hamborn, Blankenrath, and Hof, seven men and one woman are killed.

Nothing but Goodbyes

Wednesday, March 8

Frankfurt is teeming with SA and SS auxiliary policemen. In the alleyways of the labyrinthine old city all around the Römerberg, Harry Graf Kessler sees innumerable swastika flags hanging from the windows of the upper floors where mostly the more indigent common folk live.

On Kaiserstrasse he runs into a street vendor selling swastika badges, with resounding success, primarily to young boys who immediately pin them on.

One of Kessler's main reasons for stopping off in Frankfurt was to visit Heinrich Simon, editor-in-chief and co-owner of the *Frankfurter Zeitung*. Unlike in his conversation last week with Fritz Landshoff, Simon's assessments today, three days after the election, are quite pessimistic, and not just because the "Main River Line" didn't hold. In Hitler's electoral victory he sees the foundation for an unforeseeably long Nazi dominion and speaks of twenty or thirty years.

Then, in the afternoon, Kessler boards a train headed to Saarbrücken. His destination is Paris, yet he travels with complete equanimity, as is his wont. Thoughts of fleeing never enter his mind. The next morning he is already meeting friends in Paris.

*

The *Frauenstadtverband* [*Municipal Women's Association*] in Wuppertal must cancel the long-scheduled reading by Else Lasker-Schüler. The organizer writes to request she postpone her appearance until the autumn. The atmosphere in the city is too hostile for her to be able to risk keeping her invitation: "I hope, dear Frau Lasker-Schüler, that we are able to meet in the not too distant future when the stars are better aligned."

It has since also become clear that Leopold Jessner, like Gustav Hartung a week ago, must cancel the promised world premiere of *Arthur Aronymus* at the Schillertheater. The production of the Richard Billinger play at Gendarmenmarkt was his swan-song performance in this city, for which he has done so much in the theater world. He is now whipping together a tour troupe with which he intends to leave Germany and travel through Holland, Belgium, and England. There is simply no more time for Else Lasker-Schüler. Only a short time ago, in the fall, it was looking like a stirring comeback for her after her long years of mourning her son. Now, however, just a few months later, she is met only with rejections. If she is honest with herself, she has nothing to show for it all.

*

In the Reichstag election, the KPD won eighty-one seats. Today their parliamentary mandates are annulled thanks to the *Notverordnung zum Schutz von Volk und Staat*. The deputies cannot attend the opening of the Reichstag anyway, Reich Interior Minister Frick sneers at a rally in Frankfurt am Main, because they are of course in concentration camps.

In Breslau [present-day Wrocław], a propaganda march with around 250 storm troopers comes under fire from inside the union building. A twenty-year-old SA man dies, and five others are wounded.

Unexpected Attacks

Friday, March 10

It is the most beautiful day of the week in Lenzerheide – blue skies, good snow – and today of all days Erika and Klaus Mann have to return to Munich. So as not to let the glorious weather go to waste, they ascend the slope with their skis one more time first thing in the morning and lie down in the sun for a while before their downhill run. When they arrive back at the chalet, time is short, and they have to pack right away. The car ride down to Chur is hurried. A fabulous drive: the landscape shows itself from its best side, and they make their train just in time. Downhill skiing and departure have occupied them so much so that they haven't heard any news the whole morning, and the catastrophic report doesn't reach them until they buy newspapers at the border.

Hitler's government has now also appointed Reich commissioners for Saxony and Bavaria who take over police authority under the *Notverordnung zum Schutz von Volk und Staat*, and are thus de facto the new state rulers. For Bavaria that is Franz Ritter von Epp, a general with a butcher's mindset who was involved in some of Germany's dirtiest and most lethal military operations, from the colonial war against the Herero in Africa, to the battles at Verdun, to the fights of the *Freikorps* against Munich's Soviet Republic. The last tiny bit of protection the Bavarian government under Heinrich Held had offered against Hitler's despotism is now gone. As Erika and Klaus realize while reading the newspapers, their train is bringing them out of Swiss safety into the very heart of Nazi terror.

Hans Holzner, the family chauffeur who picks them up from Munich's central station, looks distraught. He is remarkably nervous, his hands atremble while putting their luggage into the vehicle. "If I may give my young patrons a bit of advice," he says with an ashen face, "exercise restraint over the next few days." Weeks later it will come to light that Holzner had been reporting the goings-on in Thomas Mann's household to the Nazis in Munich for years as an informer. He therefore knows first-hand how perilous the situation has become for the family. Like a double agent, he feels torn between his loyalties to his party and to his employers.

The city appears quiet, without much happening in the streets, but during the ride Klaus and Erika see swastika flags flying from all public buildings, and placards with statements from General von Epp posted on all advertising columns. From their Pringsheim grandparents, whom they visit briefly on their way home, they also learn nothing that might reassure them about the city's new plight.

Once home on Poschingerstrasse, they do not dawdle. They immediately request an international connection from the operator to Arosa, *Neues Waldhotel*, to warn their parents.

It turns into a complicated conversation. Erika and Klaus fear the line is bugged, so they don't want to bring up the dangers lying in wait for their father in Munich directly. But no clever circumlocution springs to mind either by which they might immediately make themselves intelligible to him. They begin with a fabricated weather report. Lately, they say, the weather conditions in Munich and surrounds have been absolutely miserable, which is not at all good for their parents' health. They had better remain in Switzerland. Besides, the entire house is turned upside down: spring cleaning, chaos everywhere. But Thomas Mann doesn't get it and doesn't intend to let such trifles hold him back; he wants to come home, to his desk, to his manuscript of the Joseph novel. No matter how much they coax him, their father remains imperturbable until the siblings finally throw caution to the wind: "It's impossible, you mustn't come. Stay in Switzerland! You wouldn't be safe here."

*

"You're coming with us now, down to the office," says one of the two officers who have opened his cell door.

Egon Erwin Kisch has been in Spandau Prison now for over a week. He has a private cell and gets half an hour of yard exercise per day, coffee for breakfast, soup for lunch, tea for dinner, and twice a week there is herring or boiled potatoes. He follows the officers in silence, sensing what is ahead.

In the office another officer calmly declares: "You're going back to police headquarters."

"Why?" Kisch asks.

"Are you a foreigner?"

"Yes."

"Well, you're probably being deported from Germany. Take your things and go with those two gentlemen there."

The two gentlemen, both from the Political Police, do not exactly give him a warm welcome. They try to intimidate him straight off, saying they'll shoot him if he tries to flee. Then they put him in a police vehicle and drive away.

They aren't kidding, Kisch has since learned, as quite a few prisoners these days are shot while allegedly trying to escape. He will not give them the slightest cause for doing so.

Nothing physical was done to him in Spandau, but on his rounds through the prison yard the shrieks of those beaten were easily audible from their detention cells. The screaming set his teeth on edge, but there was nothing he could do.

At police headquarters the jailers take him to a communal cell with fifty to sixty other prisoners, and it is here he first comes face to face with the men who have lived through the sorts of flogging orgies he witnessed acoustically. They are bruised, maimed, bandaged, bloody. They show him their wounds and talk and talk. On election Sunday or the day after, they were taken from their homes and arrested, transported to SA barracks or wild concentration camps. Some were forced to drill in the yard, dropping down into the mud and jumping up on command, down and up and down and up again until they lay unconscious. Others were forced to drink castor oil and then bend over tables with their buttocks bared. They were clubbed until their skin broke open and the laxative caused the contents of their intestines to spill out over their raw flesh.

One of the prisoners was put face to face with his son. Both were handed clubs and forced at gunpoint to strike each other. Grave threats of execution by shooting were issued again and again, and at night the watchmen would sometimes shoot blindly into the dark of the sleeping quarters for fun. Afterward everyone would lie awake for hours. The Jews among the prisoners fared the worst. They were beaten most fiercely and lined up against the wall for execution, where guns were then trained on them and fired just above their heads.

The inmates recount almost unbearable stories like these for Kisch deep into the night. The light is never turned off because more new prisoners keep being brought to the cell. But sleep is inconceivable anyhow.

*

In the first week after arriving in Arosa, Thomas Mann was still calm and confident, enjoying the relaxation after the focused labors of recent months. Since the election and Hitler's triumph, however, that has changed. He senses growing unease. It is a kind of melancholy heightened by fear that he knows in weaker forms from other experiences of leaving. But now it is much stronger, extending to panic. On a recent night it escalated into a crisis. He was unable to cope by himself and had to seek refuge with Katia, who managed with great difficulty to calm him.

As an author, he tries to reach clarity about the new circumstances by writing. He begins keeping a political diary to register his thoughts, his impressions, and above all his indignation. Perhaps one day he'll compile a *Book of Ill-Humor* from these records, he considers, or a book of his *Leiden an Deutschland* [*Sufferings from Germany*].

It is becoming clearer and clearer that an epoch of life has concluded. He must completely overhaul his existence. In the future it would probably be a good idea to shed all the obligations and offices from his life that he let himself be cajoled into, out of good-naturedness if nothing else, and to concentrate solely on his work. If he retreats into literature entirely, he provides the fewest inducements for political attacks.

The weather is gorgeous, but he feels unwell. He can neither eat nor sleep properly. The thought of thoroughly upsetting his existence, the notion of having to go into exile, puts him in a state of incessant agitation and shock.

Today a rather strange letter from Gottfried Bermann Fischer arrived from Berlin. Bermann Fischer was once a physician, but after marrying Brigitte, daughter of Samuel Fischer, he became managing director of S. Fischer Verlag and at some point will succeed the aged founder of the house. Bermann Fischer's missive does not sound like business mail from the press, however, but like an unsolicited medical consultation:

"I hear," Bermann Fischer writes, "that you already mean to abandon your course of treatment so soon. From a medical standpoint I consider that *entirely* preposterous and would view the regimen as complete only when your condition can safely be apprehended. Everything else I would regard as not quite risk-free since, at the present moment of treatment, such a sensitive nature as your own might still be subject to unexpected attacks. Hazarding your health in such a manner must be avoided if at all possible."

The wording is unambiguous. Thomas Mann figures out at once what is meant. After all, there was never any mention of taking the cure in Arosa, merely of a brief holiday. The letter is in essence doubly unsettling: on the one hand as a warning against "unexpected attacks," and on the other because Bermann Fischer thinks it necessary to issue his warning in medical disguise. He obviously assumes his mail is opened en route and read by prying eyes.

Then came the unannounced call from Klaus and Erika. At first peculiar banter, also likely intended to serve as a cover, then the rather forceful command: don't come to Munich, it's too dangerous, stay in Switzerland.

Could that be? Must he in fact not return to his own home in Munich? For decisions of such scope, he would rather not rely on his children or on Bermann Fischer. Instead, he writes to two confidants in Munich with great savvy, Lord Mayor Karl Scharnagl and the attorney Karl Löwenstein. They will be able to provide a trustworthy appraisal of the situation. But as matters are now unfolding from one day to the next, he probably has to view himself as under bodily threat. He can hardly believe it.

*

Masurenallee all around Berlin's *Haus des Rundfunks* is brimming with SA and SS. Hitler will give a speech here tonight at 8 p.m., and the men of his combat associations are cordoning off the building hours in advance. From 7 to 8 p.m., however, Hermann Kesten is supposed to read from his new, still unfinished novel *Der Gerechte* [*The Righteous Man*], a date set weeks ago that no one thought to cancel later despite all the political upheaval. Oblivious, Kesten is walking toward the radio building with his wife Toni when he suddenly realizes what they have gotten themselves into. Standing every few meters are men in brown or black uniforms with whom they would rather not cross paths. But if they do a sudden about-face here in the street and walk away now, they will draw all the more suspicion.

For over a month now they've had visas for France in their passports; they just couldn't tear themselves away from Berlin just yet. First Kesten's family had to recover from the flu, and then his sister Gina was about to become engaged, which he was also supposed to wait for. Then, two weeks ago, the buzzer rang. Kesten answered the door, and a neighbor was standing outside upset. She was trembling and whispered that the police and SA were searching her flat right then. Her husband was an editor, they had arrested him, and they were going to take him away. Since she knew Kesten was an author, she wanted to warn him in advance in case he might also be on their list. Then she ran back downstairs to her husband. He and Toni snuck out of the building by the rear staircase, but luckily it was a false alarm, and no one wanted to ransack their apartment.

And now they are walking the length of a veritable column of SA and SS men, one of whom feels entitled to check their papers every ten paces. To anyone who asks, Kesten shows his identification papers and the contractual letter from the radio confirming that he is expected today in one of the studios here. The distance along the front of the building to the entrance is long, very long, a seemingly endless path to Kesten and his wife. It is a reddish brown, somewhat drab building, still quite new, designed by Hans Poelzig, whom the Nazis are now calling an "architectural Bolshevik."

The checks continue inside the building, and Kesten is happy when he is finally sitting in front of the microphone. He reads from the novel's first chapter about a village parson who has joined the communists and openly preaches against dictatorship. Because of this his two sons abduct him and tie him to a willow tree in the forest to let him starve to death. While Kesten is reading, for a never-ending half hour, he expects the door to the studio will be torn open at any moment and one of the many men in uniform will lead him away. But nothing happens. After surviving his time at the microphone, he goes straight to the cashier's office with Toni, receives his fee, and while leaving the building must show his papers multiple times. No one detains them.

A few days later he and Toni are finally packing their suitcases. On Kurfürstendamm they run into Erich Kästner outside Café Leon, where Kästner usually works, and show him their tickets to Paris. Kästner tries once more to dissuade them: "Are we not obliged to stay? We can't just all up and leave!" But they will not be deterred. Sixteen years later Kesten returns to visit Germany.

*

On the night of March 10, the editorial offices of the satirical magazine *Simplicissimus* in Munich's Friedrichstrasse are burglarized. The next morning all the desks, shelves, and file cabinets have been rifled through and ravaged. The magazine's trademark, the red plaster bulldog *Simpl*, is in pieces. Only the manuscripts and caricatures by graphic artists Olaf Gulbransson and Eduard Thöny remain untouched. Later, in the years of the Third Reich, the pair will be held in high esteem by the Nazis and awarded prizes.

*

Yesterday and today, in numerous cities throughout the country, SPD party leaders are arrested, and buildings and editorial offices of Social Democratic newspapers are occupied and shut down. Former Reich Interior Minister Wilhelm Sollmann, for instance, is attacked in his home in Cologne-Rath. He succeeds in fending off his attackers and pushing them down the stairs. Later, three vehicles full of members of the SA and SS drive up, kick down the front door, subdue Sollmann, and kidnap him. Several storm troopers ransack the residence and leave behind devastation. At Cologne's NSDAP party headquarters, Sollmann is beaten for hours, critically injured, only admitted to a police hospital that evening, and later taken into protective custody. He first emigrates to the Territory of the Saar Basin, then via Luxembourg and Great Britain to the United States.

Final Days
Saturday, March 11

Around noon Kisch hears his name being called. He makes his presence known amid the crush of people in the overcrowded cell. One of the guards opens the barred door and leads him through the hallways of police headquarters into the administrative office. There an officer declares to him that as a Czech citizen he is being officially deported from the German Reich and must leave the country today. Kisch's attorney had urged the Foreign Ministry of Czechoslovakia to intervene with the German authorities on his behalf, and the latter obviously would like to avoid a public fuss about the arrest of the internationally renowned reporter.

Kisch is briefly allowed back into the cell where he spent the night in order to fetch his coat. Later, while in Prague working on his – yet again sensational – report about his days in Hitler's prisons, he will write that he took his leave from his cellmates with raised fist and "Red Front!" More than fifty right fists rose to return the salute with a more than fiftyfold "Red Front!"

*

Neither Erika nor Klaus heed the advice of their family chauffeur Hans to maintain as low a profile as possible in Munich. Given the considerable number of their undertakings and obligations, that would hardly be possible.

Under the watchful eye of rabid Reich Commissioner von Epp, a cabaret like the *Pfeffermühle* no longer stands a chance. Erika is under no illusions about that and starts planning her troupe's emigration. To start, she means to cancel the old contracts. After the performance break in March, the *Pfeffermühle* was supposed to start a new program in a larger building, Schwabing's *Serenissimus*, on April 1. Now she has to void the agreements she just made with the stage's owner, but he, an archetypical denizen of Munich, proves intransigent.

"You've got a contract, a contract!"

"Yes of course, we have a contract," Erika appeals to his political reason, "but we're one of those anti-, you know, ventures, and the black-lists are out, and even for you it would be, even for you ..."

The man is astonishingly impervious to such objections: "We had a deal."

"Yes, we had a deal, but it'll be shut down immediately, and we'll all be arrested. So will you!"

A warning that only elicits the man's laughter: "Me? I'm an old party member, look here, and I'll get you SA stewards for the hall, you'll be protected ..."

Erika Mann is delighted at her negotiating partner's completely twisted mindset: storm troopers are to safeguard an anti-Hitler cabaret from being arrested by the Nazi regime? What a bizarre idea! At the same time Erika realizes the kind of danger discussions with this man put her in, his obvious political naïveté tantamount to his lack of business scruples: "With SA stewards we'll do it up top notch," she promises quickly, "It's a done deal, this'll be even better."

"Yes," her interlocutor replies, "or else I'd have to take you straight to court."

"No, we'll perform," she asserts calmingly, adamantly aware that she'll be leaving the country behind her quite soon.

Her brother Klaus is also aware that not much time remains for him in Germany. He writes letters, reworks an essay to be published in the *Weltbühne*, and finishes a chanson he wrote on vacation for one of Herbert Franz's performances in the *Pfeffermühle*.

By evening the house is suddenly full. Their youngest brother, Michael, is on holiday from boarding school. Herbert Franz comes for dinner; he and Klaus haven't seen one another since their amorous Carnival days. From the city Erika brings along Magnus Henning, the cabaret pianist, plus two other friends. When Henning sits down at the piano, the evening lists all of a sudden in the direction of a spontaneous party. At thirteen years of age, Michael has no experience with alcohol and is drunk in a very funny way, to such a degree that it is difficult to put him to bed. The main thing, however, is that Herbert Franz spends the night, which makes Klaus very happy. Is a relationship in the making here, one more stable than his previous ones?

*

Joseph Goebbels receives his long-anticipated appointment as Reich Minister for Public Enlightenment and Propaganda today. The ministry was created for him and tailored to his interests. He is in charge of the press, radio, film, theater, literature, fine arts, and music. By fall, Goebbels will found a Reich Chamber of Culture subordinate to his ministry. It is structured into seven individual chambers, each responsible for one of the aforementioned cultural sectors: the Reich Chambers of Literature, of Music, of Film, etc. Whoever wishes to perform at public events or to publish, exhibit, or showcase something in Germany in the future must be a member of the respective chamber and will be constantly monitored by it. Goebbels establishes a system of almost seamless political censorship.

Departures

Monday, March 13

A day of farewells and decisions. The day before yesterday Gustav Hartung traveled from Darmstadt to Zurich because he wanted to hear a baritone there whom he might engage for his theater. But his situation has now essentially become untenable. Last Friday the four-person delegation from Darmstadt's NSDAP came to him again and threatened that the evening performance of *Fidelio* would be disrupted by the SA if it were to take place as planned under the direction of Jewish conductor Hermann Adler. And yesterday crews of storm troopers occupied the theater entrances, thereby inhibiting the performance of Ferdinand Bruckner's *The Marquise of O....* Hartung finds it difficult, but he must confess he can no longer lead his theater under these conditions. He requests an international connection at his Zurich hotel, calls his director of operations in Darmstadt, and dictates to him his letter of resignation.

*

Erika Mann sets off before noon to Arosa, to her parents. Snow-covered roads notwithstanding, she takes her car, a cabriolet. Of course it would be warmer and more comfortable to travel by train, but she has a lot to transport; at her father's request she retrieved the half-finished manuscript of *Joseph in Egypt* from his study, along with a bundle of preliminary sketches and notes he needs to continue work on the Joseph novel. She arrives in Arosa by evening. Her reports of the arrests and maltreatment of Hitler's adversaries in Munich are harrowing. Since, in their responses to Thomas Mann's written request for an appraisal of the situation, Lord Mayor Scharnagl and the attorney Löwenstein also emphatically advise against returning to Munich, the decision is made. He will remain in Switzerland for the time being.

*

Erika's companion Therese Giehse still wants to tough it out in Munich. She has rehearsals to attend at the Kammerspiele. While conversing with her peers during a rehearsal break, she makes fun of Hitler, who allegedly greatly admires her acting despite the fact that she is Jewish. She calls him a "wackadoodle" and tells the joke about the father sitting and dining with his young son. The son asks: "Father, who set the Reichstag on fire?" The father replies: "*Ess, ess,* [*eat, eat*] my boy." One of her colleagues denounces her, while another warns her about the denunciation. Without hesitation she leaves the rehearsal stage, fleeing from the theater carrying nothing more than a single bag. Magnus Henning helps her get out of the city. By evening she has reached Lermoos in Tyrol, and the following day she journeys onward to Erika Mann in Switzerland. Only sixteen years later, in 1949, will she appear on the Kammerspiele stage in Munich once more.

*

A restless soul, Klaus Mann has always traveled widely; he has practice in going away. Yesterday he declared to Erich Ebermayer in a long letter that he is giving up work on *Night Flight* and then sent telegrams to friends in Paris to announce he's coming. It was a beautiful day in early spring, which he used to take one more walk through Munich and say his goodbyes to the city. Then, today, the final letters and telephone calls. At midday Herbert Franz comes for lunch on Poschingerstrasse. Munich radio, he says, is now no longer employing Jews. After dining, they listen to music on the gramophone: *Salome* by Richard Strauss and Mahler's *Kindertotenlieder*. With the weather still clement, they sit out on the terrace for tea. They speak a great deal and are tender to one another. Then Herbert must be off to his next radio rehearsal. After this parting nothing is left for Klaus to do but pack. He doesn't want to leave. The feeling of loneliness is intense. Even years later he carries a framed photo of Herbert Franz with him.

He takes the night train to Paris. In the sleeper car he meets a very congenial American man.

*

Brecht hits the road again in Vienna. He's heard that some writers he regards highly have fled to safety in Switzerland. Perhaps his idea of a colony of émigrés, of which he has spoken from time to time whenever the topic of exile came up, could become reality in Switzerland?

He wants to suss out the possibilities in Zurich. Helene Weigel will stay in Vienna with the children for the time being. At Brecht's Zurich hotel a letter from Margarete Steffin is already waiting for him, from his Grete, and he replies promptly. The weeks following are a restless period. In Zurich he meets up with Anna Seghers and Döblin, at Lake Lugano with Hermann Hesse, Bernhard von Brentano, and Margarete Steffin, among others. In the interim he develops the ballet *The Seven Deadly Sins* with Kurt Weill in Paris, a short work commissioned for the Théâtre des Champs-Elysées and bankrolled by an English art lover for his wife, a dancer. And yet the idea of an emigrant colony in Switzerland cannot be realized; the authors' interests are too different – and the country proves too expensive. Anna Seghers and Döblin decamp for Paris, and Bernhard von Brentano remains in Switzerland. Brecht relocates to Denmark with Helene Weigel, their children, and Margarete Steffin, to the islet of Thurø, near Svendborg. For the next five years he lives there cheaply but, in contrast to his usual work habits, largely in isolation. After war breaks

Figure 28: Bertolt Brecht, Henry Peter Matthis, Margarete Steffin, and, at far right, Brecht's and Weigel's son Stefan, Sweden, 1939. From 1939 the writer Henry Peter Matthis was a board member of the Swedish Writers' Association and in April 1939 helped the Brecht family obtain entry visas to Sweden

out, he and his family are forced to flee from the advancing German Wehrmacht via Sweden and Finland to California.

*

Surrender of an Academy. The Division for the Art of Poetry convenes this evening on Pariser Platz. Its members appear helpless, as if paralyzed. Only Gottfried Benn has an objective in mind and believes he knows how to achieve it. He has prepared thoroughly for today's meeting. An official from the ministry is participating in the session as an observer; supposedly Minister Rust continues to be dissatisfied with the state of affairs in the division and expects a reorganization. Up to now, however, there has been no concrete proposal from the circle of members for how they intend to deal with the minister's political expectations. From among the out-of-towners, Rudolf Binding is in fact the only one who has come to Berlin. The others have either eschewed the travel costs, as Loerke predicted, or already given up any hope for the Academy.

The meeting begins with an impertinent move. The minister, it is revealed to the assembled, has appointed Hanns Johst as a member of their division. As a rule, new members were hitherto elected to the Academy by the existing ones as they saw fit. And yet Minister Rust has summarily flouted this prerogative in favor of his fellow party member Johst, demonstrating to those present the plight of their authority.

At this point Benn speaks up. The division's passivity is getting on his nerves, and he wants them, finally, to take charge of their restructuring themselves. His proposal: a collective declaration of loyalty so peremptory that it will eliminate any incentive for the minister to intervene further. He has prepared a text to this end, which leaves nothing to be desired in terms of unambiguity. Every member is to be presented with this query: "Acknowledging the changed historical circumstances, are you prepared to continue placing yourself at the disposal of the Prussian Academy of the Arts? Affirming this question precludes public political action against the government and obligates you to loyal collaboration on those duties of the nation that fall to the Academy by statute."

This is total political submission, the renunciation of any and all freedom of expression, or of critical distance from the government. What is palpable in these two sentences is Benn's scorn for democratic ideals, liberalism, tolerance, and diversity of opinion – and his excessive political activism. For by this attestation, members would ultimately declare their approval not only for the government's present actions, but likewise for all its future actions, which aren't yet even foreseeable.

The brutal directness of the question as Benn phrased it jibes with the fact that he intends to permit only a simple yes-or-no answer. There is to be no room for doubt or hedging on this point, just radical assent or rejection. That strikes even Rudolf Binding, himself no friend of the Republic, as sinister. For that reason, as chairperson of the meeting, he does not allow a vote on Benn's proposal, but asks each attendee individually whether he has objections to the draft. As Benn has written the declaration, however, there is no room for negotiation. Even quietly uttered misgivings would now appear like the implicit announcement of "public political action against the government," and in light of the current pursuits of the SA and SS, everyone would rather avoid exposing themselves to that suspicion.

To do the job properly, Benn's draft is then taken to the office of the Academy's president so that he can sign off on it. But Max von Schillings is not satisfied and rushes into the meeting, demanding that the question be put even more decisively and the division's surrender be even more complete. The second sentence of the question is to be slightly amended: "Affirming this question precludes public political action against the government and obligates you to loyal collaboration on those *national cultural duties that accord with the changed historical circumstances, which fall to the Academy by statute.*"

The renunciation of dissent against the government thus becomes a voluntary commitment to work for the government's interests in the future. Submission becomes an oath of allegiance. Yet even that cannot deter the attendees anymore. Not a word of resistance is uttered. They all consent to their disenfranchisement and exploitation and furthermore vote to dispatch the declaration to all members who did not attend the meeting so they can sign it.

Benn leaves the battlefield as the victor, having achieved what he wanted to achieve: after this declaration the new rulers no longer have any reason to shut down the Division for the Art of Poetry. Benn is nonetheless soon forced to realize that his victory is indistinguishable from a total loss because the Academy loses all writers with a respectable intellectual presence. At first it is Thomas Mann, Alfons Paquet, Alfred

Döblin, and Ricarda Huch who, needless to say, do not wish to sign Benn's declaration of loyalty. In a second step Jewish or politically unwelcome members, such as Leonhard Frank, Georg Kaiser, René Schickele, Franz Werfel, or Jakob Wassermann, are expelled from the Academy. The positions freed up are taken over in May by authors like Hans Friedrich Blunck, Hans Grimm, Erwin Guido Kolbenheyer, Wilhelm Schäfer, and Emil Strauß who, aside from their *völkisch* nationalistic convictions, have little to offer in the way of intellect. Benn is so appalled by this outcome that he never again sets foot in the Academy after this summer.

Still, Thomas Mann and Döblin take pains with their resignations to avoid the appearance of open protest against the regime. They do not seek confrontation – yet. Mann attests he has "no intention whatsoever of working against the government," but instead wants to focus exclusively on his literary endeavors in the future and for this reason relinquishes his seat in the Academy. Initially Döblin writes that he is fully prepared to make the requisite political statement, but in a second letter he backs off from his own concession and resigns because "as a man of Jewish ancestry under today's circumstances" he would simply be too heavy a burden for the division.

Only Ricarda Huch is uncompromising. Despite not living in exile – nor does she later leave Germany either – she has the courage to state bluntly what she thinks of the Academy's self-dismantling: that she is unwilling to give up her right to freedom of expression, that she denies the Academy's authority to compel her to make declarations of loyalty, and that she rejects Hitler's politics for a variety of reasons "in the strongest possible terms." To her surprise, however, Max von Schillings will not accept her resignation, and instead builds the conservative and popular author golden bridges to keep her in the Academy. He threatens her a bit as well, suggesting her conduct might be interpreted publicly as an expression of solidarity with Heinrich Mann and Döblin, who have since fled abroad.

Ricarda Huch must wage an outright battle to be able to leave the Academy, and she does so with great dignity and resoluteness. Since Schillings lauds her "German disposition," she makes plain what that implies: "That a German has German sensibilities I might almost regard as self-evident; but on the question of what is German and how Germanness is to act there are various opinions. What the current government prescribes as a national disposition is not my Germanness. Its centralization, its coercion, its brutal methods, its defamation of those who think differently, its boastful self-praise I regard as un-German and inauspicious." What's more, she also vehemently rebuffs Schillings' furtive threat: "You mention Herr Heinrich Mann and Herr Dr. Döblin. It is true that I did not see eye to eye with Herr Heinrich Mann, nor did I always with Dr. Döblin, but on some matters I did. At any rate, I would wish that all non-Jewish Germans so conscientiously sought both to discern and do what is right, were so open, honest, and upstanding as I have always found him to be. In my view, when faced with this baiting of Jews, he could not have acted differently than he did."

As she writes this, Ricarda Huch is sixty-eight years old, a white-haired, dapper lady and highly organized intellectual who retreated from Berlin to the more tranquil provinces in Heidelberg. At the same time, she is entirely unswerving in her determination and civil courage about defending civic freedom and human decency. Alas, she finds almost no fellow comrades-in-arms of her caliber in or outside the Academy. For her, lonesome years of inner emigration now begin.

She will survive the dictatorship and the bombing war. Her home in Jena becomes the nexus of a discussion group for Hitler detractors. Two years after the war ends, she travels to Berlin to gather material for a book about the German resistance to Hitler. She stays in a hotel on Fasanenstrasse, where she is approached in one of the corridors by a man who recognizes her and greets her, beaming: Alfred Döblin.

*

City Building Commissioner Martin Wagner, the only one to quit the Academy in solidarity with Käthe Kollwitz and Heinrich Mann, is suspended with immediate effect by Hermann Göring late this evening. Another four members of Berlin's municipal authorities must vacate their offices along with him. Over the next two years Wagner is largely unemployed. In 1935 he goes to Istanbul as a metropolitan planning consultant. Three years later he receives an offer from Harvard University and works there as a professor of city and regional planning until his retirement in 1950.

*

The *Liga für Menschenrechte* declares its disbanding. It ceases all operations in Germany.

In Schönebeck (near Magdeburg), an SPD town councilor is shot and killed. In Kiel, an attorney campaigning for city councilor for the SPD is shot and killed.

SA companies muster outside Cologne's city hall. NSDAP *Gauleiter* Josef Grohé appears on the balcony of city hall and declares Cologne's Lord Mayor Konrad Adenauer deposed. During Hitler's visit to Cologne on February 18, Adenauer had prohibited all flag decorations in the city and refused to shake the Reich Chancellor's hand. On election posters the NSDAP subsequently demanded: "Adenauer an die Mauer!" or "Adenauer against the Wall!" An old schoolmate of Adenauer's, now abbot of the Maria Laach cloister in the Eifel, temporarily accepts Adenauer into the abbey as Brother Konrad after his removal from office. By order of the city council, Adolf Hitler is named an honorary citizen of Cologne on March 30.

The Sight of This Hell
Wednesday, March 15

This morning around three hundred riot police, several dozen detectives, and SA companies gather at various Berlin police precincts and set out for Wilmersdorf. Once they reach Laubenheimer Platz, several of the men leap from their open-bed trucks and block all the access roads around the entire square. They are armed not only with revolvers, but also with carbines. Between Breitenbachplatz and Laubenheimer Strasse they cordon off three large residential blocks clustered in rings around generous lawns. Altogether the buildings contain more than five hundred apartment units. Berliners like to refer to the area as the "Hungerburg," or "Fortress of Famine."

A few years ago, the *Genossenschaft Deutscher Bühnen-Angehöriger* [*Cooperative of German Stage Workers*] and the *Schutzverband deutscher Schriftsteller* built these blocks for theater people and authors for whom life wasn't financially a bed of roses. The flats are small, their features Spartan, but these elements are compensated for by low rents, the park-like greenspace in the inner courtyards, and above all by the tight-knit community of residents who all work in related freelance professions: a metropolitan artists' colony.

Since the global economic crisis, straitened circumstances have, for most of them, become utter penury. Many can no longer pay even their meager rents and are forced to face eviction. They fight back with protest demonstrations that in their hands often take on the character of street theater and popular entertainment. Solidarity within the buildings is high; most eviction attempts are fended off. That's why, aside from "Hungerburg," the housing estate also bears the nickname "the Red Blocks." Hardly anyone lives here who doesn't identify as a Social Democrat, socialist, or communist.

Two weeks ago, just after the Reichstag fire, the first home searches and arrests took place. The very night of the fire, Johannes R. Becher, coming from downtown, ran from door to door to warn the residents, among them Karola Piotrkowska, the partner and later wife of philosopher Ernst Bloch. Bloch was out of town, so she combed through their little private library by herself, packed all Marxist books into a box, and stored it away with friends outside the "Red Block." When she returned to carry two more suitcases with treasonable manuscripts to safety, the SA was already in the building, and she had no other choice but to stash the suitcases in her attic as an expedient. Then she got dressed especially elegantly so as not to give the raiding party the faintest idea that she could be a communist. Indeed, the men rummaged through her wardrobe and underwear at least as intently as they did the bookshelves, where nothing heretical was left to find now. She thought she had weathered the danger when a storm trooper said: "Now show us your attic."

Karola Piotrkowska climbed the stairs up to the loft as though marching to her own execution. With all her force of will she attempted to suppress her fear and find a way out. Suddenly she remembered that she had on her keyring not just the key to her own storage area, but the one to the storage area belonging to her neighbor, the poet Peter Huchel. Ernst Bloch had deposited a medieval wooden sculpture with Huchel, a Madonna with child for which he couldn't find room in his own overflowing attic unit. Karola Piotrkowska knew Huchel wasn't storing anything suspicious, so she opened the padlock to his storage door, the Madonna's beatific smile radiated toward her, and after a brief glimpse into the unit the SA man retreated.

Immediately afterward she warned her partner by telephone, and Ernst Bloch absconded to Switzerland. He would later write in one of his essays, in gratitude: "Madonna helped."

Yet many residents of the "Red Blocks" had been arrested at that time already. Others wanted to flee, but they lacked money and so tried to lie low in Berlin.

Today, after surrounding and cordoning off Laubenheimer Platz, the police and SA proceed even more drastically. This large-scale raid gives a sense of how much constitutional restraint has dwindled even now, six weeks after Hitler's takeover, both among officers who are now collaborating with Hitler's private army as though it were a matter of course, as well as among citizens who identify with the Nazis.

The police and SA storm all the buildings ambush-style so that, to the extent possible, neighbors are unable to warn each other. Some of the residents succeed in barricading themselves inside to buy time and burn documents in their ovens. Still, the attackers have brought vehicles from the fire department with aerial ladders that they secure against apartment balconies in order to smash windows and climb in by that route.

For young Galician-born Manès Sperber, this proves unnecessary. He is surprised while asleep by the buzzing at his door and opens up. Like Bloch, Sperber is a communist and a Jew and has a pronounced literary ambition. A disciple of psychotherapist Alfred Adler, he is currently employed at the *Berliner Gesellschaft für Individualpsychologie* [*Berlin Institute for Individual Psychology*]. He wrote his first novel at nineteen, the autobiographical story of a young man in Vienna seeking love and the meaning of life and intending to incite a world revolution along the way. Yet after finishing his youthful work, he found it sentimental and full of pathos, and he opted to shelve it. For a few weeks now Sperber hasn't been sleeping in his flat in the "Red Block." He was coerced by party comrades into stashing two army pistols and several revolvers there, which are intended for a potential communist uprising against the Nazis, and he understands full well what it would mean for him if weapons were to be found at his home.

Last night, for once, he was unable to stay in his temporary quarters at a girlfriend's place, however, and decided to spend this one night at the "Red Block," in spite of it all. Now a plainclothes detective and two policemen, along with four SA men and a young woman with a swastika armband, are pushing their way into his rooms. The search party proceeds thoroughly, finding manuscripts, letters, and photos he kept there only because he hasn't really been using the apartment at all anymore. One of the storm troopers rummaging through his bookshelves gives a shout of excitement when he stumbles upon a book with a Russian author's name, but the young woman with the swastika on her arm points out to him that Dostoyevsky wasn't a communist.

Sperber has no bed in the flat, just three fold-out couches in the frames of which he tucks away the bedding during the day. In one of them he has hidden the weapons. He waits for a new cry of triumph any second when one of the ransackers discovers them. But the cry never comes.

The papers they've found, though, suffice for the police and SA to take Manès Sperber into custody. His escort party ushers him out of the building to one of the open vehicles with several rows of benches mounted to the truck bed. There he must take his seat beside the other arrestees, some of whom are bleeding, their lips split or sporting headwounds. Because the truck is almost full, he is forced to sit in the last row and wait. Thirty to forty curious bystanders surround the vehicle, and the SA guards explain to them that these are Bolsheviks sitting in the vehicle, criminals, arsonists, traitors to their country, pestilent boils on the German body national. One of the onlookers, an older woman, berates the prisoners, swipes at one of them, slips, hurts herself, and cries out. All at once, others rush toward the man she attacked and pommel him. A boy, still too small to be able to reach the man, jumps into the truck bed and spits in his face.

Just moments later almost all the bystanders are swinging indiscriminately at the arrestees. The men on Sperber's easily accessible rear bench in particular are enveloped by punches. The police and SA watch without intervening. While Sperber attempts to dodge the fists, he sees an old married couple moving from an adjacent road and crossing the square toward the truck. The man struggles to walk and leans on a cane. Now and then he pauses, his face red, gasping for breath. And yet he makes efforts to advance as quickly as possible into the circle of the lynch mob.

Figure 29: Raid on the artists' colony at Laubenheimer Platz, March 15, 1933. Those arrested are detained in open police vehicles

Once at the truck, he swings his cane, laying into the detainees and screaming that they are criminals, traitors, responsible for the inflation that ruined him.

Only now do some policemen shove their way between the prisoners and the madding crowd. They're not so easy to rein in, though. Unchecked, the rowdies press forward from all sides toward the truck, trying to reach the victims, until two brownshirts set out a large tin in front of the prisoners, almost as if it were necessary to pay a cover charge for the pleasure of lynching: "Fellow Germans, hurry, if you want to make donations to the SA, here's the collecting can." Hardly anyone tosses anything in, but the mob leaves the prisoners alone and begins to disperse.

All the while, raiding parties haul files, red flags, manuscripts, leftist newspapers, and especially books out of the apartments. Whatever cannot serve as evidence is confiscated anyway and treated as unclaimed spoils. The men chuck everything in Laubenheimer Platz into a pile and set fire to it, hosting a book burning on their own initiative.

After Sperber and his fellow sufferers have been sitting motionless in the cold for a good long while, the trucks finally drive off with them. They stop again at an intersection in the heart of Berlin, and the storm troopers clamber out. It is plain to Sperber what that means. They have the improbable luck of being taken to a proper prison, not to one of the "wild" camps run by the SA or SS.

Upon their arrival at the police prison, some of those beaten find it difficult to climb down from the truck. Cold and pain have made them stiff and lame. The guardsmen are impatient but not violent. Together with the others, Sperber runs through the usual procedures. He must show his identification papers, empty his pockets, render signatures. He is put in an overcrowded communal cell for five days before being transferred to a different prison where he spends a month in solitary confinement. His greatest fear is that the weapons stash in his flat could be found, because then he would go from being a fairly harmless political prisoner to a dangerous criminal who could be tried for intent to commit murder. Isolated in his cell, he vacillates for weeks between the mulish hope of being released and the fear of being pulverized inside the judicial machinery of the Nazis for his foolish choice to spend the night in the wrong place.

Still, Sperber's improbable luck holds. On April 20, Hitler's birthday, he is released from detention as a foreigner. Like Egon Erwin Kisch before him, he, too, is required to leave the German Reich without delay. A short while later, he alights from the train in Vienna.

*

SA headquarters for the *Gau* Berlin-Brandenburg is located in Kreuzberg on the fifth floor of the building at Hedemannstrasse 31. Its building sits on the corner where Hedemannstrasse terminates at Wilhelmstrasse. Not two hundred meters beyond this intersection, almost within earshot, is the main portal of Anhalter Bahnhof. It is from there that many of the emigrants leave the city, including Helene Weigel, Bertolt Brecht, Margarete Steffin, Alfred Kerr, Anna Seghers, Theodor Wolff, and Else Lasker-Schüler.

Figure 30: Berlin-Kreuzberg,
Hedemannstrasse 31,
December 1931

Even before Hitler's accession to power, SA detachments occasionally kidnapped political enemies to their home base or other locations in order to – as they called it – interrogate them. From January 30 on, the number of those randomly abducted or officially arrested will increase to such a degree that all the city's jails are overwhelmed and for a few weeks "wild" prisons will crop up in SA barracks or squad bases that are supervised neither by the judiciary, nor by the police, nor by any other public body. They are places without any justice or law. More than a hundred, perhaps even a hundred seventy of them, are scattered throughout the city. And they do not exist only in Berlin or Prussia, but in all larger cities and states in the Reich. What must arrestees reckon with who, unlike Kisch and Sperber, are not so lucky as to be foreigners or famous, or who enjoy one last shred of protection for other reasons?

There exist several such detention sites all around SA headquarters at Hedemannstrasse 31, including diagonally opposite in the buildings at Hedemannstrasse 5 and 6. In the prisoners' area there, fifteen men or more are imprisoned together. The space is completely bare except for some straw on the ground. There is an ordinance of punishments for the "interrogations," a catalog of the usual methods of torture: twenty-five to fifty "numbered" blows to covered or bared haunches, or "continuous" blows from head to toe. "Thrashings" are possible, either with bare fists or with brass knuckles. "Assimilation" means that the prisoners have to beat each other up under the watchful eyes of the sentries. Hair is torn out by the handful, drugs administered that cause diarrhea, or individual prisoners led away to mock executions. Prisoners receive almost nothing to eat and no appreciable medical care, and the hygienic conditions are abysmal.

By no means do the "inquisitions" take place solely in the secrecy of basement rooms, but in the offices of the SA as well, including in headquarters at Hedemannstrasse 31. The tortured men scream their heads off, their cries audible, as local residents report, all the way out on the street. Even emigrants hurrying to Anhalter Bahnhof to put Germany in their wake are likely not spared these screams. To put an end to his agony, the worker Paul Pabst, a member of the KPD, leaps from the fourth-floor window of the building at Hedemannstrasse 5 to his death.

Rudolf Diels – director of the Political Police in the Prussian Ministry of the Interior, from April the first commander of the Geheimes Staatspolizeiamt (Gestapa) [Secret State Police Office], and a close associate of Göring – does not want to put up with the high-handedness of the SA. In a book he will write after the Second World War, he claims to have pressed Göring and Hitler multiple times to close these wild prisons. According to his testimony, he first had to prevail against massive pushback from the leader of the Berlin-Brandenburg SA group before he could clear out the torture sites on Hedemannstrasse weeks later:

"The victims we found were close to dying of hunger. They had been locked in cramped cabinets, standing for days on end, to extort their 'confessions.' The 'interrogations' had begun and ended with beatings; a dozen men battered the victims with iron bars, truncheons, and whips every few hours. Missing teeth and broken bones attested to the ordeals. When we entered, these living skeletons were lying on rotting straw, one after the other, with festering wounds. There was not one whose body did not bear the blue, yellow, and green marks of inhuman beatings from head to toe. Many had eyes swollen shut, and crusts of congealed blood stuck beneath their nostrils. There was no groaning or lamenting any more: just a numb waiting for the end, or for more beatings. Every one of them had to be carried to the awaiting patrol cars; they were no longer capable of walking. Like big clods of dirt, strange puppets with dead eyes and wobbly heads, they clung there on the benches of the police vehicles, stuck to one another. The sight of this hell rendered the policemen speechless."

What Happened Afterward

33 Life Sketches

Max von Schillings is appointed artistic director of the Städtische Oper Berlin, joins the NSDAP on April 1, and dies shortly thereafter on July 24, 1933, during surgery for colon cancer.

Kadidja Wedekind enjoys great success with her novel *Kalumina*, but she finds neither the tranquility nor the energy to make more out of her literary talent. In 1938 she travels to the United States, works as a journalist, actor, sales clerk, and nanny, and occasionally takes another stab at a literary career, but without compelling results. In 1949 she returns to Germany, publishes a play and a novel that meet with little response, and dies in Munich in 1994.

Else Lasker-Schüler escapes to safety in Zurich on April 19, 1933. Three years later her *Arthur Aronymus* celebrates its world premiere there, with Katia and Thomas Mann among the opening attendees. In his diary Thomas Mann describes the drama as a "long, disordered, but lovable Rhenish Jew play." Else Lasker-Schüler travels to Palestine three times for lengthy periods. On her third trip, in 1939, she is blindsided by the outbreak of war and is not issued a return visa by Switzerland. She spends her final years living in a sublet room in Jerusalem. She is on friendly terms with a number of emigrants, including Martin Buber, the man who contrived the escape plan in Darmstadt for communist publisher Willi Münzenberg. She dies in Jerusalem in 1945.

Hanns Johst works his way up to become the highest literary official in the Third Reich, including as President of the Reich Chamber of Literature and of the Division for the Art of Poetry at the Prussian Academy. His friendship with Heinrich Himmler earns him the rank of an SS-*Gruppenführer*, which corresponds more or less with the rank of lieutenant-general in the Wehrmacht. Thereafter he appears in public almost exclusively in uniform. He accompanies Himmler on his travels and is eminently well informed about the murderous conduct of the SS during the Holocaust. In May 1945 he is arrested and interned in various camps until October 1948. His denazification trial drags on. The verdict that he numbered among the "Offenders" is reversed in 1955, as is his publication ban. He lives on Lake Starnberg unnoticed and unmolested until his death in 1978.

Ernst Toller is among the writers who openly and most intensively campaign against the Nazi regime. *Christiane Grautoff* refuses to work on an anti-Semitic Nazi propaganda film in 1933 and follows Toller into exile. The couple marries in London in 1935, shortly after Grautoff's eighteenth birthday. Toller suffers increasingly from depression and hangs himself in New York in 1939. Grautoff's so auspicious start in her theatrical career comes to a standstill. She appears on stage less and less frequently, marries the writer Walter Schönstedt, and settles in Mexico City, where she dies in 1974.

Oskar Maria Graf writes the famous letter of protest *Verbrennt mich!* [*Burn Me!*] after his books are spared at the book burnings on May 10. As an avowed enemy of the Nazis, he earned the right to be opposed by them. In 1938 he flees with Mirjam Sachs via the Netherlands to New York, where he delivers the eulogy at Ernst Toller's funeral ceremony the following year. Mirjam Sachs' cousin *Nelly Sachs* is unable to escape to Sweden until 1940 and receives the Nobel Prize for Literature in 1966 for her poetry. Oskar Maria Graf returns for the first time to visit Germany in 1958. He dies in New York in 1967.

Carl von Ossietzky is transferred on April 6, 1933, to the concentration camp Sonnenburg, where the SA troopers of *Sturm 33* hold sway. They beat and persecute him. In spring 1934, at Esterwegen concentration camp in Emsland, he is deployed to drain moorlands, with the obvious intention of ruining his health. From abroad Kurt Grossmann launches a campaign with Ossietzky's friends to promote him as a candidate for the Nobel Peace Prize. Involved in this effort in Norway is a young German emigrant named Herbert Frahm, who in exile has adopted the nom de guerre Willy Brandt. Ossietzky is awarded the Nobel Peace Prize in

November 1936. Shortly thereafter, now gravely ill with tuberculosis, he is transferred to a Berlin hospital. Maud Ossietzky nurses him selflessly, without shying away from the risk of infection. He dies on May 4, 1938, at the age of forty-nine. Federal Chancellor Willy Brandt receives the Nobel Peace Prize for his eastern policy in 1971.

George Grosz is unable to tap into the artistic successes of his German years in the United States. His late work is often apolitical; he paints landscapes and still lifes. During the war the SS takes possession of the flat on Savignyplatz belonging to his parents-in-law and pockets the rent without suspecting that Grosz had stored numerous drawings and other works there. After returning to Berlin in 1959, he finds them intact, in the same crates in which he had packed them twenty-six years earlier.

Gustav Hartung works in Swiss theaters as an actor and director. In 1945 he returns to Germany, becomes head of the Heidelberger Kammerspiele, and dies a short while later on February 14, 1946.

Erich Maria Remarque emigrates from Switzerland to the United States in 1939. While in exile he writes another eight novels, though none of them live up to the success of *All Quiet on the Western Front*. He is a womanizer, carrying on affairs with, among others, Marlene Dietrich, Greta Garbo, and Paulette Goddard, whom he marries in 1958. Remarque's sister Elfriede, a resident of Dresden, is denounced in 1943 for making anti-Nazi statements and sentenced to death by Roland Freisler, president of the People's Court. Remarque does not learn of her execution until after the end of the war.

Gottfried Benn is repeatedly impugned as a modernist poet in the Third Reich, despite his considerable contribution to the *Gleichschaltung*, or political alignment, of the Academy as well as several essays in which he enthuses about the changed historical state of affairs following Hitler's rise to power. In 1935 he joins the Wehrmacht as *Oberstabsarzt*, an officer surgeon of the medical staff, the "aristocratic form of emigration" in his view. In 1938 he is expelled from the Reich Chamber of Literature and receives a publication ban. After the war ends, he resumes working as a physician in Berlin and is again barred from publishing until 1948. In

1951 he receives the Büchner Prize, one of most prestigious West German literary awards, and two years later the Order of Merit of the Federal Republic of Germany, First Class.

Klaus Mann writes a personal letter to Gottfried Benn in May 1933, warning him he will reap only ingratitude, ridicule, and persecution from the Nazis, not recognition. Benn replies to him publicly in a newspaper article, which he also reads over the radio; Klaus Mann and the other emigrants must finally realize that the National Socialists' ascension to power is not about a change in the "form of government, but about a new vision for the birth of mankind, perhaps an ancient, perhaps the last, grand conception of the white race, probably one of the grandest realizations of world spirit ever." In September 1933 Klaus Mann founds the exile magazine *Die Sammlung* [*The Collection*] in Amsterdam. It is published by the Dutch press Querido, the German-language division of which *Fritz Landshoff* heads from 1933 to 1940, transforming it into one of the most important publication venues for German exile literature. In 1938 Klaus Mann emigrates to the United States and joins the U.S. Army. His contributions as a correspondent for the military magazine *Stars and Stripes* include an interview conducted with the now-captive Hermann Göring in 1945. After his discharge from American military service, he is unable to find his footing in the German literary scene again. Unlike Gottfried Benn, he receives no prizes or decorations. He dies in Cannes from an overdose of sleeping pills in 1949.

Erika Mann goes on tour with her cabaret *Die Pfeffermühle* in Switzerland and in many other European countries, starting in 1933. When she is expatriated by German authorities, she marries the homosexual writer W. H. Auden and thereby receives British citizenship. From 1937 she lives in the United States. After the *Pfeffermühle* is disbanded, *Therese Giehse*, who now sees no further employment opportunity for herself as an actor, breaks up with Erika Mann and relocates to Switzerland. Erika remains in the United States and disabuses the American public about the Hitler regime's crimes on long lecture tours. Between 1943 and 1946 she travels throughout Europe and the Middle East as a war correspondent for various newspapers. In 1952 she leaves the United States with her parents and settles near Zurich with them.

Thomas Mann initially remains in Switzerland with Katia in 1933. At first, he abstains from making political statements. In 1936 he makes a public break with the National Socialist regime and is expatriated. In 1938 he relocates to the United States with his wife. The couple first live in Princeton, then in Pacific Palisades, outside Los Angeles. In the summer of 1951, he must testify before the *House Committee on Un-American Activities*; he and Katia leave the United States in 1952 and move to Switzerland.

Helene Weigel, Bertolt Brecht, and *Margarete Steffin* seek protection after the outbreak of war not in the Soviet Union, but in the United States. In 1941, however, their escape leads first to Moscow, where Margarete Steffin dies of tuberculosis. Weigel and Brecht continue their travels via Vladivostok to California, where Brecht works for the Hollywood film industry. In 1943, in collaboration with Fritz Lang, he is able to complete the film *Hangmen Also Die!,* which is loosely based on the assassination of the chief architect of the Holocaust, Reinhard Heydrich, in Prague. Helene Weigel has no opportunity to work as an actor, aside from a handful of performances in silent roles. In 1947 Brecht must face questioning by the *House Committee on Un-American Activities* in Washington, D.C., and departs for Zurich a few days later. In 1948 he resumes his stage work in Berlin. Helene Weigel becomes artistic director of the Berliner Ensemble, Brecht the principal stage director.

Erich Mühsam is never released after his arrest. SS men murder him on July 10, 1934, in Oranienburg concentration camp.

Nelly Kröger and *Heinrich Mann* marry in 1939 and flee to the United States the following year. Nelly Kröger cannot overcome her alcoholism and takes her own life in 1944. Heinrich Mann lives in Santa Monica, not far from his brother Thomas, who provides him financial support. In 1949 he is elected the founding president of the Deutsche Akademie der Künste [German Academy of the Arts] in East Germany. He dies on March 11, 1950, just before his planned return to Berlin.

Pierre Bertaux never launches a magazine with Heinrich Mann, but does prove his extraordinary talent in other fields. During the war he becomes one of the leading heads of the French Resistance and, in 1949, the director of the *Sûreté nationale*, the French intelligence agency. He loses his position in 1951 after a close friend of his from Résistance days is involved in a spectacular jewel heist and avoids arrest for a long time. He later teaches German Studies at the Sorbonne and publishes several books, including on Hölderlin and Goethe.

Rudi Carius takes part in the Spanish Civil War as a volunteer on the communists' side. He does not learn of Nelly Kröger's death in the United States until he resumes contact with Heinrich Mann after the end of the Second World War.

Erich Kästner remains in Germany both because he does not wish to leave his mother behind and in order to gather eye-witness material about life in the Third Reich as a topic for a future novel. When he stops over in Zurich on his journey from Merano, he meets with Anna Seghers and other authors who entreat him not to return to Germany. But his mind cannot be changed. In subsequent years he will never be admitted to the Reich Chamber of Literature, despite making several attempts, and can thus only publish under a pseudonym. After 1945 the notebooks in which he collected records about life under National Socialism sit idle: "The Thousand-Year Reich does not have the stuff for a great novel."

Mascha Kaléko emigrates to the United States in 1938. She returns to Germany for the first time in 1956; her books are published to great success once again, and her debut, *Das lyrische Stenogrammheft*, is reprinted. In 1959 she is set to receive the Fontane Prize from the Berlin Academy of the Arts, but after learning that jury member Hans Egon Holthusen was in the SS, she withdraws her candidacy. After that she relocates to Israel for her husband's sake. Until her death in 1975, she scarcely attracts any further literary attention in Germany.

Theodor Wolff journeys to Berlin one more time before the Reichstag election on March 5, casts his ballot, and then leaves the country with his family. From 1934 onward he lives in Nice and Sanary-sur-Mer. Hermann Göring makes him an offer to return to Germany as editor-in-chief of the *Berliner Tageblatt*, but Wolff refuses. In 1943, at the age of seventy-five, he is arrested in Nice and deported to Sachsenhausen concentration camp, where he takes ill. On September 23, 1943, he dies in a Berlin hospital.

Alfred Döblin settles provisionally in Paris in 1934 and then flees to the United States, where he is employed for a time as a screenwriter in Hollywood. After the end of the war, he is one of the first writers in exile to return to Germany and works for the French military administration. He no longer fits into Germany's literary life, however; his new books are failures. In 1953 he moves back to France.

Ricarda Huch resides in Jena from 1936 onward. Two years later she and her son-in-law Franz Böhm are denounced for harboring views friendly to Jews. Her renown is so great that the Minister of Justice drops the case against her and Böhm. The third and final volume of her comprehensive *Deutsche Geschichte* [*German History*], however, is not permitted to be published. On her eightieth birthday in 1944, she receives congratulatory telegrams from Hitler and Goebbels, and she is awarded the Raabe Prize. After the war the French occupational authorities likewise refuse their imprimatur for the third volume of *Deutsche Geschichte* on account of its critical remarks about the absolutism of Louis XIV. In 1947 she takes part in the First German Writers' Congress in Berlin as honorary president. She dies not long afterward in Schönberg, outside Frankfurt am Main.

Oskar Loerke loses his position as Academy secretary, which he fought for at great self-sacrifice, as soon as the end of March 1933. But he remains a member of the Academy and an editor for S. Fischer Verlag, which also publishes another five volumes of poetry by him. He dies in 1941.

Gabriele Tergit initially emigrates to Prague and Palestine. In 1938 she relocates permanently to London. Since 1933 she has been carrying the manuscript for her great social novel *Effingers* in her luggage, but makes slow progress on it during her years on the run. When it is able to be published in West Germany in 1951, it does not find many readers, nor does she find an entry point into the German journalism of the postwar era either. Instead, for twenty-five years she works in London in a voluntary capacity as treasurer and secretary for the PEN Club of German-language writers in exile. She dies in London in 1982.

Afterword

"The memory of the past will serve no purpose if used to build an impassable wall between evil and us, identifying exclusively with irreproachable heroes and innocent victims and driving the agents of evil outside the confines of humankind. This, though, is precisely what we usually do."

Tzvetan Todorov*

For the destruction of democracy, the antidemocrats did not require any more time than the length of an ample annual vacation. Those who left a state under the rule of law at the end of January returned four weeks later to a dictatorship.

That is more or less what happened to Lion Feuchtwanger, one of the most successful novelists of the Weimar Republic, who had already set off on a lecture tour of the United States in November 1932. In New York he met Eleanor Roosevelt, wife of Franklin D. Roosevelt, who had been elected president a few days earlier, an acquaintanceship that would later prove life-saving for Feuchtwanger. It was Eleanor Roosevelt who in 1940 would not only mobilize her husband, but move heaven and earth to send American aid to Feuchtwanger on his dramatic escape from the Gestapo out of Marseille to Spain.

On January 30, 1933, it is a legation counselor from the German embassy who delivers Feuchtwanger the news of Hitler's swearing-in. And at a dinner on the same day, the ambassador, Friedrich von Prittwitz und Gaffron, strongly urges him not to return to Germany. As both a Jew and the author of the novel *Success*, in which he caricatures Hitler's political ascent, Feuchtwanger was high up on the list of authors the Nazis would have simply loved to send to prison or, better yet, straight to kingdom come. Two years earlier Feuchtwanger had had a villa built for

---

*Tzvetan Todorov, "Memory as Remedy for Evil." *Journal of International Criminal Justice*, 7, no. 3 (2009): 447–62, here 461.

himself in Grunewald, one of Berlin's poshest residential areas, just a few hundred paces from Alfred Kerr's villa. Still, he takes the ambassador's warning quite seriously, allows his booking on a German steamship for the return journey to Europe to lapse, and instead takes a French ship. When he finally joins up with his wife in Austria, news reaches him from his secretary that five SA storm troopers ransacked his villa. Apparently, they were well briefed about the date of his arrival in Europe. Since they did not happen upon him and his wife, they pillaged his villa in disappointment, smashing the furniture to pieces, beating the staff, and shooting at the caretaker.

From America, Feuchtwanger bade goodbye with one simple line: "Hitler means war." He is forced to give up his home in Berlin as well as the majority of his fortune and settle in Sanary-sur-Mer, the fishing village not far from Marseille. In subsequent years Sanary will become a capital of German literature, on account of so many emigrants living here or stopping off during their escape: Wilhelm Herzog, Joseph Roth, Bertolt Brecht, Ferdinand Bruckner, Stefan Zweig, Heinrich Mann, Annette Kolb, Theodor Wolff, Hermann Kesten, Egon Erwin Kisch, Thomas Mann, and his children Erika and Klaus. Only a few managed to salvage more into exile than what would fit into one or two suitcases; the totalitarian overpowering of democracy had happened too fast.

The fate of the Academy of the Arts provides a representative sense of how scant the resistance of German institutions was at the time. And only six weeks later the forces of civilization proved so weak that random passersby on Laubenheimer Platz assailed defenseless persons with one accord while the police watched good-naturedly. The preciousness of democracy and justice is evident once they begin to disappear.

Naturally there are contradictions and uncertainties in the accounts of the time period narrated here. Writers and artists are not bookkeepers of their own pasts. Some did not record their memories until many years or decades later and thereby botched this or that historically verifiable date. Such are the errors I have tacitly corrected here. In writing later, other authors were so flagrantly aiming to politically whitewash their conduct during those weeks that I disregarded their reports. The most vivid and convincing records to me were diary entries, notes, or letters that arose in parallel with the events. In instances of doubt, I trusted them most of all.

But much of what happened then and is documented cannot be substantiated sufficiently to withstand judicial scrutiny. To give one example: it is both plausible and confirmed by witness testimony that the SS captain Hans Maikowski and the police officer Josef Zauritz were shot and murdered on January 30, 1933, at the behest of Joseph Goebbels. After the war ended, however, the parties concerned were dead, and there was no interest in pursuing any further legal investigation. Goebbel's involvement has therefore not been proven with the utmost conclusiveness. Available evidence and statements seem to me sufficiently persuasive, however, to portray his involvement in the matter as historical fact. I have proceeded similarly in other cases.

The daily reports about politically motivated acts of violence in these initial days and weeks of Hitler's reign I have taken primarily from the *Vossische Zeitung*, the *Frankfurter Zeitung*, and the *Berliner Morgenpost*. At the same time, homicides were all I was able to incorporate in any systematic way. The number of clashes resulting in injuries was too large for me to be able to mention them all within the scope of this book. In the weeks leading up to the election on March 5 alone, sixty-nine people are said to have been murdered for political reasons and several hundred injured.

Bibliography

Asmus, Sylvia, and Brita Eckert, eds. *Rudolf Olden: Journalist gegen Hitler – Anwalt der Republik*. Leipzig and Frankfurt am Main: Deutsche Nationalbibliothek, 2010.

Barbian, Jan-Pieter. *Literaturpolitik im Dritten Reich*. Munich: Deutscher Taschenbuch-Verlag, 1995.

Barth, Rüdiger, and Hauke Friedrichs. *Die Totengräber: Der letzte Winter der Weimarer Republik*. Frankfurt am Main: S. Fischer, 2018.

Bauschinger, Sigrid. *Else Lasker-Schüler: Biographie*. Göttingen: Wallstein, 2004.

Bemmann, Helga. *Erich Kästner: Leben und Werk*. Berlin: Ullstein, 1998.

Benn, Gottfried. *Essays und Reden in der Fassung der Erstdrucke*. Frankfurt am Main: Fischer Taschenbuch, 1989.

Benn, Gottfried. *Prosa und Autobiographie in der Fassung der Erstdrucke*. Frankfurt am Main: Fischer Taschenbuch, 1984.

Benn, Gottfried, and Egmont Seyerlen. *Briefwechsel 1914–1956*. Edited by Gerhard Schuster. Stuttgart: Klett-Cotta, 1993.

Benn, Gottfried, and Thea Sternheim. *Briefwechsel und Aufzeichnungen*. Edited by Thomas Ehrsam. Munich: Wallstein, 2006.

Benz, Wolfgang, and Barbara Diestel, eds. *Der Ort des Terrors: Geschichte der nationalsozialistischen Konzentrationslager*. Vol. II: *Frühe Lager, Dachau, Emslandlager*. Munich: C. H. Beck, 2005.

Berger, Günther. *Bertolt Brecht in Wien*. Berlin, Bern, Vienna: Peter Lang, 2018.

Bloch, Karola. *Aus meinem Leben*. Pfullingen: Neske, 1981.

Blubacher, Thomas. *Die vielen Leben der Ruth Landshoff-Yorck*. Berlin: Insel, 2015.

Blubacher, Thomas. *Gustaf Gründgens*. Leipzig: Henschel, 2013.

Blubacher, Thomas. *"Ich jammere nicht, ich schimpfe": Ruth Hellberg: Ein Jahrhundert Theater*. Göttingen: Wallstein, 2018.

Bracher, Karl Dietrich. *Die deutsche Diktatur: Entstehung, Struktur, Folgen des Nationalsozialismus*. Berlin: Ullstein, 1997.

Brecht, Bertolt. *Love Poems*. Translated by David Constantine and Tom Kuhn. Foreword by Barbara Brecht-Schall. New York: Liveright Publishing Corporation, 2015.

Brecht, Bertolt, and Helene Weigel. *Briefe 1923–1956.* Edited by Erdmut Wizisla. Berlin: Suhrkamp, 2012.

Brenner, Hildegard, ed. *Ende einer bürgerlichen Kunst-Institution: Die politische Formierung der Preußischen Akademie der Künste ab 1933.* Stuttgart: Deutsche Verlags-Anstalt, 1972.

Brentano, Bernard von. *Du Land der Liebe: Bericht von Abschied und Heimkehr eines Deutschen.* Tübingen and Stuttgart: R. Wunderlich, 1952.

Bröhan, Nicole. *Max Liebermann: Eine Biographie.* Berlin: Jaron, 2012.

Bronsen, David. *Joseph Roth: Eine Biographie.* Cologne: Kiepenheuer & Witsch, 2018.

Debrunner, Albert M. *"Zu Hause im 20. Jahrhundert": Hermann Kesten.* Wädenswil am Zürichersee: Nimbus Kunst und Bücher, 2017.

Decker, Gunnar. *Gottfried Benn: Genie und Barbar.* Berlin: Aufbau-Verlag, 2006.

Decker, Kerstin. *Mein Herz–Niemandem: Das Leben der Else Lasker-Schüler.* Berlin: Propyläen Verlag, 2009.

Delmer, Sefton. *An Autobiography. Vol. 1: Trail Sinister.* London: Secker & Warburg, 1961.

Delmer, Sefton. *An Autobiography. Vol. 2: Black Boomerang.* London: Secker & Warburg, 1962.

Diels, Rudolf. *Lucifer ante portas.* Stuttgart: Deutsche Verlags-Anstalt, 1950.

Distl, Dieter. *Ernst Toller.* Schrobenhausen: B. Bickel, 1993.

Döblin, Alfred. *Autobiographische Schriften und letzte Aufzeichnungen.* Edited by Edgar Pässler. Olten and Freiburg im Breisgau: Walter-Verlag, 1977.

Döblin, Alfred. *Briefe.* Edited by Walter Muschg *et al.* Zurich, Dusseldorf: Walter-Verlag, 1970.

Döblin, Alfred. *Briefe II.* Edited by Helmut Pfanner. Zurich, Dusseldorf: Walter-Verlag, 2001.

Döblin, Alfred. *Schriften zu Ästhetik, Poetik und Literatur.* Edited by Erich Kleinschmidt. Olten and Freiburg im Breisgau: Walter-Verlag, 1972.

Döblin, Alfred. *Schriften zu Leben und Werk.* Edited by Erich Kleinschmidt. Olten and Freiburg im Breisgau: Walter-Verlag, 1986.

Döblin, Alfred. *Schriften zur Politik und Gesellschaft.* Edited by Hans Graber. Frankfurt am Main: Fischer Taschenbuch, 2015.

Dove, Richard. *He Was a German: A Biography of Ernst Toller.* London: Libris, 1990.

Drobisch, Klaus, and Günther Wieland. *System der NS-Konzentrationslager 1933–1939.* Berlin: Akademie Verlag, 1993.

Düsterberg, Rolf, ed. *Dichter für das "Dritte Reich."* Bielefeld: Aisthesis, 2009.

Düsterberg, Rolf. *Hanns Johst: Der Barde der SS: Karriere eines deutschen Dichters*. Paderborn, Munich, Vienna, Zurich: Schöningh, 2004.

Dyck, Joachim. *Benn in Berlin*. Berlin: Transit, 2010.

Dyck, Joachim. *Der Zeitzeuge: Gottfried Benn, 1929–1949*. Göttingen: Wallstein, 2006.

Ebermayer, Erich. *Eh' ich's vergesse: Erinnerungen an Gerhart Hauptmann, Thomas Mann, Klaus Mann, Gustaf Gründgens, Emil Jannings und Stefan Zweig*. Munich: LangenMüller, 2005.

Eggebrecht, Axel. *Der halbe Weg: Zwischenbilanz einer Epoche*. Reinbek bei Hamburg: Rowohlt, 1981.

El-Akramy, Ursula. *Transit Moskau: Margarete Steffin und Maria Osten*. Hamburg: Europäische Verlagsanstalt, 1998.

Fallada, Hans. *A Stranger in My Own Country: The 1944 Prison Diary*. Translated by Allan Blunden. Cambridge, UK: Polity, 2015.

Fechter, Paul. *Dichtung der Deutschen: Eine Geschichte der Literatur unseres Volkes von den Anfängen bis zur Gegenwart*. Berlin: Deutsche Buch-Gemeinschaft, 1932.

Fest, Joachim C. *Hitler*. Translated by Richard and Clara Winston. New York: Harcourt Brace Jovanovich, 1974.

Feuchtwanger, Lion. *Ein möglichst intensives Leben: Die Tagebücher*. Berlin: Aufbau, 2018.

Feuerstein-Praßer, Karin. *Die Frauen der Dichter*. Munich: Piper, 2015.

Fischer, Lothar, and Helen Adkins. *George Grosz: Sein Leben*. Berlin: Bäßler, 2017.

Flügge, Manfred. *Heinrich Mann*. Reinbek bei Hamburg: Rowohlt, 2006.

Flügge, Manfred. *Traumland und Zuflucht: Heinrich Mann und Frankreich*. Berlin: Insel, 2013.

Fuld, Werner, and Albert Ostermaier. *Die Göttin und ihr Sozialist: Christiane Grautoffs Autobiographie: ihr Leben mit Ernst Toller*. Bonn: Weidle, 1996.

Giehse, Therese. *Ich hab nichts zum Sagen*. Reinbek bei Hamburg: Rowohlt, 1976.

Goebbels, Joseph. *Die Tagebücher*. Edited by Elke Fröhlich. Part I: *Aufzeichnungen 1923–1941*. Vol. 2/III: *Oktober 1932–März 1934*. Munich: K. G. Saur, 2006.

Görtemaker, Manfred. *Thomas Mann und die Politik*. Frankfurt am Main: S. Fischer, 2005.

Görtz, Franz Josef, and Hans Sarkowicz. *Erich Kästner*. Munich, Zurich: Piper, 1998.

Graf, Oskar Maria. *Gelächter von außen: Aus meinem Leben 1918–1933*. Munich, Leipzig: List, 1994.

Gronau, Dietrich. *Max Liebermann: Eine Biographie.* Frankfurt am Main: Fischer Taschenbuch, 2001.

Gross, Babette. *Willi Münzenberg: A Political Biography.* Translated by Marian Jackson. East Lansing: Michigan State University Press, 1974.

Grossmann, Kurt R. *Emigration: Geschichte der Hitler-Flüchtlinge 1933–1945.* Frankfurt am Main: Europäische Verlagsanstalt, 1969.

Grossmann, Kurt R. *Ossietzky: Ein deutscher Patriot.* Frankfurt am Main: Suhrkamp, 1973.

Grosz, George. *George Grosz: An Autobiography.* Translated by Nora Hodges. Berkeley: University of California Press, 1998.

Grupp, Peter. *Harry Graf Kessler 1868–1937.* Munich: Beck, 1995.

Haase, Horst. *Johannes R. Becher: Leben und Werk.* Berlin: Das europäische Buch, 1981.

Hackermüller, Rotraut. *Einen Handkuß der Gnädigsten: Roda Roda.* Vienna, Munich: Herold, 1986.

Hanuschek, Sven. *"Keiner blickt dir hinter das Gesicht": Das Leben Erich Kästners.* Munich: Deutscher Taschenbuch Verlag, 2003.

Harpprecht, Klaus. *Thomas Mann.* Reinbek bei Hamburg: Rowohlt, 1995.

Hecht, Werner. *Brechts Leben in schwierigen Zeiten.* Frankfurt am Main: Suhrkamp, 2007.

Hecht, Werner. *Helene Weigel: Eine große Frau des 20. Jahrhunderts.* Frankfurt am Main: Suhrkamp, 2000.

Heer, Hannes, Sven Fritz, Heike Drummer, and Jutta Zwilling: *Verstummte Stimmen: Die Vertreibung der "Juden" und "politisch Untragbaren" aus den hessischen Theatern 1933 bis 1945.* Berlin: Metropol, 2011.

Heine, Gert, and Paul Schommer. *Thomas Mann Chronik.* Frankfurt am Main: Vittorio Klostermann, 2004.

Herlin, Hans. *Ernst Udet: A Man's Life.* Translated by Mervyn Savill. London: Macdonald, 1960.

Herzog, Wilhelm. *Menschen, denen ich begegnete.* Bern, Munich: Francke, 1959.

Hof, Holger. *Gottfried Benn: Der Mann ohne Gedächtnis.* Stuttgart: Klett-Cotta, 2011.

Ishoven, Armand von. *The Fall of an Eagle: The Life of Fighter Ace Ernst Udet.* Translated by Chaz Bowyer. London: W. Kimber, 1979.

Janßen, Karl-Heinz. *Der 30. Januar: Ein Report über den Tag, der die Welt veränderte.* Frankfurt am Main: Edition Freitag, 1983.

Jasper, Willi. *Der Bruder: Heinrich Mann.* Frankfurt am Main: Fischer Taschenbuch, 2001.

Jasper, Willi. *Die Jagd nach Liebe: Heinrich Mann und die Frauen.* Frankfurt am Main: S. Fischer, 2007.

Jens, Inge, ed. *Dichter zwischen rechts und links: Die Geschichte der Sektion für Dichtkunst an der Preußischen Akademie der Künste.* Leipzig: Kiepenheuer, 1994.

Jeske, Wolfgang, and Peter Zahn. *Lion Feuchtwanger: Der arge Weg der Erkenntnis.* Munich: Heyne, 1986.

Jüngling, Kirsten. *"Ich bin doch nicht nur schlecht": Nelly Mann.* Berlin: List, 2009.

Kapfer, Herbert, and Lisbeth Exner. *Weltdada Huelsenbeck: Eine Biografie in Briefen und Bildern.* Innsbruck: Haymon, 1996.

Kästner, Erich. *Der tägliche Kram.* Zurich: Atrium Verlag, 2013.

Kebir, Sabine. *Helene Weigel: Abstieg in den Ruhm.* Berlin: Aufbau Taschenbuch, 2002.

Keiser-Hayne, Helga. *Erika Mann und ihr politisches Kabarett "Die Pfeffermühle" 1933–1937.* Reinbek bei Hamburg: Rowohlt, 1995.

Kesser, Armin. "Tagebuchaufzeichnungen über Brecht 1930–1963." *Sinn und Form* 58, no. 6 (2004): 738–59.

Kessler, Harry Graf. *Das Tagebuch. Neunter Band 1926–1937.* Edited by Sabine Gruber and Ulrich Ott. Stuttgart: Cotta, 2010.

Kessler, Harry Graf. *The Diaries of a Cosmopolitan: Count Harry Kessler, 1918–1937.* Translated by Charles Kessler. London: Weidenfeld and Nicolson, 1971.

Kesten, Hermann. *Deutsche Literatur im Exil: Briefe europäischer Autoren 1933–1949.* Vienna, Munich, Basel: K. Desch, 1964.

Kesten, Hermann. *Meine Freunde, die Poeten.* Berlin, Vienna: Ullstein, 1980.

Kisch, Egon Erwin. *Der rasende Reporter.* Berlin, Weimar: Aufbau, 1990.

Kisch, Egon Erwin. *Mein Leben für die Zeitung. Part 2: 1926–1947.* Berlin: Aufbau, 1993.

Klee, Ernst. *Das Kulturlexikon zum Dritten Reich: Wer war was vor und nach 1945.* Frankfurt am Main: S. Fischer, 2007.

Klein, Michael. *Georg Bernhard: Die politische Haltung des Chefredakteurs der Vossischen Zeitung.* Frankfurt am Main: Peter Lang, 1999.

Kluy, Alexander. *George Grosz: König ohne Land.* Munich: Deutsche Verlags-Anstalt, 2017.

Knopf, Jan. *Bertolt Brecht: Lebenskunst in finsteren Zeiten.* Munich: Carl Hanser, 2012.

Köhler, Wolfram. *Der Chef-Redakteur Theodor Wolff.* Dusseldorf: Droste, 1978.

Kollwitz, Käthe. *"Ich will wirken in dieser Zeit": Auswahl aus den Tagebüchern und Briefen, aus Graphik, Zeichnungen und Plastik.* Berlin: Ullstein, 1993.

Körner, Torsten. *Ein guter Freund*. Berlin: Aufbau, 2001.

Kühn, Dieter. *Löwenmusik: Essays*. Frankfurt am Main: Suhrkamp, 1979.

Kurzke, Hermann. *Thomas Mann: Life as a Work of Art*. Translated by Leslie Wilson. Princeton: Princeton University Press, 2002.

Lahme, Tilmann. *Golo Mann: Biographie*. Frankfurt am Main: S. Fischer, 2009.

Landes, Brigitte. *Im Romanischen Café: Ein Gästebuch*. Berlin: Insel Verlag, 2020.

Landshoff, Fritz H. *Amsterdam, Keizersgracht 333, Querido Verlag: Erinnerungen eines Verlegers*. Berlin: Aufbau Taschenbuch, 2001.

Lasker-Schüler, Else. *Briefe 1925–1933*. Edited by Sigrid Bauschinger. Frankfurt am Main: Jüdischer Verlag, 2005.

Lemke, Katrin. *Ricarda Huch. Die Summe des Ganzen*. Weimar: Weimarer Verlagsgesellschaft, 2014.

Lethen, Helmut. *Der Sound der Väter: Gottfried Benn und seine Zeit*. Berlin: Rowohlt, 2006.

Loerke, Oskar. *Tagebücher 1903–1939*. Edited by Hermann Kasack. Frankfurt am Main: Suhrkamp, 1986.

Lorey, Annette: *Nelly Mann: Heinrich Manns Gefährtin im Exil*. Würzburg: Königshausen & Neumann, 2021.

Lühe, Irmela von der. *Erika Mann: Eine Lebensgeschichte*. Reinbek bei Hamburg: Rowohlt, 2009.

Mann, Erika. *Briefe und Antworten*. Vol. I: *1922–1950*. Edited by Anna Zanco Prestel. Munich: Spangenberg, 1984.

Mann, Golo. *Reminiscences and Reflections: A Youth in Germany*. Translated by Krishna Winston. New York: Norton, 1990.

Mann, Heinrich: *Der Haß: Deutsche Zeitgeschichte*. Frankfurt am Main: Fischer Taschenbuch, 1987.

Mann, Heinrich, and Félix Bertaux. *Briefwechsel 1922–1948*. Frankfurt am Main: S. Fischer, 2002.

Mann, Katia. *Meine ungeschriebenen Memoiren*. Edited by Elisabeth Plessen and Michael Mann. Frankfurt am Main: S. Fischer, 1999.

Mann, Klaus. *Briefe und Antworten*. Vol I: *1922–1937*. Edited by Martin Gregor-Dellin. Munich: Heinrich Ellermann, 1975.

Mann, Klaus. *Der siebente Engel: Die Theaterstücke*. Edited by Uwe Naumann and Michael Töteberg. Reinbek bei Hamburg: Rowohlt, 1989.

Mann, Klaus. *Der Wendepunkt: Ein Lebensbericht*. Edited by Frederic Kroll. Reinbek bei Hamburg: Rowohlt, 2014.

Mann, Klaus. *Der zehnte März 1933*. https://www.monacensia-digital.de/mann/content/titleinfo/31263

Mann, Klaus. *Tagebücher 1931–1933*. Edited by Joachim Heimannsberg, Peter Laemmle, and Wilfried F. Schoeller. Munich: Spangenberg, 1989.

Mann, Thomas. *Briefwechsel mit seinem Verleger Gottfried Bermann Fischer 1932–1955*. Edited by Peter de Mendelssohn. Frankfurt am Main: S. Fischer, 1973.

Mann, Thomas. *Ein Appell an die Vernunft: Essays 1926–1933*. Edited by Hermann Kurzke and Stephan Stachorski. Frankfurt am Main: S. Fischer, 1994.

Mann, Thomas. *Essays: Achtung, Europa!: 1933–1938*. Frankfurt am Main: S. Fischer, 1995.

Mann, Thomas. *The Magic Mountain: A Novel*. Translated by John E. Woods. New York: Alfred A. Knopf, 1995.

Mann, Thomas. *Reflections of a Nonpolitical Man*. Translated by Walter D. Morris and others. New York: New York Review Books, 2021.

Mann, Thomas. *Tagebücher 1933–1934*. Edited by Peter de Mendelssohn. Frankfurt am Main: S. Fischer, 1977.

Mann, Thomas, and Heinrich Mann. *Briefwechsel 1900–1949*. Edited by Hans Wysling. Frankfurt am Main: Fischer Taschenbuch, 1995.

Martynkewicz, Wolfgang. *Tanz auf dem Pulverfass: Gottfried Benn, die Frauen und die Macht*. Berlin: Aufbau, 2017.

Medicus, Thomas. *Heinrich und Götz George: Zwei Leben*. Berlin: Rowohlt, 2020.

Meissner, Otto. *Ebert, Hindenburg, Hitler: Erinnerungen eines Staatssekretärs 1918–1945*. Esslingen, Munich: Bechtle, 1995.

Mendelssohn, Peter de. *Der Zauberer: Das Leben des deutschen Schriftstellers Thomas Mann*. Second Part: *Jahre der Schwebe 1919 und 1933*. Frankfurt am Main: Fischer Taschenbuch, 1997.

Merseburger, Peter. *Willy Brandt*. Stuttgart, Munich: Deutsche Verlags-Anstalt, 2002.

Mittenzwei, Werner. *Das Leben des Bertolt Brecht oder Der Umgang mit den Welträtseln*. Vol. 1. Frankfurt am Main: Suhrkamp, 1987.

Mittenzwei, Werner: *Der Untergang einer Akademie: Die Mentalität des ewigen Deutschen*. Berlin und Weimar: Aufbau, 1992.

Moreno, Joaquín, Gunnar Szymaniak, and Almut Winter, eds. *Ferdinand Bruckner (1891–1958)*. Berlin: Weidler, 2008.

Mühsam, Kreszentia. *Der Leidensweg Erich Mühsams*. Berlin: Harald-Kater-Verlag, 1994.

Münster, Arno. *Ernst Bloch: Eine politische Biographie*. Hamburg: CEP Europäische Verlagsanstalt, 2012.

Nottelmann, Nicole. *Die Karrieren der Vicki Baum*. Cologne: Kiepenheuer & Witsch, 2007.

Parker, Stephen. *Bertolt Brecht: A Literary Life*. London: Bloomsbury, 2014.

Patka, Marcus G. *Egon Erwin Kisch: Stationen im Leben eines streitbaren Autors*. Vienna, Cologne, Weimar: Böhlau, 1997.

Petersen, Jan. *Our Street: A Chronicle*. Translated by Betty Rensen. London: V. Gollancz, 1938.

Petit, Marc. *Die verlorene Gleichung: Auf den Spuren von Wolfgang und Alfred Döblin*. Frankfurt am Main: Eichborn, 2005.

Prater, Donald A. *Thomas Mann: A Life*. Oxford, New York: Oxford University Press, 1995.

Prokosch, Erdmute. *Egon Erwin Kisch: Reporter einer rasenden Zeit*. Bonn: Keil, 1985.

Regnier, Anatol. *Du auf deinem höchsten Dach: Tilly Wedekind und ihre Töchter: Eine Familienbiografie*. Munich: A. Knaus, 2003.

Regnier, Anatol. *Jeder schreibt für sich allein: Schriftsteller im Nationalsozialismus*. Munich: C. H. Beck, 2020.

Reiber, Hartmut. *Grüß den Brecht: Das Leben der Margarete Steffin*. Berlin: Eulenspiegel, 2008.

Rosenkranz, Jutta. *Mascha Kaléko: Biografie*. Munich: Deutscher Taschenbuch-Verlag, 2007.

Roth, Joseph. *Briefe 1911–1939*. Cologne, Berlin: Kiepenheuer & Witsch, 1970.

Roth, Joseph. *Joseph Roth: A Life in Letters*. Translated and edited by Michael Hofmann. New York: Norton, 2012.

Roth, Joseph. *The Radetzky March*. Translated by Michael Hofmann. London: Granta, 2002.

Rudolph, Katharina. *Rebell im Maßanzug: Leonhard Frank*. Berlin: Aufbau, 2020.

Rühle, Günther. *Theater für die Republik: Im Spiegel der Kritik*. Vol. 2: *1926–1933*. Frankfurt am Main: S. Fischer, 1988.

Rühle, Günther. *Theater in Deutschland 1887–1945: Seine Ereignisse – seine Menschen*. Frankfurt am Main: S. Fischer, 2007.

Sahl, Hans. *Memoiren eines Moralisten: Das Exil im Exil*. Munich: Luchterhand, 2008.

Schaenzler, Nicole. *Klaus Mann: Eine Biographie*. Frankfurt am Main: Campus, 1999.

Schärf, Christian. *Der Unberührbare: Gottfried Benn – Dichter im 20. Jahrhundert*. Bielefeld: Aisthesis, 2006.

Schebera, Jürgen. *Damals im Romanischen Café: Künstler und ihre Lokale im Berlin der zwanziger Jahre*. Berlin: Das Neue Berlin, 2005.

Schebera, Jürgen. *Hanns Eisler*. Mainz: Schott, 1998.

Schebera, Jürgen. *Vom Josty in Romanische Café: Streifzüge durch Berliner Künstlerlokale der Goldenen Zwanziger.* Berlin: Insel, 2020.

Schmidt, Renate. *Therese Giehse.* Munich: LangenMüller, 2008.

Schnetz, Wolf Peter. *Oskar Loerke: Leben und Werk.* Munich: Junge Akademie, 1967.

Schoeller, Wilfried F. *Alfred Döblin: Eine Biographie.* Munich: Carl Hanser, 2011.

Schymura, Yvonne. *Käthe Kollwitz: Die Liebe, der Krieg und die Kunst.* Munich: C. H. Beck, 2016.

Skrodzki, Karl Jürgen. *Else Lasker-Schüler.* https://www.kj-skrodzki.de/lasker.htm

Sperber, Manès. *The Unheeded Warning: 1918–1933.* Translated by Harry Zohn. New York: Holmes & Meier, 1991.

Sternburg, Wilhelm von. *"Als wäre alles das letzte Mal": Erich Maria Remarque.* Cologne: Kiepenheuer & Witsch, 1998.

Sternburg, Wilhelm von. *"Es ist eine unheimliche Stimmung in Deutschland": Carl von Ossietzky und seine Zeit.* Berlin: Aufbau, 1996.

Sternburg, Wilhelm von. *Joseph Roth: Eine Biographie.* Cologne: Kiepenheuer & Witsch, 2009.

Sternburg, Wilhelm von. *Lion Feuchtwanger: Ein deutsches Schriftstellerleben.* Berlin: Ullstein, 1987.

Sucker, Juliane, ed. *Gabriele Tergit.* Text + Kritik 228 (2020).

Suhr, Elke. *Carl von Ossietzky: Eine Biographie.* Cologne: Kiepenheuer & Witsch, 1988.

Tergit, Gabriele. *Etwas Seltenes überhaupt: Erinnerungen.* Berlin: Ullstein, 1983.

Tergit, Gabriele. *Vom Frühling und von der Einsamkeit: Reportagen aus den Gerichten.* Frankfurt am Main: Schöffling & Co., 2020.

Tetzner-Kläber, Lisa. *Das war Kurt Held.* Aarau and Frankfurt am Main: Sauerländer, 1961.

Ullrich, Volker. *Adolf Hitler: Ascent 1889–1939.* Translated by Jefferson Chase. London: Bodley Head, 2016.

Ullstein, Hermann. *The Rise and Fall of the House of Ullstein.* New York: Simon and Schuster, 1943.

Uzulis, André. *Hans Fallada: Biografie.* Berlin: Steffen, 2017.

Vietor-Engländer, Deborah. *Alfred Kerr.* Reinbek bei Hamburg: Rowohlt, 2016.

Völker, Klaus. Theodor Tagger als Theaterunternehmer und Regisseur. In *Ferdinand Bruckner (1891–1958).* Edited by Joaquin Moreno, Gunnar Szymaniak, and Almut Winter. Berlin: Weidler, 2008.

Walter, Hans-Albert. *Deutsche Exilliteratur 1933–1950.* Vol. 1: *Bedrohung und Verfolgung bis 1933.* Darmstadt und Neuwied: Luchterhand, 1972.

Walter, Hans-Albert. *Deutsche Exilliteratur 1933–1950.* Vol. 1.2. *Weimarische Linksintellektuelle im Spannungsfeld von Aktion und Repression.* Stuttgart: J. B. Metzler, 1978.

Walther, Peter. *Fieber: Universum Berlin 1930–1933.* Berlin: Aufbau, 2020.

Walther, Peter. *Hans Fallada: Die Biographie.* Berlin: Aufbau, 2017.

Wedekind, Tilly. *Lulu: Die Rolle meines Lebens.* Munich, Bern, Vienna: Rutten & Loening, 1969.

Wendt, Gunna. *Erika und Therese: Erika Mann und Therese Giehse – Eine Liebe zwischen Kunst und Krieg.* Munich: Piper, 2018.

Wessel, Harald. *Münzenbergs Ende: Ein deutscher Kommunist im Widerstand gegen Hitler und Stalin: Die Jahre 1933 bis 1940.* Berlin: Dietz, 1991.

Wildt, Michael, and Christoph Kreutzmüller, eds. *Berlin 1933–1945.* Munich: Siedler, 2013.

Zuckmayer, Carl. *A Part of Myself.* Translated by Richard and Clara Winston. New York: Harcourt, Brace, Jovanovich, 1970.

Zuckmayer, Carl. *Aufruf zum Leben.* Frankfurt am Main: S. Fischer, 1995.

Zuckmayer, Carl. *Geheimreport.* Edited by Gunther Nickel and Johanna Schrön. Göttingen: Wallstein, 2002.

From among the newspapers and periodicals of the time period depicted, I primarily utilized the *Vossische Zeitung,* the *Frankfurt Zeitung,* the *Berliner Morgenpost,* and the *Weltbühne.* I retrieved data about weather at the time from the website *chroniknet.de* and Paul Schlaak: *Das Wetter in Berlin von 1933–1945. berlingeschichte.de/bms/bmstxtoo/ooo9gesd.htm,* among others. I was able to verify countless details in the databases of the Akademie der Künste (Berlin), the *Deutsche Biographie, Künste im Exil,* the Institut für Frauen-Biographieforschung (Hannover and Boston), the Stiftung Deutsches Historisches Museum, and *Wikipedia.* I owe thanks to those who created these portals.

Index